Student Power

Student Power

PRACTICE AND PROMISE

Glorianne Wittes, Joan Chesler, and Dale Crowfoot

Research Project on Educational Innovation
Educational Change Team
University of Michigan

CITATION PRESS   NEW YORK   1975

Library of Congress Cataloging in Publication Data

Wittes, Glorianne.
    Student power, practice and promise.

    1. Student particpation in administration.
2. Self-government (in education) I. Chesler, Joan.
II. Crowfoot, Dale. III. Michigan. University.
Research Project on Educational Innovation. IV. Title.
LB3092.W5   373.1′2   74-28095
ISBN 0-590-09584-6

Published by Citation Press, Library and Trade Division,
Scholastic Magazines, Inc.

Editorial Office: 50 West 44th Street, New York, New York 10036.
Printed in the U.S.A.

Library of Congress Catalog Card Number: 74-28095

Cover design by Constance Ftera

1 2 3 4 5 79 78 77 76 75

Contents

Acknowledgements

The Research Project on Educational Innovation's core staff took responsibility for the research design, data collection, and case study chapters. Members included, in alphabetical order: Joan Chesler, Dale Crowfoot, Perry Cunningham, C. Beth Duncombe, Susan Golden, Patricia Wilson Graham, Betty Neal, Penny Owen, and Glorianne Wittes. Ms. Wittes also served as coordinator of the Project. Further analyses of the major issues were undertaken by Ms. Wittes, Chesler, Crowfoot, and Golden. Mr. Cunningham provided valuable methodological analyses, for which we are very grateful. Ms. Neal, as executive secretary for the Project and team researchers, undertook various responsibilities during the field work stage of the study and the typing of the manuscript.

Members of the site teams deserve great credit for their excellent work. In addition to the nine mentioned above, they were: Deborah Cowing, Kurt Hansen, Ro Lee, Roslyn McClendon, Verdis McManus, Robert Orr, Louis Piatrowski, and Julie Wittes.

We are especially grateful to the students and staff members of the schools we investigated. Their collaboration and participation were outstanding and of utmost value and made the depth of this study possible.

Finally, our colleagues on the Educational Change Team, University of Michigan, sparked our imaginations during the conception and implementation of this study, for which we are grateful. During its brief two years of existence (1970–72) the Educational Change Team engaged in a variety of research and training activities designed to shed light on the issues and alternatives in school conflict and change. A central concern of the multi-racial, interdisciplinary group of scholars and activists was the extent of racism and youth oppression in American schools. This study was an outgrowth of that concern, an attempt to discover some schools that were grappling with the problems and testing solutions.

Funds for this study were provided by the U.S. Office of Education under contract number OEC-O-70-3322(505) of 1970, under the auspices of the Educational Change Team.

Special appreciation is also extended to Barbara Carter, educational journalist, writer, and editor, who transformed our original lengthy research report into the present professional book for educators.

Foreword

This is a book about issues in contemporary education with a focus on student power. It is a book about schools that are committed to finding ways to increase the individual and collective power of the students they serve. It is a book that is concerned with both the processes of innovation and the impact of innovation on students and staff alike. It is a book that speculates and interprets, but its observations are drawn from case studies of six real schools in action.

Quite frankly, we are excited about this book. Our teaching and consulting experience and the literature published prior to this volume have convinced us that our approach to this study is unique and valuable.

We examined six innovative alternative schools that had set as a prime priority the building of student power and participatory governance. We were curious to see if it worked. Was participatory government really achieved in these schools? If so, were students able to alter their learning environment? Were they benefiting more than in traditional schools? What was the nature of these benefits? What were the difficulties in gaining student power? What were the rewards? Were the students less alienated and the schools less oppressive than traditional schools? How did administrators and the teaching staffs adjust to their less authoritarian roles? Did the traditional racism in schools decrease?

We essentially wanted to know what might be learned from the experiences of schools at the very frontier of new political arrangements. We wanted to compile information that would be useful to others who were implementing new structures in their schools.

HOW THE SCHOOLS WERE SELECTED

We selected for intensive study a small sample of highly experimental public and private schools, with particular emphasis on schools that were not yet popularized. Although there was a large range of experimental schools and programs proliferating in the early 1970s, certain limitations narrowed the selection process. First, since the focus of our study was on participatory forms of school governance and curriculum, we focused on schools with student rather than community participation and control. Second, the study was designed to provide operating models for middle- and long-range change in secondary schools. Third, we concentrated on predominately white and interracial schools and did not investigate alternative schools for blacks; we felt that that task was more appropriate for a group of black scholars.

The selection process was aided by our collaboration with the Association for Supervision and Curriculum Development's informal study of approximately 900 schools, 136 of which had apparently made innovations in their governance structures. Extensive telephone interviews, reviews of materials, information from underground newsletters, exchanges of letters, and pilot visits narrowed the choice for our extended study down to the six schools:

1. A large multi-racial public high school in Seattle—Franklin High School

2. A much smaller interracial public school-without-walls in Chicago—Metropolitan (Metro) High School

3. A school-in-a-school in a New England public high school—called here "Dillington" school-in-a-school, a fictitious name

4. A mini-school in the public high school in Berkeley, California—Community High

5. A small private school in semi-rural Massachusetts —Sudbury Valley School

6. Another small private city school—Milwaukee Independent School

We begin the book with Franklin High School, the most traditional, and conclude with Milwaukee Independent School, which was created by students themselves. Between the two extremes lie all the critical issues of educational reform.

ASSUMPTIONS AND METHODOLOGY

Inherent in all research, but often unstated, are the assumptions and perspectives of the researchers. We assumed that the organization of most schools contains a fundamental dichotomy between student and staff roles. We assumed that students had little or no influence in making decisions about how their schools were run, not only regarding rules and regulations for student behavior but, more importantly, in substantive areas such as curriculum, faculty selection, class scheduling, and the like. We further assumed that various interest groups based on role, status, or cultural differences existed within schools and that conflict between these groups was endemic. We assumed that students' and staffs' satisfaction with themselves and each other contributed significantly to the functioning of a school. We assumed that curriculum and teaching processes reflected the basic ideology of the school in practice, if not in intent. We further assumed that there were stresses for both students and staff who were operating in an experimental milieu that was foreign to their past experience, however much they may have desired innovation.

After determining as many of our assumptions as possible, we tried to develop an objective methodology to gain information about the cultural and the educational processes in each of the six schools. To broaden our adult, university-biased observations, high school-aged individuals worked on the methodology and became part of each research team. Three to six adults and students, with a racial composition appropriate to each school, spent five days at each site. They used a variety of documentation methods to collect data including: (*1*) individual and group interviews (Some respondents were selected at random and others because of their experience in the program.); (*2*) observation of classes, meetings, and activities in the halls, lounges, and outside the building; (*3*) analyses of documents and records such as minutes of meetings, program proposals and evaluations, and printed articles; and (*4*) questionnaires administered to school participants.

In each case study the research focused on areas related to our assumptions. These included:

1. The history of the innovation, impetus for it, and pressures helping and hindering it;
2. The general atmosphere of the school;
3. The governance structure and the extent to which students were an integral part of it;
4. The school curriculum and the roles of teachers and students in determining it;
5. The values, goals, satisfactions, and dissatisfactions of members;
6. The informal influence structures and processes of control.

Intergroup relations, counseling of students, and teacher training were also investigated.

Each school reviewed the first draft of its case study and made additions or corrections. Three schools responded with comments and clarification of details, which have been incorporated; one school did not reply; and two schools chose not to comment, one asking not to be identified in the published report. In deference to this request, we substituted its name and location with the fictitious name of "Dillington" High School-in-a-School. For this publication, we renewed contact with each school through phone calls and letters, to determine its current stage of development. This more current information has been integrated into each case study.

ANALYSES AND COMPARISONS

Part Two contains the analyses of the major issues that emerged from the case studies. We found striking similarities among the six schools in many areas such as leadership, initial development, relations with administrators and the community outside the school, and uncertainty among staff and students about their new roles.

We also discovered a mixed bag of problems and solutions. Student power didn't mean the same thing in the different schools, and size seemed to influence the degree of student control. The kinds of decisions made by students, teachers, administrators, parents, and interested community people varied considerably as did the amount and kinds of power shared by these groups. In all cases there were students who did not care or know how to handle freedom and responsibility, and conflict between a "do your own thing" ethos and the desire for community was inevitable. Curiously enough, in the largely white, middle-class schools where the students had the most freedom, we found the least concern about developing more pluralistic education.

We think our analyses will shed light on these difficult problems and will indicate trends and guidelines for future innovators.

GLORIANNE WITTES
JOAN CHESLER
DALE CROWFOOT

Student Power

PART ONE

On the Spot

Observations and
Interviews

Franklin
High School,
Seattle *By Joan Chesler*

Franklin High School, a big, old four-story building in southeast Seattle, is like many large innercity schools, except for its new governing Senate composed primarily of teachers, students, and parents. Over the past decade its tenth- to twelfth-grade student population has undergone rapid racial and socio-economic change. In May 1971, about half (47 percent) of its 1,500 students were white, a fourth (26 percent) were black, and nearly a fourth (24 percent) were Oriental. The remainder (3 percent) were Filipino, Chicano, and American Indian. Most of the students live in the surrounding community—the legal attendance area—but a small percentage, both black and white, have transferred in to attend a desegregated school.

Ten to fifteen years ago Franklin was in a solidly middle-class neighborhood. Now it is inhabited by middle- and lower-income residents. The whites who remain apparently support racial balance at Franklin. Still, the number and percentage of black students increases yearly. The Oriental population is somewhat more stable, although a number of families from Hong Kong have resettled in the area, and there is tension between the "new" Chinese and the "old." Some other Oriental students, new arrivals from the Philippines, Samoa, and Japan, speak little or no English and require a special program in school. The turnover rate of the student body as a whole is unusually high. In 1970–71, it was 67 percent, or twice the normal 33 percent.

The teachers remain a more stable group, 40 percent of them having taught at Franklin for ten years or more. While most of the eighty-nine teachers were white, there were eleven blacks and five Orientals as well as one Filipino and one Chicano. More non-white teachers have been added since, bringing their number to a third of the staff. Of the eight administrators and counselors, two were black and none Oriental. The staff is traditionally educated and certified, 60 percent having B.A.s and 40 percent with M.A. degrees or their equivalent. The majority (70 percent) belong to the Seattle Teachers' Association, an affiliate of the N.E.A.

On the whole, the teachers appeared to be friendly, warm, and concerned. Those under thirty seemed to have an easy and *sympatico* rapport with their students, although close, personal friendships between students and teachers were rare, in part because the student-teacher ratio was high—one to twenty-two—including counselors and special service personnel. The administrators and counselors, a hand-picked group, were, for the most part, outstanding, talented, and committed.

Even with 1,500 students enrolled, the school was orderly. Throughout the day students not in class could meet upstairs in the student cafeteria for snacks and television or go outside in good weather. While the building is old and typical, the interior at least is cheerful. Classroom walls were enlivened with posters and prints. Overall, the pulse of the school was measured and moderate—it did not buzz, nor did it crawl. The depressing effect of Seattle's economic recession was readily apparent. Where earlier years had been disrupted with racial and political confrontations, 1971 was quiet.

INTERGROUP RELATIONS

A white school-community liaison agent described race relations as "careful—we tolerate each other." Most whites perceived little tension and little racism. As one white student described it:

> Well, there's . . . always some kind of racial fight, but they aren't really racial. They're just like one-to-one and stuff like that. Franklin isn't that way.

While white students reported "some" interracial mixing, black students perceived "little." Although blacks who desired social relationships with whites seemed to be able to establish them, many black students told black interviewers that they felt more hassled and discriminated against than their white or Oriental counterparts. There was more mixing between whites and Orientals, they said, then between whites and blacks.

Not surprisingly, black, white, and Oriental students perceived the extent of racism in the school differently. In a questionnaire, more than half the black students said they felt left out of activities because of their race; but few Oriental students (16 percent), and even fewer whites (6 percent), felt blacks were discriminated against. Black students were also more sensitive to discrimination against others. For example,

17 percent felt that whites were sometimes excluded, whereas only 6 percent of the whites and 3 percent of the Orientals agreed. Although black students considered some teachers prejudiced, more black students believed the staff was more aware of racism at school than whites or Orientals.

Most white teachers interviewed seemed quite satisfied with their relationships with black students. The more successful in this regard had conveyed their concern for black students by providing relevant curricula, individualized instruction, and independent study. They were open to alternative perceptions of social reality and were fair and firm in enforcing rules.

The white teachers who were less able to reach black students appeared to either overlook the pervasive effects of racism and treat all students alike or to expect less of blacks (and more of the Orientals). Some felt the first requirement of a satisfactory relationship with black students was order and quiet.

White students found it easier than teachers to have friendships with black students because they were peers. Interracial relationships, from the white students' point of view, were satisfactory on athletic teams and in various school and class activities. Yet a white student didn't expect the races to mix much on account of their different experiences: "Blacks have just gone through a whole different trip than whites have." Whites used the term interracial *mixing* far more than interracial *friendships*.

White girls, however, spoke casually about dating blacks:

> You are talking to a girl who has a black boyfriend. It's not unusual at all here at Franklin.

> It's no big thing. You see it all the way down the halls. You see interracial couples and everything.

A white teacher felt that the white girls "are damned if they do, and damned if they don't. . . . There's not much you can do as a teacher." Less frequently, white boys dated black girls. Because of the dating pattern, black girls often found themselves in serious conflict with some of the white girls and black boys. The administration responded with informal counseling of both black and white girls as well as by transferring several white girls.

The Orientals' relations with whites and blacks were somewhat less strained, although a fourth of the Oriental students said they felt discriminated against. While the three races tended to stay separate, Orientals and whites mixed more frequently than Orientals and blacks. The Oriental students were perceived as the school's "intellectuals" because of their academic standings and their presence on all major committees. The stereotype, many said, created a "halo effect"—a quiet Oriental was seen as "studious"; a quiet white or black was thought of as "just sitting there."

This pattern was beginning to change, however. Some Orientals were no longer academically oriented, tending to identify instead with hippie and Third World life styles. Although one Oriental teacher called them "crazy bastards who think they're white," some Oriental students felt relief in being freer to choose among a wider range of life styles. Their rebellion against being stereotyped and their apparent rejection of the need for respectability in whites' eyes seemed to make these tough "new" Chinese appear all the more attractive to others. One Oriental boy smiled as he told our Oriental interviewer that some Chinese groups were "whipping the ass" off blacks and whites. "I guess they know who's cool now," he said. Oriental girls have also rebelled by dating black males, to the anger of their parents and of black girls as well. Several Orientals acknowledged hostility from black students, but tensions between the two groups, on the whole, were covert.

Black students were more concerned with intragroup feelings than intergroup relations. Their focus was on black unity and their relationships with black teachers. Some were upset that a number of black teachers seemed "out of it," offering no informal means of support and making it harder than necessary for the black students. They were snobbish, aloof, and resistant to influence:

> You can't talk to them. They pump all that white stuff into you. . . . Talking to blacks is like talking to one of "them."

Many black students preferred to work with white teachers or counselors, although the preference was not universal. There was widespread agreement that black students not only needed to support one another more but also needed more support from the school in guidance, encouragement, skill training, and vocational development.

For some black students it was as much a question of class as it was of race:

> It's all based on class. . . . You bring the rich and poor together, and it's going to be hard for the poor people. . . . It's a known fact that rich people have a better chance of learning. . . . All these poor people coming in . . . they're not going to learn really.

The black faculty at Franklin, for the most part middle class, were by training and empathy more prepared to teach those who—regardless of race—were academically motivated and verbally skilled. As the school included more and more lower-income students, with different educational values and social interests, all teachers and counselors found their allegiances and skills severely challenged, especially the black teachers, from whom black students expected special support. As it was, the black staff was not a close group. Because of their small number and newness in the system, they were worried about their own job security. They didn't share ideas or feelings with one another, one black educator reported, and they didn't trust each other.

Most students liked their teachers but simultaneously criticized their outmoded curricula and inappropriate methodologies. Classes were boring, some said, and teachers apathetic. Most teachers did feel their energies were decreasing as their frustrations mounted but blamed students' laziness, poor motivation, and disinterest to account for their lack of participation. Commonly teachers reverted to the "tried and true" methods of instruction instead of teaching students to participate more actively in their own education by using more strenuous methodologies such as open discussions, simulations, and field trips.

While the majority (63 percent) of students indicated that teachers respected and listened to them, only about half as many (37 percent) felt that teachers really understood and helped them. Most student-teacher relationships were limited, apparently, to specific material under scrutiny or to disciplinary matters. While laughter and wisecracks were exchanged, no anger was. Most students did not ask for help, and conversation flowed more from teachers to students than vice versa.

Students seemed to feel that the administrators and counselors were fair but contacted them only when they were in trouble or had a problem. Several students expressed the need for more continuous contact.

Some teachers, of course, had achieved excellent rapport

with students. But their rapport sometimes provoked other teachers' suspicions and envy, polarizing some members of the staff:

> The polarization is even greater [now] than when we
> tried to reduce it years ago.

Teachers could sometimes be heard arguing in the lounges and lunchrooms about educational policy and curriculum, yet those who clashed, continued to ride in the same car pool and go fishing together. Perhaps only those with longstanding friendships could express political and educational differences. In general, one teacher said, there was little open disagreement. The norm was "don't pick on fellow teachers —just let things ride." Another declared:

> If there are sides, there's a small group that still hopes
> something can be done, and a larger group . . . kind of
> smiling at them as if it's a hopeless task.

Older teachers, who had taught at Franklin for ten or more years, expressed discomfort with the changes since 1968—a new principal and more flexible rules. They sensed a lack of direction and leadership. They wanted the principal to relate to them the way they themselves related to their students. They were in the minority, however. Most teachers were satisfied with the principal's style. Many, in fact, appreciated the lack of administrative interference in their teaching.

THE INSTRUCTIONAL SETTING

Franklin's curriculum included all the standard courses of a typical high school. Honors sections were scheduled in the English and Math Departments, and advanced elective courses were offered in other departments. In addition, there was English As a Second Language for the newly arrived foreign students, the FEAST program—a course in the mass production of foods, Afro-American History, the Minority Experience in American History, Law and Society, Japanese, Far Eastern History, and the African Ensemble in the Music Department. Only the Math Department offered individualized options for advanced or able students who had difficulty with the English language.

Students and teachers agreed the range of course offerings was adequate for college-bound students (some 60 percent of the student population), but not for those who planned to take jobs immediately after high school. Some teachers thought family pressures were forcing some students who would be more suited for vocational training to take college preparatory courses; others felt that if a wider variety of interesting vocational programs were offered, students would take them. (Occupational training and career guidance have since become Franklin's first priority.) Some black students felt they were counseled into vocational programs when they could succeed in college.

Teachers were more dissatisfied with the curriculum than students. Nearly 60 percent of the students said they were satisfied; only 25 percent of the teachers were. Quite a few teachers felt that the school wasn't doing "a good job" for average students, the quiet, "invisible" ones who have "learned to play the game well." Others felt the "capable students" had been "blighted!"

> They don't rebel. They accept. They do the tasks, they get the grades, but they're completely uninteresting people.

Black students voiced some concerns about both the range and content of the courses offered. One felt the course in

American Contemporary Problems, for example, rarely discussed problems relevant to blacks. When issues of significance to blacks *were* raised, the white students talked or laughed and did not contribute. When black students brought up black problems, he added, they were told those problems would be handled later. Another was angry that there were no black literature classes. The African Ensemble course was popular, however. A security guard praised it as "something to show that blacks have real talent."

The development of black talent was a prime concern of one black administrator. In her conversations with black students, she repeatedly said:

> You really aren't anywhere, no matter how much moving and shaking you do, nor how many things you innovate . . . until we have our own lawyers who can become judges and policy makers who can be movers and shakers in the whole delivery of justice. . . .

To accelerate development of black students' motivation, she pointed to the need not only for more black teachers but for more skilled teachers, both black and white, who asked the right questions and didn't let their students get away with not working.

In general students and teachers both agreed that courses were repetitive and not properly sequenced. Students offered a variety of explanations for the boredom so prevalent in classes, especially in the required courses. Some students faulted the teachers:

> You're putting traditional teachers in a nontraditional school, and it doesn't work. You need teachers to fit the school.

> It's too easy to get good grades. I never have to work.

Other themes were touched on: student and teacher styles were not optimally matched; relevance and contemporaneity were occasionally overworked; and teachers needed to provide a clearer, more challenging structure of expectations and demands.

More teachers than students thought that courses had built-in racial and class biases and were not related to life outside the school. More students than teachers thought their specific interests were not adequately represented in the curriculum. Teachers thought the school was doing a very good job preparing students for college, but students rated it only average. Both agreed students should have more influence on curricula.

Highly motivated students benefited from the more freely structured classes and readily acknowledged their responsibility for their own education:

> Franklin hasn't failed me, because it offers the opportunities, and if I don't take them, then it's my fault.

Only in the advanced classes, however, did students exercise some minimal influence over the content of courses. In the advanced Spanish classes, for example, students choose the novels they read. In theory, one student said:

> Most teachers will do what you want them to, but not always in practice.

> Remember our teacher, sixth period? She told us, "You pick the subjects you want for this quarter, and I'll teach it to you." And so everybody was picking out the subjects that they wanted, and she turned around and said, "I'm going to teach you creative writing." And after going through all this big thing.

Several teachers tried letting students teach class for one or two days at a time, probably to make very specifically prepared presentations. Only one teacher considered teaching students how to teach or that to take responsibility for their learning was a curricular goal. He felt that the formal content should be "secondary to getting kids to think and make decisions."

Some students felt they were too lazy to work on bringing about needed changes unless the class was so terrible that it was worth the hassle. The changes students most often suggested were: adding more electives, particularly in vocational areas, and courses in ecology and human relations because "people at this school are really starting to get into people." Teachers were more concerned with the broader educational context. One suggested eliminating the grading system; another, introducing a broad interdisciplinary approach to the liberal arts. Many teachers expressed the need to coordinate curricular innovations and, even more emphatically, the need to establish clear, cohesive priorities.

DEVELOPMENT OF THE SENATE

Before the change in governance, Franklin had been the scene of considerable unrest. The three major racial groups had barely tolerated one another. The former principal had been labeled a racist. Most students had felt uninvolved in school affairs. The situation came to a head in the spring of 1968 when a spontaneous and loosely organized coalition of black students confronted the administration with a number of demands, and a group of parents and teachers moved to oust the principal. Several changes followed. A grievance procedure for dissatisfied students was set up. The faculty formed a "soul search group." A new principal was installed the next fall.

By the spring of 1969, a cabinet to advise the principal had been established, which was composed of students and teachers elected by their peers, and two workshops funded by the state's N.E.A. had been attended by all the staff as well as by some students and some community members. Shortly after, students in the Principal's Cabinet were given voting rights—something never done before in the school district. The forerunner of the Senate to come, the Cabinet brought about a number of changes including: an optional pass-fail system, a pilot program enabling students to evaluate their teachers, the establishment of student and teacher lounges, the formation of a student-teacher-administrator committee to write an attendance policy, and the painting of the school interior in bright and cheerful colors. Yet the Cabinet had no formal powers; it was advisory only.

During this period the idea of power-sharing emerged as a potent vehicle for improving school conditions, particularly the idea of teachers and students as well as community representatives sharing power with the school administration. Teachers looked for models in other schools and learned of none. As the faculty grew increasingly interested, one of the counselors contacted a trainer accredited by the National Training Laboratory who worked at the University of Michigan. He agreed to lead a workshop and, as orientation, sent a taped discussion about the various issues facing participants in a shared-power structure.

About sixty students, teachers, and administrators, along with several school guards, attended the first session; about 150 community persons and students turned out for the next evening's open house. Task groups worked on curriculum, school governance, teacher evaluation by students, and students' rights. Several reported that this January workshop was the "key encouragement" for the Senate's development.

The liberals among the students, teachers, administrators, and community members continued working together as a planning group. Through the summer of 1970, the planning group, whose thirty active members were divided almost evenly between students and staff, attended two labs that focused on the skills, concepts, and issues involved in change. Initially the adults feared that the students would vote as a bloc. However, no solid student bloc developed. Instead student-teacher and student-community alliances emerged. All in all, the group seems to have worked well together as the plan for a Senate took shape, and a Constitution was presented to the school. The principal would retain his authority, but the Senate would share in decisions affecting such vital matters as curriculum, student-teacher relationships, and discipline. Many said, "It won't work," and some felt the teachers hadn't time to participate adequately, yet there was no real or organized opposition.

Students favored the Senate because they wanted new courses, the opportunity to select their own teachers, and the right to speak directly to teachers about their teaching methods and classes. Teachers wanted a greater voice in policy-making and curriculum.

In November 1970, the Senate's Constitution was ratified, first by the students then by the teachers and administrators. The Seattle City School Board and the central office also approved it, having supported the concept from the beginning. The teachers' union raised no objections, for although student evaluation of teachers was threatening, it was not an integral part of the governance structure.

Elections to the Senate were held in January 1971. Although student leaders reported that they had difficulty persuading teachers to run, and teachers said the same about the students, all positions were filled. Several weeks later the Senate began its work.

As the school's formal policy-making body, the Senate's membership was drawn from all groups that played a role in the school. Of its thirty-three members, sixteen were students, eleven were staff (nine teachers, one administrator, and one member of the noncertified staff), and five were members of the neighborhood community. In addition, the principal served as an *ex-officio* member of the Senate's Executive Committee and attended all Senate meetings.

The election of each group differed. Community representatives were elected by the Citizen's Advisory Council of the school. Most of these elected in 1971 were parents of Franklin students, although this was not a prerequisite. Staff members were elected by their peers, as were the students, but half the students were elected for specific "position seats" and half were elected "at large." The unusual format, according to the Constitution, was designed to "allow all minority and/or interest groups a fair chance of being elected to the Senate." Racial balance, without a quota system, was the goal, but a goal that was never made explicit or clear. Not surprisingly, then, after the first election, whites were over-represented. The distribution improved in later years as the white student population decreased.

Members serve for one year, although they can be dismissed if they miss three consecutive meetings. By May 1971, despite poor attendance records, this option had not been exercised. In later years it was, and absentees voluntarily forfeited their seats.

The Constitution established four standing committees: Curriculum, Student-Staff Relationships, Due Process and Hearings, and an Executive Committee. The last, composed of the principal, Senate officers, and standing committee chairmen, functions as a decision-making body between Senate meetings, draws up the agenda for Senate meetings, and supervises the nomination and election of Senate members for the following year.

In addition, an ad hoc Ways and Means Committee was appointed to study the problem of extortion and physical violence, and a temporary committee was drawn together to organize support for an upcoming levy, which passed in June.

THE FIRST SIX MONTHS

By May 1971, after its first six months of operation, the Senate had made some headway. The Committee on Due Process and Hearings (three students, one certificated staff member, and one community member) had drafted a Students' Bill of Rights, which was subsequently approved by the Senate. It had also held hearings on the matter of undercover narcotics agents enrolled as students and documented the system's ineffectiveness in preventing the sale and use of narcotics during school. As a result, letters from the Senate were sent to the Seattle School Board, the Mayor, and the Superintendent informing them that no one—narcotics agents included—would be allowed in the school under false pretenses. While committee members were proud of their research on undercover agents, at least one felt the work had resulted in little more than "an idle threat"—a letter only. No official response was ever made, but undercover agents have not been sent to the school since.

The Committee on Student-Staff Relationships, which must

be chaired by a student and include at least two students and one faculty member, had set up a subcommittee to study the attendance policy, and it concerned itself with the smoking policy as well. It ruled that the two teachers' lounges should be divided between smokers and nonsmokers, but had been unable to find an indoor area where students could legally smoke. This angered several students and teachers, adding to their cynicism about the Senate.

The Curriculum Committee, potentially the Senate's most powerful group, had neither exercised nor tested its areas of influence. Students who wanted to introduce new courses or change scheduling had not tried to work through the committee nor been encouraged to. Students and teachers on the committee had been unable to agree on what were its legitimate concerns. Meeting only three or four times, it had taken little initiative and—more importantly—had not challenged the authority of the faculty's Instructional Council, with which it was supposed to have a close link. The Committee was still inactive in 1973.

Most Senate members were dissatisfied with the problems they had chosen to work on. They had found no gut issues, none with strong emotional appeal. The narcotics agents issue was meaningful to some, but not for long. The smoking rule for the teachers' lounges was viewed as significant by some because the teachers accepted the Senate's authority, but most teachers thought it petty, silly, and a waste of the Senate's time.

In general, that first spring Senate members felt discouraged by their slow progress and by the unglamorous, difficult administrative tasks they were involved in. It upset them that, "very few people follow the Senate or are interested in it." Some in the original planning group, who had worked hard over the two years, were worn out. Some Senate members feared the slow, dull tone of the Senate was a product of its structure and function. Others were sure it was just a slump, the natural anticlimax of a new organization getting into gear. The principal saw it as growing pains:

> I'm not discouraged myself . . . but the faculty and students—they expected the thing to go into orbit right away. . . . I think we are begining to realize that genuine involvement of people in policy-making is much more complex a process than most people perceive it to be. . . .

Many agreed it was a slow learning process. A teacher on the Senate said:

> I guess what we've experienced is the cumbersomeness of democracy. You lose patience. You want things to happen faster.

A member of the noncertificated staff spoke the same way:

> Well, it seems that we're really not getting any place. There's so much talk, and we haven't really come up with anything of importance. . . . I think the reason is that we were doing, and we had to learn how to do things, the mechanics of running these meetings.

Learning the mechanics proceeded by trial and error. For example, the committees met irregularly and inefficiently at first. By May, however, they had established regular meeting times during lunch hours, gave one course credit to students who attended, and found this was working better. Students and teachers who could not attend after school were able to during lunch times. Leaders emerged, and gradually committee members—students and teachers—were learning to organize themselves and work together.

Tests of Power. School members not involved in the Senate, however, questioned the real extent of the Senate's power. By May 1971, there had been little or no resistance to any of the Senate's decisions; the letter on undercover agents had caused no ripples, the teachers had complied with the smoking policy set for their lounges, and the administration had bent over backwards to be helpful and supportive. But the tests of power had been few and limited.

Several reasons for this were suggested. One administrator believed that neither teachers nor students wanted too much power because they were not willing to take on major responsibilities. The inactivity of the Curriculum Committee, when everyone thought curriculum revision was a top priority, was cited as evidence.

Others felt the Senate had not tested its powers because students and teachers didn't know what power meant or how to use it. A student member of the Senate pointed to the difficulty:

> Just because we have shared power . . . doesn't mean we can solve problems any more effectively than a principal can. I'm just discovering that now.
>
> I've learned that . . . it's easier to identify the problem than to come up with a solution. . . . The solution gets all bogged down in personal problems of people —all sorts of things come into play.

Some suggested it was because the Senate had no "bad guy" to resist. A community representative explained:

> One of the most serious difficulties we have in trying to assert our power in this school is that the principal is such a great guy. We miss the enemy terribly. If we just had the bad villain who was doing everything wrong, then we could say, "Boy, we're going to do it

this way, he's doing it all wrong. . . ." But with such a fine, saint-like person like him, he's for everything we're for. . . . It's just the terrible immovability of the bureaucracy that defeats you and confuses you. He's with you all the way. . . .

The Senate president agreed:

The students have nothing to fight against, or rally around, or work against. The administration does almost anything you want them to. We have an open campus, people smoke where they want—except in the classroom—there's no dress code or hair length, you can skip fifteen classes, very few kids get suspended. Everybody is satisfied with what they have. They don't need the Senate.

While the principal voluntarily agreed to share his power with the Senate on an informed basis, his authority had been left intact. A student explained the planners' strategy:

I went down to the school district lawyer. When he looked me in the eye and said, "The principal can't delegate his powers to a group like that. It won't work; we won't allow it. . . ." I said, "Frankly, how can we get around this?" He said, "Well, what you can do is get a verbal agreement from your principal that he will agree with any decision the Senate makes." And it just so happens that we have the type of principal who would do that. . . . [He] is going to be here for a while and if we can establish the responsible body that makes good decisions and that represents Franklin . . . then the next principal . . . will have to deal with the Senate. The downtown office will not send a principal who cannot live with the Senate as [our principal] has lived with it.

The principal agreed with the strategy because he felt that

confrontation with the School Board might jeopardize the entire concept. Initially, almost all of the Constitution's planners agreed, but now some are upset by the result:

> We have a bad psychological base. There's a little paragraph in the Constitution that says the principal's function will not change. So that, in a sense, we're. . . behaving *as if* we're some sort of an advisory body, which shouldn't challenge the administration because we'll get turned down anyway. (Teacher)

> [The Senate] should be free to think out and make policy without considering whether it will or will not be vetoed by the principal. I don't feel that you can get any free expression when you always on one side are thinking, "Will it get by?" . . . It's kind of like a company union. (Senate radical)

> The school isn't a shared power school. (Student president)

While some Senate members felt restricted by the principal's broad legal powers, some found security in knowing the principal could reverse any decision he disagreed with. The administrators are widely perceived as the most powerful group in the school, and the fact that the principal's legal powers remain unchanged has only increased others' perception of his already substantial power. What would the principal do if he disagreed with a policy decision?

> Well, to the degree that I can, I'd let the Senate make the mistakes—if I thought they were mistakes—we'd go ahead with it. If I thought that it would be an irretrievable mistake, then I wouldn't let them. I would exercise the authority which is vested and which I can't delegate—as the School Board explained it to me—to not move in that direction but to get the Senate to come up with an alternative.

As a member of the Executive Committee, the principal recommends items for the Senate's agenda but tries not to lead or dominate. He finds this a difficult balance to achieve:

> I'm not the one that determines the agenda, really. But I realize that as a member of the Senate it's my responsibility to bring in a share of the agenda. The dilemma is I've got to be sure that by referring agenda items to the Senate that I don't dominate it. . . . The Senate has sort of got to find its role itself, rather than being told what its role is by me in the way that I bring agenda items to them.

Some believe the Senate's insecurity about its power *vis-à-vis* the principal stems from the simple fact that since he voluntarily shared his authority with the Senate, the Senate never really wrested power away from him and therefore never tested the limits of the principal's power in the process of power sharing and redistribution. As a result, each current issue in part must test the power relationship between the principal and the Senate—especially since it rests on informal agreement. Yet by 1973, no power tests had developed.

Another area of potential conflict is between the Senate's Curriculum Committee and the faculty's Instructional Council. Any policy changes passed by the Senate related to the instructional program "must also be approved" by the Council, a powerful (and exclusive) body:

> It makes suggestions, which are very, very often accepted. They run the mechanics of the school. They're the strongest body that we have, with the exception of the Senate, and they may be stronger because they have tradition to back them up.

Although the existence of the Senate clarified the faculty Council's role as a *recommending* body, the Council feels it should persist as a separate body until the Senate gains far more power in the school. Council members perceived no conflicts of interest until that time arrives. Yet the Council is seen as "conservative, bent on maintaining the status quo," and the Senate seems more oriented toward change.

Several policies with clear curriculum implications had been sent to the Senate for approval: a revised attendance policy, which permitted up to fifteen absences from class, and a restructured six-period rather than seven-period day. The principal had supported their inclusion on the Senate's agenda. By 1973, a restructured day permitting long and short periods had been passed—and rescinded after one semester, when the District found it too costly. The attendance policy was still in a draft stage.

Questions about the legitimacy of grading, the relevance of the courses offered, and the quality of instruction had been discussed only briefly—and then dropped.

Within the Senate itself, students and teachers agreed, the administrators, again, formed the most powerful group. Students and teachers had only moderate influence, they said, and community representatives little. By 1973, it is worth noting, students' interest in shared power, as an issue, had waned.

A few were disillusioned and angry that the administration still had the most powerful role in the Senate. One who had been active in initiating the Senate declared:

> I'm disillusioned—decided to stay out of it. I know where the power is. To me it's just another establishment deal. . . . The fact that you have students on there—you know it's the good students. You don't see any of the really poor students, they wouldn't be caught dead on something like that.

Some felt the administration was covertly manipulating them:

> I think the issues are being selected. I feel there's a
> great deal of manipulation to allow and . . . people
> behind the scene making power plays.

Yet, as noted, there were some—older, more traditional teachers—who felt the Senate had left the principal too little power:

> I have some reservations about . . . the dilution of
> authority, so that *no one* is responsible and that noth-
> ing ever gets done and no one is at fault and no one is
> responsible for any action and it comes from a vague
> sort of a group out there which is the Senate—com-
> munity, students, administration, faculty—a vague sort
> of group. . . . It ultimately becomes *no* leadership.

The findings of our questionnaire showed that more students than teachers thought teachers had a great deal of influence, and—interestingly enough—more teachers than students thought students had a great deal of influence. Both wanted their own group to have more.

Degrees of Participation. The degree of participation in the Senate varied with each group. Students did not participate as much as adults. One student attended few meetings, spoke little, and, as she put it, "sat back and let the program ride." Students mentioned several barriers to their participation in the Senate: it was too time-consuming; it was boring, ineffective, "a drag." Yet they approved of its existence: "I haven't used it yet, but I'm glad it's there."

Students and teachers disagreed about how much students gained from participation in the Senate. Teachers thought students had learned more than the students themselves reported. Many student members did not seem to believe that the Senate was a viable body or that it would benefit them.

Some felt they lacked the skill, energy, and personal power to make it really work. Some did not trust the adults and so did not participate. Most student members addressed teachers by their last names, while teachers called the students by their first. Although some students were more informal when invited to be, their informality lasted only as long as the Senate sessions; afterwards they returned to using the teachers' last names. When students heard teachers addressing the principal by *his* last name, in turn, it corroborated the hierarchical structure of relationships already present in the Senate.

Teachers and staff members admitted they dominated the Senate sessions, but added they didn't know how else to make it work. Some spent "fifteen hours a month, easily" on Senate and subcommittee meetings and found it "time-consuming much beyond our original expectation." Tired and drained, they hoped to structure the time into the school day, perhaps by giving teachers class load credit for participation. (Teachers were later given clearance to use their duty period for Senate work.) Many felt that as an extra-curricular activity the Senate was not as effective as it might be and perhaps doomed to failure. A few of the activist teachers planned to return to full-time teaching as soon as their term was over.

Parental or community involvement was also difficult and time-consuming. Only two or three parents participated in the Senate, mainly in the discussion about drugs. One school-community liaison agent reported he had never discussed the Senate with parents. He felt that the parents generally were unaware of the Senate's existence.

The one representative of the noncertificated staff had a special problem. She had asked to have an alternate replace her when she could not attend, but the Senate did not grant her request, although the administrators were allowed alternates. The Senate wrestled briefly with the contradiction, then dropped it as other work proceeded.

Who Represented Whom? There was strong agreement among those in the Senate that members represented only themselves and not their constituencies—if any. Ostensibly the sixteen student members represented the entire student body of 1,500 as a whole, nine teachers their eighty colleagues, and the five community members "the" community, despite its wide diversity. But since no groups or blocs had been organized to support different political stances (and still had not by 1973), Senate members assumed they were elected to represent their own personal ideologies.

Most members, it was agreed, represented "liberal" interest in change. Some outside the Senate were suspicious of the members' motives; whites suspected them of wanting change for change's sake; blacks suspected them of not having black interests at heart. Many blacks, for example, stated that for them the Senate was not vital.

> The Senate definitely is not important for black students.

> They don't come because it won't do any good. All we do is talk about smoking. I signed up because I thought it was going to be different.

> Whites run the whole show.

In face of the broader social problems black students contend with, the issues the Senate selected were seen as petty and insignificant; only the questions raised by the undercover narcotics agents involved the interest of black students.

Since members felt they represented no group or bloc but only themselves as individuals, they rarely represented or advocated any group's interest. The assumption was, "We're all in this together, so let's work on problems whose solutions will benefit everybody." This made it difficult for a black to be "black enough" to represent all blacks. It prevented the Asian Coalition for Equality representative from voicing a single-interest viewpoint. It inhibited the noncertificated staff member from voicing her opinion on "educational matters" because she felt only teachers and administrators knew enough. In fact, she was never asked her viewpoint precisely for that reason.

One student member of the Senate complained that students weren't bringing issues to the Senate, despite the fact that some had problems the Senate could work on. But for Senate members to represent their possible constituencies effectively, the flow of information to and from the Senate would have to improve. Most found communication between the Senate and the rest of the school poor. The Senate published its minutes, but the minutes recorded decisions only—not the discussions. The daily bulletin publicizing Senate meetings and events had limited effectiveness.

Impact of The Senate. In discussing the impact of the Senate on its members, one student said:

> In a traditional classroom I'm more dissatisfied now. Maybe it's because of my age or because I'm on the Senate. Now I'm asking, "Why are we doing all this?" . . . . It's made me doubt a lot of things. Because if you begin to doubt why the principal should have all the authority, then you begin to doubt why the teacher should have all the authority. . . . But there's a danger. . . . You've got to be careful that students don't try and control things that they're not able to control. Teachers still know an awful lot— they sure know a lot more than I do.

Several students said they had learned how to obtain *real* information and not rely on rumor or hearsay. To investigate the regulations on smoking and the principal's legal authority, for example, they had gone to the central office and the school's legal counsel, and they had learned how vague some regulations really were. Many said they had learned how to work through official red tape and how to organize politically.

The Senate's impact, however, was restricted to its members. The larger school-community knew little about it and was not affected much by its activities or decisions. Some students confused the Senate with the old Student Council, but most had some general notion of what it was. All the teachers knew of the Senate's existence, but most considered themselves poorly informed about its activities. A majority of students (nearly 70 percent) thought the Senate made decisions about curriculum, but less than half the teachers (40 percent) agreed. Only a third of the teachers and a fourth of the students thought the Senate made decisions about the evaluation of teachers and classes. Even fewer believed the Senate made decisions about testing and grading, hiring teachers or administrators, or the school budget.

The majority felt that students had neither increased their political skills nor gained any more control over what they were learning. Only a few students, and none of the teachers, believed the Senate affected students' interest in school.

As the 1971 spring term ended, many in the Senate were tired, discouraged, and pessimistic, although some hoped the Senate would prove more powerful in coming years. As a whole, the school was quiet. Students "are tired of yelling and demanding," a teacher said. "They're tired of complaining, and they're tired of learning, and they're tired of living."

Franklin's atmosphere today is neither political nor academic. It's a place, a job, unhassled, occasionally warm, sometimes even exciting. "If you want to learn here, you can," college-bound as well as turned-off students said. For students the tone is primarily social. The easygoing, permissive atmosphere is one reason they enjoy or tolerate Franklin. Even students who hate school think Franklin is better than most, though "you can't hardly do anything." For them, the freedom and leniency of rules under the new Senate do not counteract the oppressiveness of the institution itself.

Metro
High School,
Chicago By *Glorianne Wittes*

On State Street, heading away from the lake and the spaciousness of Chicago's Michigan Avenue and within sight of the el, among small, forlorn stores, burlesque houses, and dingy hotels, sits the headquarters of Metro (Chicago Public High School for Metropolitan Studies Center). The old office building gives no indication it houses a school. There are no locked doors or fences, no "Visitors Report to the Office" or "No Trespassing" signs. Metro values its intimate connection with the community and encourages visitors and informality.

Inside all is bright, comfortable, and airy. The school occupies three floors, and most partitions have been removed to form large open spaces, divided by desks and chairs into work or lounging areas. The walls, painted coral, orange, bright blue, or yellow, are covered haphazardly with grafitti, photographs, paintings, notices, and newspaper clippings. Anyone wishing to can add a contribution.

It is a homey place where one immediately feels relaxed

but alert. The space is arranged to foster interaction, informality, and a sense of community. People can relate as people rather than teachers, students, and peers. There are no closed classrooms or private offices. Intimate seating arrangements provide space for quiet conversation around office desks, coke machines, and lunch tables. Passersby are not sealed off, but privacy seems to be respected.

The second and fourth floors of the building are used as study and office areas. The third floor is the common lounge for staff and students alike. Here, among coke machines, card tables, picnic tables, and record players, Metro students cluster in groups of two, three or more, joined from time to time by teachers who come to chat or "play." Occasionally it is hard to spot the teachers since some look no older than the students.

The general feeling is one of vitality and purposiveness. Even when no formal classes are in session, students' "off hours" are not spent aimlessly but seem directed at having fun or learning. Teachers appear less relaxed in their leisure moments, but they spend them with the students rather than by themselves. Polarization between black and white students is immediately apparent, but where blacks and whites *do* interact, it is with spontaneity and ease.

Students are amazingly cordial toward visitors, almost as if they are receiving them in their own home. Communicative, gracious, and completely unperturbed, they either incorporate guests into their conversations or politely ignore them as they go on with their business. The staff, initially, is more reserved.

The atmosphere—social, unstructured, permissive—exudes warmth. People slap each other affectionately on the back. Teachers put an arm around a student's shoulder or hug a student in exuberance or camaraderie. First names are used consistently. Anger is also freely expressed, verbally and non-verbally, appropriately and inappropriately—it's all accepted.

It is Metro's principal who sets the tone of accessibility and warmth. Known as Nate to one and all, he strolls through the lounges and study areas, rapping with teachers, students, file clerks, and visitors. His desk, in an open office area, is usually surrounded by people. The fact that he is black allows him a rapport with black students seldom seen in traditional schools, and this rapport extends to whites as well.

OUTSIDE CONSULTANTS

Experimental schools are occasionally started by educational innovators who develop a proposal and then seek out a school system in which to implement it. Metro was launched with this strategy. A group of young consultants at the Urban Research Corporation in Chicago designed a model for an urban school-without-walls and, after six months of negotiation, persuaded the Chicago Board of Education, and Chicago businessmen as well, to support it within the public school system.

Metro opened in February 1970, after a summer pilot program had proved successful. Its 150 students—50 percent white and 50 percent nonwhite (largely black)—were drawn by lottery from the metropolitan area. By its second year there were 350 students and a faculty of twenty-one, of whom 50 percent were nonwhite. The Urban Research consultants were not only involved in designing the school but in selecting the staff and students, developing the administrative procedures, contacting participating organizations, and planning curriculum and staff development. Yet, to their credit, they managed to remain in a consultant role rather than assume a controlling one.

The Urban Research team offered a particular advantage in one strategic area. A major problem for Metro has been its relationship to the district school superintendents and the central administration, whose imposition of traditional procedures and denial of adequate autonomy have been constant issues of strain. However, the Urban Research team's contractual role as consultants to the school board, rather than employees, helped Metro circumvent many roadblock procedures during its early development. The consultants were able to deal directly with the general superintendent, for example, rather then people at the district level, which the principal of Metro could not have legitimately done.

By the spring of 1971, the Metro staff felt it had gained enough experience to run Metro without the consultants' help. The crisis of a temporary eviction in March had brought the consultants' power to the foreground, and although the staff and the consultants worked together harmoniously during the crisis, the relationship began to deteriorate rapidly afterward. Some resented the consultants, others defended them. There was considerable variance among the teachers about the U.R.C.'s continuing role, as the following comments show:

> I guess I'm ambivalent about U.R.C. . . . . The guys are pretty sharp people. . . . Frequently the workings of the school have almost been halted by them . . . or we've had to go through incredible kinds of things to go around decisions they've made. I feel they're not really receptive to listening to what we say . . . and come on strongly with their own ideas, which I personally find a hindrance.

I guess there is a strong feeling that the staff's priorities and U.R.C.'s priorities are different.

U.R.C. makes recommendations. Instead of going up the line, they go around the end. This has been a source of real irritation and a source of a lot of problems that hopefully might be worked out once we're on our own.

I think that the way their roles are set up is a role that is called for. . . . In a sense there's a parent-child war, where the child has to rebel. He feels his own power; he might get mad at times.

Metro's principal gave unstinting praise to the U.R.C. team for their guidance but felt their job was done. The consultants themselves were certain, and had been from the very beginning, that their function in Metro was to facilitiate its independence and reduce its reliance on outsiders. They had, in fact, restricted their new contract to a six-month rather than a year-long period, so as not to force a longer relationship. They had anticipated their eventual rejection by the staff. They even valued it, despite the sadness they felt at having to let go, as their comments reveal:

You're not successful if you haven't helped staff to kick you out. This is a symptom of their growth.

If you're fortunate enough to get strong-willed, opinionated teachers, then their growth to autonomy should be transferable. It should communicate itself to board and parents and show them as strong and self-sufficient.

This is hard for me, much as I value it happening. I've so much of myself invested in this school. This points up the useful role we play here as scapegoat, middleman . . . but it's painful!

In the spring of 1971, the consultants announced that when their contract ended in June they were leaving the U.R.C. to start their own firm in Chicago (Center for New Schools). This relieved the staff who had thought the consultants would try to negotiate a new contract and retain leadership of Metro's directions indefinitely. Recognition of their motives in leaving Metro renewed the staff's appreciation of them, even though they did not want a *continuing* contract with any consultant group.

PARTICIPATING ORGANIZATIONS

Metro's relationship with participating organizations has been marked by mounting enthusiasm by the organizations. Some, such as Illinois Bell, Peoples Gas, Western Electric, and various cultural institutions, came into the program immediately. Their immediate support helped convince the board that a school-without-walls was a pragmatic possibility. Some organizations hesitated, letting others run the risk before taking the plunge themselves. Some were skeptical that they or the students had anything to gain by such participation. The difficulties they anticipated were real.

For example, what happens when employees are freed to teach students who show up once or twice and never again? Or what happens when students' boisterousness, dress, or even the color of their skin offends some employees or clients? How well will the program be coordinated? Will there be adequate communication and supervision between Metro and the participating organizations? Metro was also concerned about such issues and devoted considerable time to their solution.

Despite the difficulties encountered, the number of partici-

pating organizations has grown from 60 to 140, of which 65
are businesses. They now conduct about 40 percent of Metro's
classes. A Participating Organizations Council has been meeting regularly since April 1971, to develop closer relationships
between the organizations and the school and to increase the
resources available to the school.

"I was sceptical in the beginning," recalled the Curator of
Education at the Shedd Aquarium, "but it's been a most en-
lightening thing for me and my staff. Participating organizations are profiting with the students, or maybe more than the
students.

"No apologies are needed by Metro for anything," an
N.B.C. executive said. "It's fantastic. I challenge the Board of
Education to insure that this program continues!"

There has been some argument whether or not Chicago
can support more Metro-type programs or a vastly expanded
Metro. Some of the Metro staff, including the principal,
fear they may end up fighting over the same resources.
Others in the participating organizations feel there are count-
less resources in the city yet to be tapped and that there is
considerable room for expansion. Metro participants, however, do not see their school as a spawner of other little
Metros. They feel that no single model, however successful,
can answer all the needs in education. They would like to
expand Metro to two or more autonomous, *small* centers,
each experimenting with new variations of curriculum and
governance, but not until Metro's relationship with the central
administration is considerably improved.

> We can't take care of what we have without all kinds
> of heartache. To add more would be suicidal until the
> Central Office learns to support what they've already
> got.

EARLY STRUGGLES WITH THE
CENTRAL ADMINISTRATION

A Temporary Eviction. Metro's eviction from it's headquarters by the fire department in March 1971, underscores the kind of bureaucratic behavior that hampered its development during the first year. Eviction posed serious problems. Without a headquarters, the communication link between students, teachers, and participating organizations was broken. Immediately upon hearing of the fire department's order to vacate, Metro requested the board to bring the present quarters up to code standards as quickly as possible and to provide temporary classroom space elsewhere. It also outlined its requirements for a new headquarters, in case one would be needed.

Three ad hoc committees composed of students and teachers were set up to hunt for temporary classroom space and permanent headquarters space as well. Consultants, parents, and members of participating organizations joined in the search. Within forty-eight hours after their eviction, they had found 181 "classrooms" where they continued to meet until the crisis was resolved in May. Class locations had to be telephoned to students individually each morning by their teachers. It was truly a school-without-walls—and an administrative nightmare.

Metro tried to use the crisis and the consternation of the Metro community of students, staff, parents, and participating organizations to force some changes in relationships with the central administration. A new representative Policy Board was formed to serve as its official voice and to act as bargaining agent with the school board. Through this, it was expected, Metro would have an apparatus to replace the Urban Research consultants' informal influence with the superintendent and board. The Policy Board's first task was to improve operating procedures between Metro and the central administration. On April 2, in a letter to the superintendent, it offered several solutions to both Metro's procedural and space problems and requested a meeting with the superintendent and his immediate deputy no later than April 6, so that a central headquarters space might be occupied in time for the school term beginning April 12. The superintendent, however, passed the matter down to the area and district superintendents, the very ones in the hierarchy whom Metro had seen as impeding its progress and whose authority had frequently been bypassed before; the meeting with them was not arranged until April 15. While the superintendent was supportive of Metro, he chose to back the current structure rather than create new procedures for Metro's operations. The procedures requested by Metro included an experimental schools expediter to replace the area and district superintendent's office and more financial autonomy.

The space crisis was resolved with Metro's return early in May to its original headquarters, which had been brought up to code requirements. The procedural problems, however, remained.

Delayed Accreditation.　Metro's yearlong lack of accreditation was caused by the central administration's delay in processing Metro's letter of application to the North Central Association. Most of Metro's students and staff thought the delay was deliberate. The Urban Research consultants attributed it to the reluctance of the board to approve and sign Metro's accreditation letter because, according to the board, it was too "wordy" and needed drastic revision. When the letter was finally approved, with only slight changes, it was too late for the North Central Association to act upon it at its annual meeting in April. Thus accreditation was delayed a year.

The worst consequences of the fiasco, however, were averted. The superintendent arranged for the graduating seniors to receive diplomas from their original high schools. After Metro was accredited in 1972, they received diplomas from Metro as well and now have two to hang on the wall.

Two Centers in One. In the fall of 1971, Metro expanded. It was a precarious business. Two hundred new students and ten new staff were to have moved into a new center, housed in a separate location. The old students and staff were to remain in the original center. The centers were to be completely autonomous, each with its own curriculum and programs. But the board did not come up with a separate site, and a compromise was reached to house the two centers on separate floors of Metro headquarters, with the third floor used as a common lounge and study quarters. The compromise threatened to split the staff apart.

In practice the two centers idea never worked out. They became competitive, as students played the two faculties against each other, and jealousy and rivalry mounted between the staffs. Moreover, the physical proximity prevented genuine differentiation and autonomy. By the end of the school year there was no longer any semblance of two separate centers, and the staff was left with many wounds to heal.

THE METRO PROGRAM

Metro's planners believed that the possibilities for a meaningful education are enhanced when education occurs in real life situations, including the businesses, cultural institutions, and neighborhoods of the city. Students, they felt, can learn from people with varied skills and interests—lawyers, electricians, artists, newspaper reporters—and gain from them a rich and individualized education. Thus, Metro's curriculum is organized around three forms of educational experience: (1) individual job placements, (2) learning units, and (3) counseling groups.

While the program is designed to use the entire community as a learning laboratory, the basic unit is considered to be the "fairly small learning community of teachers and students . . . to which the students relate." This community of learners is to provide "both constant support and constant evaluation feedback to the student regarding his directions for learning." Students are involved in making the basic decisions concerning their learning, and the diversity of their backgrounds is considered an educational resource in itself and part of the program.

The school year is divided into four cycles, each ten weeks long. The school day is made up of four periods, and students are expected to enroll for a minimum of sixteen class periods per week, including a counseling group and physical education. This schedule allows four class periods during the week for independent study or individual placement. A student may enroll for more than sixteen class periods if he chooses.

According to Metro's catalog:

> A typical student could begin his day interviewing inmates at a state prison as part of a course in law and justice. He then heads for the Loop, where his counseling group meets in a conference room provided by Montgomery Ward. He ends the day photographing buildings as a part of a class in city planning. His next day could consist of math lab experience at Metro

headquarters, a class in electronics at the telephone company, and a free period at the library or relaxing at Metro headquarters.

A second student could have a completely different set of experiences chosen to suit his interests and his ability. His program might consist of a journalism course taught in part by practicing reporters, a physics course using lab facilities at the University of Illinois, a placement in a quality control laboratory at a chemical company, and a course in improvisational theatre at Second City.

Individual Placements. Students are given an opportunity to find out about a job or career in which they might be interested. Individual placements have been made in secretarial pools, animal hospitals, zoos, preschools, industrial laboratories, community organizations, political campaigns, and lawyers' offices, for example. Ideally, the student is given some real responsibility in the organization and an opportunity to understand how it functions overall.

We found that almost all students valued their individual placements for the opportunity they gave to experience the world of work in practice rather than in theory. Many thought the placements made Metro less a school and more an important apprenticeship.

Learning Units. Opinion was more varied on the learning units, the basic part of the program. The units are taught by members of participating organizations as well as the school staff. Some deal with traditional subject areas such as geometry and chemistry. Some deal with basic skills such as reading. More than half deal with topics not usually covered in a high school curriculum such as studying the current art show at the museum, or the laws of probability with a group of insurance actuaries, or learning filmmaking from television producers, or community problems from neighborhood organizations. Except for a few distribution requirements, a student is free to choose whatever he wants from about one hundred courses in Metro's catalog.

All of the students with whom we talked enjoyed the diversity of the units and the leeway allowed for meeting distribution requirements. English requirements, for example, could be met through Poetry of Rock, Game Theatre, Language and Survival, and Acting Workshop; Social Studies requirements through The Drug Problem, Black America, Legal Problems of the Oppressed, Parent Management, and the Stock Market and the Economy; Science requirements through individual lab assistantships in the corporations and museums of the city; Math requirements through individual study; and Language requirements through Speaking Spanish the Native Way, to name but a few. Students also engaged in a variety of independent study electives in such activities as tutoring services, merchandising, and record and film production.

To some, however, such freedom of choice had its drawbacks, as an Urban Research consultant explained in a memo to the Metro staff:

> Ideally, Metro offers enough choice in its catalog so that every student can end up with a program that is close to what he wants. Much of our claim of student freedom rests on this assumption. Our observations suggest that the process does not quite work.
>
> We've been working with the idea that the students can handle the paper bureaucracy as competently as the teachers do. It just isn't so; information needs to come in many forms.

First many students do not really read the catalogues. They pick courses from the time sheet just by title.

After many have picked what they want they "fill in" in order to have an allowable level of free time.

Many students are not really aware of the option of independent study or independent placements. Some have vague ideas of things they might like to find out about but don't know how to approach teachers about it.

Students often feel compelled to take things for credit distributions. Sometimes they do not give as much consideration to these courses as to others.

Some students will avoid courses with teachers they don't know.

Some students are afraid of new things . . . maybe we need to clarify the possibility of change early in the cycle. Rather than change, many students assume they'll cut when it turns out they don't like it.

Most students, however, felt they fully utilized the options available to them and also influenced considerably the choices offered. They seemed to regard their individual latitude of choice as evidence of their collective power over decisions about what will be taught and who will teach it. A minority, however, disagreed:

They make it seem like you have power, but you don't. They give you a sheet with maybe thirty or forty or sixty classes on it. They let you make your choices . . . but still, they make up that sheet you decide from.

A few students had wanted a student-led black studies course but were denied permission because the faculty had already designed a black studies course with "expert" leadership.

> We are trying to start up a black studies program cul-
> ture center, and we wanted a room, and we asked for
> a lot of things. But they didn't give it to us because
> they were starting another class in black history with a
> man that had been going to college.

The situation may be atypical, but it touches on the difficulty Metro encounters in encouraging student initiative and
responsibility when the staff unintentionally overdirects and
controls. Some students doubted that Metro was sincere in
its efforts to involve them in educational leadership: "Teachers are still adults, and Metro is still a school."

For the majority of students, a major feature of the curriculum was the freedom it provided them to move about the
city:

> We have classes all over the city. Any place that you
> can imagine we're likely to have a class—in high
> schools, dope centers, skid row. Wherever there is
> something you can learn, Metro is liable to have a
> class. Right now we have a class at the park, at least I
> do, a tennis class. A lot of classes are held in the park
> in the summer because it's a good atmosphere to be in.
> You're a lot more ready to learn something there.
> Better than sitting in a classroom all day.

On the other hand, Metro's community-based program did
present problems to some students, at least to those who
complained about transportation difficulties in poor weather
and of a certain feeling of loneliness and instability experienced because of the diffuseness of the program:

> The whole school is very transient. The kids don't
> have much time to congregate in one place. . . . A lot
> of kids . . . might see completely different people in
> each class and really never get to know anyone. But

> I'm sure these cases must be few because from what I
> can see most of these people *do* have friendships and
> people they are close to.

The diffuseness of the program may also work against
Metro's desire to foster friendships across ethnic lines. It is
easier to "stick" with someone you already know well in an
environment that keeps one on the move than to establish
new friendships with strangers.

A "feel" for the experiential nature of some of Metro's
learning units is readily gained from the two examples given
here from the student publication, *The Metro Free Press:*

> "Chicago Through the Novel: Halls of Justice" by
> Paula Levy
>
> The lobby of the Family Court Building, Ogden and
> Roosevelt Road, is a depressing place. Children and
> teenagers, many handcuffed together, lining the drab
> walls and filling the hard benches. The luckier ones
> have their parents with them.
>
> Members of Metro's Chicago Through the Novel
> class . . . sat in the jury box and observed several hear-
> ings. They heard the judge place a fifteen-year-old boy
> in St. Charles Reform School because he had nowhere
> else to go. . . . The students watched the boy leave. He
> was very calm and polite—perhaps overly so. A few
> minutes later, a commotion was heard in the hall. . . .
> The boy had tried to escape.
>
> At least one of the students noticed the painting on
> the dull wall behind the judge, the painting of fair-
> haired children playing by a stream that runs through
> flowered hills. At least one of the students wondered
> how many of the children who stood before this paint-
> ing had ever seen gurgling streams or flowered hills.
> And at least one of the students thought, "There has
> to be another way!"

"The Ghetto Game: From Ghetto to Power" by Mary
Lou Green

Here at Metro the students can have a class by the
name of ghetto game. The ghetto game is a game of
power, money, votes, jobs and education. . . . You can
see how in many situations, racial or economic, you
can learn how to gain power, votes, money or friends.

There are four team colors in the game: white,
yellow, blue, and red. Roger W. is on the yellow side,
and I'm on the white side, and I was running for
mayor. I asked for the yellow votes, they said no; I
asked for the red votes, they said no; I asked for the
blue votes, the said yes; so I was the mayor. Roger W.
got mad and began to call the people that were on the
white team "honky." We started calling them yellow.

If you haven't signed up for this class, and you want
money, and you want to learn how it feels to be in
power, or how it feels to help someone get an education, take my advice and get in soon.

That many of Metro's classes were not highly structured
was an asset for some students and a liability for others.
Students seemed to receive much individual attention and
help from the teaching staff, but they were expected to take
responsibility for their own learning and to ask for assistance
when they needed it. While the goals for students were
clearly presented, there was opportunity for negotiating about
how a student might accomplish them. The teachers, though
well grounded on subject matter, were not didactic and did
not force their knowledge upon students who were unwilling
or unable to take it.

Counseling Groups. Counseling groups, the third component
of Metro's curriculum, were a source of considerable aggre-
vation. The idea, adopted directly from Philadelphia's

Parkway School, was to offer a basic social unit that would serve as a stabilizing force. The counselor, a consistent figure to whom students could go throughout the year for assistance, was to take broad responsibility for the education of fifteen to twenty students. The group would allow students of diverse backgrounds to understand and appreciate each other. In addition, it would provide a forum in which to discuss school problems.

Originally the groups were scheduled to meet for two hours twice a week. No credits were given for the time. At first, they were characterized by discussions of political interests and personal problems. When a number of students stopped attending, teacher-counselors responded in various ways. Some organized group projects such as field trips or parties at their homes. Others tried to modify the discussion approach, since many students resisted personal discussion topics. But many teachers, unable to bring together such heterogeneous groups, were frustrated and uncomfortable. Some blamed the nature and goals of the groups; others blamed themselves. Some felt they could relate more to students in a class.

After the first cycle, several changes were made. The groups met only one afternoon a week, and they were encouraged to develop activities that depended less on verbal interaction. They took on a number of housekeeping tasks such as informing students of schedule changes, distributing bus tokens, and filling out forms. They were also asked to focus more on student participation in school governance.

In the spring of 1971, however, students and staff were still frustrated and confused by the groups. The staff felt the design had been imposed on them by the Urban Research consultants. Some feared that they, in turn, were imposing it on the students.

The counseling groups suffered from two main problems. First, from the beginning the staff lacked an adequate understanding of the groups' functions. Second, some of the staff lacked the sophisticated skills needed to implement the counseling goals. Metro's principal considered counseling groups a confusing misnomer, because it implied a kind of social work by highly trained counselors. Certainly, confusion was evident in the statements of the staff:

> If I have a vague idea of what a counseling group is, the kids must have an even vaguer one. So do you force something on them to give them an idea of what the possibilities are, and take it from there, which is not what I want to do. . . . You have to have some kind of experience, some kind of knowledge beforehand.

> I must confess it wasn't really clear to anyone for many, many months. . . . Nobody knew what it was all about. I tried to make it an educational experience first—took my kids to art museums and things like that. And then, an immediate rebellion, because some kids realized other groups were playing softball.

The fact that counseling groups offered no credit and were a required course added to the difficulties. As two teachers commented:

> We tried to get away from giving grades, you know, but the kids would ask if we were giving credit for this. When I said no, there was this rebellion.

> It's ridiculous. . . . It is the only forced class at Metro. Kids are required to come. How can they relate openly to a teacher-counselor who is in an authoritarian position of forcing them to come?

Students were as negative about the groups as the teachers. Counseling groups were a place to go for bus tokens or class schedules but a "drag" otherwise. Many students resented being forced to "split" from their regular friends to spend time with students they hardly knew in a group that failed to foster new friendships between students of diverse backgrounds.

Personal counseling is something that most students regard as a private talk with a favorite teacher and not as a counseling group with a preassigned counselor with whom they might not relate. Yet they find the system open enough to allow them to seek out the kind of counseling they prefer. Three staff members, who comprise the Student Supportive Services, provide counseling for students who are frequently absent from classes. Avoiding truant officer techniques, they try to assess the cause of a student's absenteeism and help him create a program that can motivate this attendance. The group has found the approach successful.

Black students, on the whole, did not see any bias in the counseling process, nor were our interviewers able to discern any bias in the sense of vocational tracking. A black staff member, however, felt the counseling groups were failing to help black youngsters deal with the multi-ethnic realities of society. For example, they were not helping black students to appreciate their black identity nor white students to deal with theirs. "The staff blames society," he said, "but they will not accept responsibility themselves for what they must do."

Since our visit in 1971, the counseling groups have dropped their broad goals of fostering multi-ethnic friendships and racial awareness. They are no longer seen as a vehicle for personal counseling. By 1973, they were reduced to meeting one hour a week.

Evaluation. Students do not receive grades at Metro. At the end of every ten-week cycle, each student sits down with each of his teachers to review his work. Together they complete an evaluation and decide if the student is to receive credit, or partial credit, or credit withheld (allowing him another chance), or no credit. Long before the final judgement, however, the teacher and student have reached a common understanding of what was expected of each other during the course. From time to time along the way, the student had reviewed his progress with the teacher. He had also participated in planning further activities for the course, since the goals of the course and students' understanding of what was expected of them had also been reviewed periodically to see whether either needed altering.

Students took evaluation seriously. They responded with honesty and a willingness to act upon self-criticism. Some opted for no credit when they felt credit was underserved or partial credit when they wanted to work harder in another "go-around."

Metro is one of the few innovative schools to undertake a comparative evaluation of its students. A long-term comparison between 110 Metro students and 110 students attending other schools has been conducted by the U.R.C. team, funded, in part, by the Research in Urban Education program of the College of Education, University of Illinois. Short-term evaluations have also been made to clarify current trends.

To correct the shortcomings of conventional evaluation approaches, three principles were emphasized: (1) evaluation should measure the process as well as the results of educational programs, (2) experimental and nonexperimental approaches should be used, and (3) the evaluation should provide continuous feedback to help improve the program as it goes along.

Evaluation by outside consultants has been one of Metro's most outstanding features. The continuing analysis and feedback, in the form of memos to the staff, agenda items on faculty meetings, and written reports, have helped to insure continuing change and growth.

Attendance Policies.   During the first cycle, it was discovered that poor attendance was jeopardizing Metro's relationship with participating organizations. As a result, a common understanding was reached that students had a responsibility to attend class and that instead of cutting, they should either try to change a class they are dissatisfied with or drop it.

Class attendance improved somewhat after this, but enforcement of the agreement was inconsistent. Teachers who see attendance as solely the students' responsibility did not enforce the policy. Some considered mere enrollment in a class sufficient basis for credit. Others provided absentees with independent study to do outside of class. Still others refused to give students credit for classes not attended and work not done.

The inconsistency has added to the confusion about where the responsibility for a student's education lies. In himself? In the faculty? Or in both? Many black students thought teachers should bring truant-prone students into line. Some black students, they felt, needed firm direction, and teachers should accommodate their teaching styles to the need. They saw crediting absentees as a reverse form of racism rather than mature and responsible behavior:

> Like for me, what I would need to learn math is to sit down and have someone with a baseball bat over my head making sure. But that wouldn't go for learning in English. That would only go for certain subjects and certain people.

> We need different styles of teaching. Like sometimes
> there should be someone who says, "Sit your ass
> down."

> You can graduate from Metro and still not know any-
> thing. If you have a good relationship with a teacher
> you can get credit for it. The teacher should take time
> out from every class and work individually with every
> student.

Some teachers felt they must avoid authoritarian measures
if they were to win students' trust. Others thought that
laissez-faire practices diminished trust if interpreted as a lack
of concern and regard. Many students, however, brushed
both arguments aside, preferring "different strokes for different folks."

GOVERNANCE

To give students a significant role in decision-making has
been one of Metro's chief aims. Although the importance of
power-sharing is continually emphasized, it is limited in
practice.

Metro has had a succession of governing bodies since it
began. Initially meetings of the total student and faculty body
were held to make policy decisions and determine daily operations. As a governing mechanism, the all-school meeting
proved enormously difficult. The staff found the process and
the numerous everyday operating decisions took more time
and energy than they had to give. Students found it confusing
and tedious. Their attendance dropped drastically. By the fall
of 1970, the staff found itself making decisions as a faculty
group. Although they invited interested students to partici-

pate, only the most politically aware and verbal students responded. Soon the all-school meeting was abandoned.

It was replaced by a more representative body made up of delegates from the counseling groups and the staff. Only one meeting of this body was held, however, before it too disbanded. Students felt it had been imposed on them and never set a date for another meeting.

In the spring of 1971, another plan was proposed. This time people were to form Like Groups of five and six students, along with teachers and friends. Each group would send a delegate to an official decision-making body called the Administrative Board. Small groups with common interests would, it was hoped, provide a good basis for representative government. Once again, this effort at structured participatory democracy failed. There was no continuity of membership at meetings—each time different group representatives would attend. In addition, each meeting was assigned to a different chairman. Again, school governance was left largely to the staff.

Surprisingly enough, our study revealed that there was disagreement about whether Metro actually had a formal governance structure that spring. Some 60 percent of the teachers and 40 percent of the students thought there was such a structure; 38 percent of the teachers and 56 percent of the students thought there was none; some had no opinion. In fact, Metro had *two* governance bodies, one formal, the other not. The first was the Policy Board, mentioned earlier, that represented faculty, students, parents, and participating organizations. However, it had just been set up, and many may have not been aware of it yet. The second was an informal faculty group that made the day-to-day operating decisions of the school.

The Policy Board. The Policy Board had eight members—
two staffpersons, two students, two parents, and two representatives of participating organizations. It was empowered to
make decisions regarding curriculum and evaluation procedures, to select the principal (certified by the board of
education), to advise him on staff selection and budget, and
to direct the expenditures of donated money.

Parents on the Policy Board represented the Metro Parent
Action Council, which had its own set of purposes and by-
laws. On occasion, parents and teachers on the Board have
clashed. When, for example, the school board proposed to
transfer tenured teachers from other parts of the system to
replace Metro's nontenured teachers, the staff was unalterably opposed. Such a policy, they said, could be disastrous,
since Metro teachers were handpicked for specific attributes.
The parent representatives, however, claimed the teachers put
their own self-interest above Metro's.

The staff members on the Policy Board were in a somewhat ambiguous position. They represented a faculty already
organized as a body in faculty meetings to run the day-to-
day operations of the school. If the faculty and Policy Board
were to compete for authority over the same area, the role of
the staff representatives on the Policy Board would have been
difficult.

The student members of the Policy Board were the only
ones who did not represent an organized body. They were
not accountable to any group as a group and since Metro's
students are not organized as a body, their task in representing student opinion was formidable.

The members of outside organizations on the Policy Board
represented the Participating Organizations Council, a nonprofit corporation made up of thirteen members and Metro's
principal. Its purpose was to develop a closer relationship

between the school and participating organizations. It administered funds donated for Metro and advised the principal on matters of interest to the participating organizations. The Council, like the Policy Board, was established in the spring of 1971.

As already noted, the request of the Policy Board for an experimental schools expediter to whom it could be held accountable, rather than the area and district superintendents, was turned down. Thus the Policy Board had to operate within the bureaucratic hierarchy of the public schools. It did not survive long. It was disbanded in the 1972–73 school year. Metro's principal took over its major functions, working with the parents' and the participating organizations' Councils, which have both grown in strength.

The Faculty Group. Metro's teachers have developed an increasing ability to function as a decision-making group. The eviction crisis sparked a demand for more flexibility, and teachers became more willing to delegate authority. Not only did they accept decisions informally arrived at, but, as one teacher explained, they could trust those who reversed such decisions when occasion demanded:

> It's hard to say how a decision gets made and carried out. Whoever is there at the time has to do it. . . . You may be sitting at lunch . . . and one or two of you gets an idea. Then you present your idea to the group. Half of them say they have not thought about it, half think it sounds okay. Then two or three people start implementing it. . . .
>
> Sometimes you have to make decisions when you don't have a whole group together. . . . But a lot of times it's like in the class. . . . You tell people to make their own decisions and then they don't. So you come

up with something, and sometimes it's accepted, sometimes not. That's what I see happening, probably because of the power that I have felt . . . our own powerfulness. . . .

During the crises we made a decision one day that
just wasn't sensible the next day. It was a direction,
not a decision. . . . If a decision was made and the
person who was supposed to carry it out found that
we didn't have enough information when we made
that decision, it would hardly be sensible to have it out
again with twenty people—you have to make your
own decision.

Decisions are made and entrusted to people to carry
out, and they have to use their judgement. It may con-
tradict what the decision is. If there was a priority in
everyone making the decision, we wouldn't have time
to teach classes.

Should more willingness to delegate authority develop, it
could lead to new, more organic, and less forced forms of
participatory democracy.

Student Power.   Students, on the whole, felt they had considerable power over individual decisions—over the courses they
selected, their attendance, the amount of work they did, and
their evaluations. But they did not believe their collective
power was great. Only a fourth thought students had "a
great deal of influence" over decisions. Only a fifth of the
teachers agreed.

While the staff was disturbed by the failure to involve students in decision-making, students were apathetic about it.
Most felt the staff advocated student interests and made
"good" decisions. Some felt students were informally con-
sulted, in counseling groups or in the lounge, before decisions were made:

> This school is run by the principal. A lot of times he
> makes it seem like the kids are doing it, but he runs it.
> That's okay though. . . . He acts on what he thinks is
> best for us, like what we say is important. If the major-
> ity of us really want something, he'll go all out to get
> it for us.

> I don't think altogether students have a lot of au-
> thority . . . but they do . . . give us a chance to speak
> at meetings and tell them what we want. And they put
> it into action if they feel it's right for that situation.

One or two students considered Metro an adult-run school
that gave students little power beyond the freedom to choose
among adult-approved alternatives. Courses not approved by
adults, they said, would not be introduced.

Metro's principal is not particularly concerned about the
lack of student power or involvement:

> Students will become involved when they find a need
> to. . . . When a school is functioning, and functioning
> well to a certain degree, it doesn't matter who is doing
> it as long as it is being done well. . . . You can't force
> students to become involved any more than you can
> force teachers to become involved. . . .

He believes the staff must learn the ins and outs of decision-
making first:

> We cannot expect students to do anything that we
> ourselves cannot do. . . . And when staff is able to run
> through an agenda, arrive at decisions, and feel secure
> in what they're doing without frustration setting in,
> then you'll find them bringing in students. But when
> you find staff at each other's throats and decisions not
> being made, and then students coming and throwing
> in some controversial things, it only creates a worse
> situation.

The staff revealed somewhat more adherence to their original idea of participatory democracy. While some confessed that they found the difficulties of decision-making compounded when students were present, many felt their long period of trial and error had made them more ready to tackle active student involvement.

The Urban Research consultants were concerned about the slow development of student power in the face of benevolent authority. They reported, in the summer of 1970, on the pattern they saw developing then:

> We often heard students . . . with minor dissatisfactions . . . rationalize nonactivity by a ledger kind of operation—the good outweighs the bad by so much that I don't want to rock the boat. It may be that the staff . . . are preempting most student concerns. . . . Staff might want to weigh the relative importance of the content of decisions versus the benefits of the process of student decision-making. Metro may be in danger of fostering its own brand of alienation—preparing students for a benevolent paternalism.
>
> Most often when students talked about student government and what it might do, they spoke of taking care of problems. Many saw it only as a punitive agency. Others saw its scope limited to diddley things like getting a candy machine. It was difficult for students to imagine what it might do.
>
> In classes too students tend to be passive . . . many teachers try to get their classes to join in cooperative planning . . . as an option offered to students. It might be better viewed as a skill to be taught like any other educational goal. It is not enough to just offer it; students have little experience or developed desire in this area.

Rules and Regulations.   Metro's commitment to student power was based on the hope that students would discipline and regulate themselves. Students, however, have relied on adults to take primary responsibility for the orderly running of the school. Metro's do-your-own-thing ethos has made students even more reluctant than usual to reprimand anyone's behavior or set limits to it. They were willing, by default, to allow— in fact, demand—that authority be exerted by adults.

Yet their need for autonomy conflicted with their need to look to adults for control and discipline. As a result, they sent confusing messages to the staff: on the one hand, "Let me learn and behave in *my* own way, don't impose your thing on me vis-à-vis my behavior or my attitudes," and on the other, "Don't neglect me. Give me some confines in which I can move, and don't let me abuse these confines."

Students also gave conflicting messages to one another: "We are a community and we are responsible for this school. Therefore we must police ourselves," and "Hey, leave me alone, Man! You're no adult! You've got no right to lay on me."

The staff, on the whole, were as unclear as the students in the area of discipline. They had not yet found a way to introduce structure and discipline into the context of freedom and the seesaw between "freedom to grow" and "freedom to be neglected."

Metro's increased size has made it more difficult to depend upon friend-to-friend policing where self-policing fails. While the student newspaper is increasingly used to admonish students and staff, in general, for their lack of self-discipline and responsibility, personal confrontation has been avoided.

Communication Patterns.   Metro depended far more on informal than formal communication. There were, of course, formal avenues of communication—the bulletin boards, the student press—but certain vital information, such as the agenda for faculty meetings and the decisions made there, was not formally published. Such information drifted back slowly to the student body through the grapevine. Except in times of crises when the staff went out of its way to involve students, issues were decided before most students heard about them. They learned to participate in school governance on an ad hoc basis only, in times of crises. Many were turned off from the business of school governance altogether.

Neither the staff nor the students, apparently, recognized how much participation depends on access to information. The staff may have been too busy, the students too unorganized, to set up a formal mechanism for reporting regularly on matters of school governance.

INTERGROUP RELATIONS

The traditional roles of both students and teachers, which generally serve to maintain distance between them, have been redefined at Metro. A student may serve as a teacher in one class, a helper or tutor in another, and fulfill an administrative function as well. Teachers, in turn, often serve as resource persons or facilitators and may come to student-led classes as learners.

Intergenerational Relations. Metro teachers tried hard not to appear to students as the sole source of authority, despite their expertise. Students were encouraged not to accept their judgements as final and to question and debate them. Yet, despite their efforts, most students still regarded the teachers as adults who must be responded to as the source of all knowledge, sanctions, and rewards.

Few believed teachers really meant to share power, despite the rhetoric. Few considered teachers their colleagues or confidantes:

> At Metro there is the feeling that the teacher is on the same level as you, but mentally there is still that hold-back. I feel more free talking to them here. But still it's a teacher.

Because personal information is not, for many students, the "stuff" one shares with adults, the counseling groups have also foundered on the generation gap.

The teacher-as-friend role, so dear to Metro teachers, has made their teacher-as-teacher role difficult. Teachers were "pulled between their role as friends and their role as teachers," one of the Urban Research consultants noted, and their tendency to be unclear about their expectations of students has not helped students who seek direction and guidance from adults.

The student-parent relationship at Metro has been somewhat stormy. Most students resented parent participation. They thought parents were far too conservative about education and feared they would jeopardize the program. At one point, Metro's students marched on a parents' Council meeting to protest its involvement in school affairs. While many students admitted that their parents supported Metro as an alternative to Chicago schools and recognized the political support parents can give Metro in its struggle with the school board, they continued to resist parents' direct involvement in the school's daily life. However, the parents' Council can be expected to take an active role and may do considerable checking with their constituents.

Student Relations. Metro students have grouped themselves along two lines: (*1*) old and new students and (2) black and white students. New students, who entered after Metro's first semester ended in June 1971, were seen by old students as "less committed to Metro," "less able to take responsibility," and were blamed for a decrease in community spirit. That old and new students were separated, two floors apart, when the new center was added, contributed to the animosity. Several students wished there had been a two-week acquaintance period at the beginning of the school year to help new students capture the flavor of Metro's community ethos. Unlike old students, who had helped to create Metro, new students had come into something already created and felt somehow outside the community. All students agreed that Metro's increased size had made student relationships more impersonal:

> Last year people didn't stand on ceremony with each other. We'd be able to hang around with anyone, just walk up to people you don't know and start talking or going out to lunch together and get to know them. This year its like my old school. You just don't go up to people you don't know or they'll think you're out of your head. You stick with the kids you already know.

As Metro's size increased, black and white students have pulled apart and become surprisingly polarized. In the lounge, black students played cards, danced, or rapped in small groups among themselves, and white students did the same. Friendly interaction occurred between whites and blacks, but none of it was prolonged. Black and white students often worked together on projects in class, and there appeared to be little racial tension. Most students accepted the polarization as inevitable, the consequence of society's rigid patterns. Yet some spoke wistfully of "last year when things were different, and we were closer, no matter what our race or backgrounds."

Many black students viewed interracial friendship, and dating especially, as a repudiation of their black identity:

> We had this meeting and . . . they got around to the subject of why are whites and blacks separating themselves. Then one black girl got up and shouted at this other black girl for hanging around with a lot of white kids.

Some black students resented whites trying to act like blacks and blacks like whites:

> The black students go to Metro with the white students and the white students try to change and act like a black person. They get up there and they get soul shades and they do dances like we do. And the black people try to act like white people and do what they do . . . like say hello and trying to give a regular handshake to a white person, who instead drops his hand for a soul brother shake!

Most staff members recognized the racial polarization and deplored it, but some considered it beyond their power to influence. They echoed the white students who spoke of their inability to break down Metro's racial barriers.

In a survey of the faculty's attitudes, made by a black and white teacher on the staff, several suggestions were made to deal with the problem of racial polarization—expand black contacts, hire more black staff to provide more black direction, and change the counseling groups. Metro opened as a result, in the fall of 1971, with an enlarged black staff (representing 50 percent of the faculty) and plans to change the counseling groups. Still, in 1973, the polarization remained.

Conceived as a multi-ethnic school, Metro has attempted to

introduce black culture into its curriculum, through black history and other black-oriented courses, and to provide learning experiences for its students in Chicago's black communities. However, the total program, the methodology, and the philosophy of education remained white-conceived and implemented from a white reference point. Metro is not a multi-ethnic school, though it is composed of multi-ethnic groups. It has not facilitated black and white students and staff to diagnose and articulate those areas of *common* concern that can unify them nor those where black and white separateness can be valuable and constructive. Until it develops a genuine multi-ethnic pluralism, Metro's black-white polarization can only increase.

VALUES AND SATISFACTIONS

Our interviews and questionnaires probed into the nature of students' and teachers' values and dissatisfactions with Metro, since we considered these germane to an understanding of Metro as a school.

Student Satisfactions and Dissatisfactions. Students came to Metro for a variety of reasons—to escape traditional schools, to try something new, or because their parents insisted. Most found Metro a warm, friendly, and educationally stimulating place to be. Seventy to eighty percent of the students believed Metro's teachers "really understood" the problems they have in school and helped them to do their best in schoolwork. More students, in fact, rated teachers more friendly and approachable than they rated other students.

Many students expressed pride and satisfaction in the

process by which they participate in staff selection. No teacher is hired by the faculty or administration alone, but must be interviewed by a committee that includes students as well. A student described the process:

> I was on a committee last year to choose teachers for this year. We were three students and three teachers. Applicants came in, and we took turns asking questions. . . . Then they played a game with sticks in pairs. Each tried to beat the other person to the last stick by picking them up one by one. We asked the teachers to play the game with us while everyone was watching. We'd know the trick to it, of course, so we'd win every time. The object was the different ways these teachers would act together and by themselves. Some teachers would dominate and take over and not listen to anyone else. Some really would want to try it again. . . . That gave us a pretty good idea of how they acted with kids.

One vote apiece was allowed the teachers and the students. The game described apparently helped to identify teachers who have a supportive style, show comfort with students, and ease in the learner role.

The feature of Metro that students most often praised was the freedom to take responsibility for their own learning. As one student said:

> I'd stress the element of responsibility. . . . They leave your education up to you. . . . There are no guidelines. The teacher is there if you want him, but you have to make your own decisions. It's really fun to set your own schedule and pick your own teachers.

While many students appreciated the freedom to learn what

they wanted to in an unhassled environment, others appreciated it because it allowed them to do little or nothing academically. One student spoke of having drifted happily through the year without any sense of pressure or punishment, although he confessed he had had enough of "that trip" and was resolved to apply himself the next semester.

Students also praised Metro for encouraging them to initiate and teach classes but admitted that few students had done so. Still, several student-initiated classes have been held, including, for example, a photography class and a reading course.

For the most part, Metro students focused on the present rather than the future:

> We're not concerned with that [preparing for the future]. We're all concerned with now. . . . Most students at Metro feel this way. They're not really concerned with what their occupation is going to be . . . you're taking classes for now. . . . The best thing you learn is . . . something about today.

Metro students were far more interested in their own personal growth than in Metro's development as an institution, yet they would do nothing to harm Metro. There were strong taboos against taking dope on school premises, for example, or acting up in ways to draw the anger of participatory organizations:

> If we go into a place . . . and start messing things and not showing respect. . . that's really a bad name for old Metro. We have to learn to cope.

Students expressed some dissatisfaction about their peers and their teachers and about the diffuseness of Metro's program. Some were angry at the apathy they saw in other students. This was very prevalent amongst the aspiring, hard-working black students interviewed who felt that their apathetic black peers were not developing the skills they needed to contribute to their futures, their families, or their race.

Despite their unqualified liking and regard for staff, many students, as already noted, were critical of teachers who granted undeserved credit to students who hadn't even attended class. In addition, many felt teachers' standards were much too low and failed to motivate students to their real potential:

> What bothers me about Metro is that teachers are satisfied with *whatever* you turn in. They don't prod you to try harder.

Some students recognized that behind a teacher's *laissez-faire* policy lay the fear of appearing authoritarian. The struggle to find the right balance between freedom and direction has already been discussed. While students believed that some of them might be "turned off" by a teacher's seeming authoritarianism, they thought even more are harmed by a *laissez-faire* policy.

Students also complained that communication processes were inadequate. As already noted, information about faculty meetings was left to the grapevine. In addition, students were not always informed when classes were shifted or changed. In fact, students were in favor of having more of their classes in Metro's headquarters, because they all wanted more stability and continuity in their school experience.

Staff Satisfactions and Dissatisfactions. Metro required teachers with idealism and with some clear notion of what they wanted to accomplish, according to the principal. Its teachers seemed committed to working in a free and open environment that, unlike traditional schools in their view, did not suffocate and oppress either themselves or their students. They found Metro very much to their liking:

> You walk into this huge floor . . . with desks . . . and kids all over and you feel immediately a sense of people being close to each other, feeling good about what they're doing. Everyone is busy. . . . The main thing is that everyone is happy with what they are doing. . . . The whole atmosphere has complete openness . . . the physical setup, the people, the interchanges, everything.

What features of Metro did they emphasize?

> The theme of versatility . . . the range of classes given by some ancillaries to student-run classes. In my class in parent management I hope to give students a power base and help them to make logical decisions concerning the power relationship between parent and child. I've never had any experience with this course, and am uneasy giving it, but I feel it's important so I live with my uneasiness.

> The ease of discussion between students and teachers on a subject such as sexuality and masturbation . . . the openness of the student-teacher relationship . . . the individuality of the staff, and the many different types of people with whom students can identfy.

> The lounge, the pot luck, the classes, especially those in the city . . . the easiness of Metro, but . . . real work being done.

Teachers rated high the friendliness and approachability of all groups—students, administrators, teachers. Interestingly enough, students rated their teachers' effectiveness higher than the teachers themselves did, and students enjoyed their work more than the teachers assumed. Metro's principal felt the teachers were too hard on themselves and may not even have perceived their accomplishments.

Metro teachers valued the trust and autonomy they received from their principal, and most appreciated the responsibility he had given them for the day-to-day administration of the school as well as major policy decisions, even if it meant, "You have to be willing to stick around some nights until 11:30 P.M. to get things done in our own haphazard way." Only a few questioned whether the principal might be holding himself back too much from an active role. The principal, however, believed in shared power:

> Schools like this should be able to run without administrators or older people. I'm the head teacher. . . . If I'm not here, the school should function without having to wait on me to make the decision. This is what is slowly coming about. And they recognize now that they can go ahead and do things. . . . When you give people the right to choose, they'll be dedicated, committed.

The principal usually backed the staff in its decisions, but when Metro's issues with the Board of Education came up, he reserved the role of ultimate authority. The staff accepted his authority here because they appreciated the risks invoked to his career:

> Besides being one of *the* brightest principals around, let's face it, depending on how we come out of the Metro thing, the principal's career could be over, or really flourishing! He's laid it all on the line.

Teachers were divided by personality clashes and leadership struggles within the faculty, stemming from differences in attitudes because of racial background and basic educational philosophy and goals. They were ambivalent about the kinds of investments Metro required of them and concerned that they were doing an inadequate job of teaching students career skills.

Many were starting to feel burned out, exhausted, and depressed at the energy and thought required in planning, teaching, administrating, and relating to students, participating organizations, the central office, and each other. Their commitment to Metro made heavy overtime the norm:

> My whole life revolves around my relationships with people here. . . . Like tonight I'm playing handball with one of the kids . . . my wife and I really haven't done much outside of here.

There was, however, a sense of anxiety that one must either conform to overwork at Metro or be rejected:

> It requires more commitment here than the regular school—it's not just a way of making money but is a significant part of one's life. . . . Since getting married I've had to cut back on the time I give and I feel bad about being less involved. I often wonder how teachers feel about it—am I seen as less committed?

Teachers who would not put in overtime were often called "deadwood" by the staff, although excessive overwork could lower morale and the staff's capacity to function.

The staff tended to concentrate on its problems and ignore its successes. Thus it had not developed a system to share its positive experiences in a supportive way, a lack felt particularly by teachers who feared that their innovative approaches might be inadequate. Pleas for such a feedback system were made:

> *Why is it that we have all found time to consult with outsiders about what we are actually doing and yet not to share our experiences with each other?* Many of us are doing exciting, creative things here at Metro, but there is little positive sharing among ourselves except when it comes to problems.
>
> I would like to propose that on Tuesdays and Thursdays during lunch, we set up a place for staff to meet with the decided purpose of presenting the good and bad things each of us has done—the things we think have worked, and a possible why, if we even suspect what it might be. Perhaps we could enact our vision of visiting each others' classes and truly begin to build ourselves into a support system for each other.

Metro's strengths are many. It has achieved a difficult feat —it has broken down the traditional barriers between students and staff and replaced them with a remarkably candid, warm, informal, and respectful relationship between the two generations. It has allowed students and staff to experience a diversity of roles—teaching, learning, and administration are treated as interchangable functions—and this is an education in and of itself.

Metro's curriculum is exciting for the students whom it does reach and gives them the feeling of being integrated with life, not divorced from it. They are able to use their learnings beyond the classroom and are stimulated into independent study and work. Metro's ability to unify its students, staff, and parents against external threats has been outstanding. The sense of ownership people feel about their school is rare. In addition, Metro's use of the Urban Research Corporation team (as consultants, scapegoats, and negotiators) may serve as a model for other experimental programs.

Finally, Metro has a built-in capacity for self-assessment and evaluation, which constantly regenerates its program. Therefore it is not likely to grow stagnant or mediocre.

However, critical issues remain. Metro's organization of learning does not equitably favor all students. Its curriculum, methodology, and decision-making have all developed in a way that tends to favor white or middle-class students. The absence of a genuine multi-ethnic education has contributed to the growing polarization between black and white students.

Metro's governance and communication structures do not adequately share power with students nor teach them political skills, despite its commitment to participatory democracy. Students are not aware of what their political roles might be, individually or collectively, in the decision-making process.

The Policy Board proved to be ineffective. The divided staff has yet to learn how to support each other and reduce Metro's potential for "burning out" its staff with excessive demands for overtime.

On Metro's side, however, are a committed staff and students, a politicallly astute principal, and the mounting enthusiastic support of its participating organizations.

"Dillington" School-in-a-School, New England

By C. Beth Duncombe, Penny Owen, and Glorianne Wittes

The attractive town of "Dillington," with its modest homes and businesses, has a real New England flavor. On a quiet tree-lined street sits the old, red brick high school, its hallways adorned with antique fixtures and turn-of-the-century treasures and gifts to the school.

The town was originally a river port but a mercantile and industrial class later emerged that prevailed over the supremacy of the shippers. Today "Weskegan" University is also located in the town, and the population consists of both the working class and University faculty members.

There is conflict between the university and townspeople. The university is viewed by many as elitist and is resented whenever it acquires more property near the campus, further reducing the tax base of the town. There is also conflict between the Italian and black communities. Most of the second- and third-generation Italians have worked themselves into the middle class. They have gained political control, while blacks have moved into their old ghetto area. The Italians appear to have little understanding that the situation for blacks is different from the one they faced in their earlier years.

Despite its historical character, "Dillington" High is struggling to bring education to the level of the students' changing concerns and life styles. Its new experimental school-in-a-school (SIAS), actually separate and down the street, is proof. Yet there is considerable discontent among its staff and board of education members about the status of the high school itself:

> "Dillington" High School is a reflection of a community which does not value education for education's sake. (Teacher)

> They [the voters] are willing to support the cost of new buildings but not willing to support the increase in school operating budget. (School board member)

> The school system is top heavy with bureaucracy. (Teacher)

At present, "Dillington" High School includes grades nine through twelve. Of its 555 students, 91 percent are white, 8 percent are black, and the remainder are Chicano and American Indian. About half the students are Catholic, a third Protestant, and 10 percent Jewish. With thirty-five teachers, the teacher-student ratio is approximately one to sixteen. The average per pupil expenditure in 1969–70 was $934.

The school is oriented toward comprehensive education, and students are grouped or tracked according to ability and achievement without their consent. Two percent of the student body participate in work-study programs.

There are two black teachers; the rest are white. More than half the faculty (53 percent) have masters degrees, and the rest have BAs. The bottom salary for a BA with no teaching experience is $7,400, while a teacher with an MA degree and ten years experience earns $10,900. The teachers' union has been active; it staged a strike in 1969.

The board of education has nine members, including one black. The majority are Republicans, elected as such, but there is little voting along party lines, except on budget matters. In 1970 the board negotiated an agreement with the teachers for higher salaries, but the city council vetoed it. When the board called for a referendum to the city council, it lost by a four to one majority.

TRADITIONS AT THE HIGH SCHOOL

To understand "Dillington's" school-in-a-school, one must begin with the parent high school. Our first contact with "Dillington" High took place in the teachers' lounge, which was described to us by a teacher as:

> An incredibly catty, bigoted, selfish place. Teachers don't share or help each other. They don't do their best for the students either. They . . . do a lot of bitching, but never . . . where it can do any good. There is a tremendous amount of politics played in the lounge.

Our next acquaintance was with students in their social study hall, where they have recently been permitted to go when they don't have classes to listen to records, play cards, or simply socialize. Smoking is prohibited, but students can now also leave the building during their free time and can be seen milling around the entrance smoking cigarettes and eating candy bars.

Faculty reaction to this new freedom of movement was mixed. Some feared that such a veering away from tradition might reduce the emphasis on academic education. Tradition, however, still reigned in classroom teaching styles, rules, suspensions, and graduation requirements. During a recent school year, for example, fifty-four students were suspended, ten for acts of insubordination such as challenging a teacher or using "threatening" language to staff members. Small classes, some with only eight to ten students, were taught by the lecture-recitation method, with a lot of quizzes and tests. Nothing appeared to be more important to both students and teachers than exams. There was a very determined drive by the administration, teachers, and many students toward academic excellence.

Yet one could not help but perceive the high degree of apathy at "Dillington" High. Students and teachers alike seemed to walk through the school day as if it were a chore, and there seemed to be none of the old-fashioned high school spirit and pep. A new principal had given the student government opportunities for taking a larger part in the school administration, but the students claimed not to be interested. The principal commented:

> Everybody by and large is apathetic, and I believe the faculty is reluctant to see outside their little four-walled classrooms. They are not really involved in the extracurricular activities, unless it's a personal relationship or a personal request. There are some faculty members to whom this does not apply.

One teacher, to whom the school seemed waterlogged with tradition, still dreamed that the *esprit de corps* that used to exist could return:

> We do now have a great deal of freedom from the
> administration, but there is little cooperation or con-
> tinuity in the educational program. However, teachers'
> morale is better than last year. We are not satisfied
> yet, but optimistic.

Racial tension has been a continuing problem. In May 1970,
a violent confrontation between students broke out, and
police were called in. Several students were arrested, and
police were stationed in and around the school for weeks.

One teacher reported that signs of tension had been building up, but the administration did not react until too late,
when it then overreacted. Another commented:

> Demands that were made were not unique to the
> school: black studies, black student union, more black
> teachers, soul food in the cafeteria. I don't think there
> were any truly unique problems in the school.

The superintendent attributed the disturbance to lack of
confidence in certain members of the faculty and maybe even
himself. Many accused the administration of unequal punishment of whites and blacks.

The board did little beyond holding a public hearing,
which exposed the obvious hatred between blacks and whites
as extremists from both sides attended. A citizens committee,
however, was organized and recommended, among other
things, the formation of a youth council, the development
of a black studies program at both elementary and secondary levels, and the recruitment of black teachers and administrators. Its recommendations were immediately implemented.

Since May 1970, there have been no further racial out-
breaks, but all problems certainly have not been solved. To
one black student, the school is "a prison camp" where

minorities are oppressed. "At first we've been having to deal
with the whitey, and now we've got to deal with those god
damn Italians. Man, it's a bitch." Most black students interviewed felt that the demands they had made had not, and
would not, be met, even though the administration had committed itself to the changes:

> There is open bias from the administration down to
> the cafeteria. Blacks won't ever get anywhere until we
> learn to fight back. (Student)

> There is open resentment **toward** blacks at "Dilling-
> ton." I have observed open hostilities between the races,
> and black students have told me that they feel un-
> welcome and alone at the school. (Teacher)

Yet others were not sure racism was an issue (or even, perhaps, what racism is):

> I am not sure if I am qualified to say. I have only one
> black in my class, and he is a "borderline black."
> (Teacher)

> Black, poor white, and foreign-born kids should co-
> operate in the learning process for the simple reason
> that it is offered. Every student has the right to flunk.
> There is no way that you can get the student to put
> forth any real effort. (Student)

The principal appears to be of two minds:

> I don't believe there is racism in the true context of
> the word, because if there were, I would have gotten
> rid of the person on the spot, if we could have sub-
> stantiated that type of claim. To say that there are
> teachers in this building who love blacks and who go
> out for blacks and feel that the blacks have really been
> dealt dirty, I'm sure that we have that kind of teacher,

just like the one who thinks the blacks have been given everything. . . . But I don't think there is a teacher who purposely hurts a kid in school.

If we did anything specific this year, it was for Martin Luther King. We brought in a great speaker, and they had a program that was black-centered . . . It was an excellent presentation—really well done. I think the kids respected the occasion, the way it was for Martin Luther King, and the black kids were thinking that at least they were getting a great national hero to be acclaimed. But other than that, we didn't do anything.

I know one thing: that no black kids are ever referred to the office. I don't know if the teachers are dead scared of referring them or what. I just feel that we have a good group of black students in the school. They are not aggressive, they're not real nasty kids, not noisy blacks. I've seen a school with noisy blacks.

I think there is a black-white issue because there are blacks and whites in the school and the fires could end up in a blaze at any time.

The racial confrontation of 1970 may not have brought significant changes to "Dillington" High, but it did at least help to consolidate the pressure building up behind a new idea—a mini-school—the plans for which were already in the works.

HOW THE SCHOOL-IN-A-SCHOOL BEGAN

In the fall of 1969, a new philosophy of education was being examined by a dozen teachers from both "Dillington" High and Woodrow Wilson, the other high school in town, who were taking a course on affective education at "Weskegan" University. Finding it difficult to test their ideas in the traditional classroom setting, they began to discuss the ideal way to run a school.

Six of the group, including the director of the university's Master of Arts in Teaching (MAT) program, met regularly to work out their "fantasy" of an experimental mini-school of one hundred students and five teachers, assisted by university student teachers. The director was impressed when, at an educational meeting attended by the local superintendent, two students talked about what was wrong with school. Everything they said paralleled the planning group's rationale for reform. The following week, the director completed his first paper outlining the concept of a school-in-a-school and presented it to the superintendent.

The superintendent presented the idea to the school board early in 1970. It was accepted, according to one board member, only because the funding for the project was not to come from local funds. (The project actually cost the board about $12,000 in 1970–71; the rest came from federal Title III funding.)

The two high school principals and the assistant superintendent of secondary education were invited to two meetings with the director. Here they asked detailed questions about the board concept he had outlined, not all of which he was prepared to answer. The principal of Woodrow Wilson made it clear that he had other priorities; the "Dillington" principal was still unsure. But because the director had taught a course at "Dillington" and had ties with the faculty, including five "Dillington" teachers who were taking his course on affective education, he was invited to present his plan to the "Dillington" faculty as a whole.

Although he was not a stranger, his idea was poorly received. Teachers were skeptical about changes in their secure teaching roles. Many felt the school had enough problems, without running experiments; others rejected the concept completely. The principal (who has since resigned) accepted the faculty's response. Yet after the presentation, three teachers decided to lend some aid. As one of the planning group recalled, "This was just what I was looking for."

The next step was not as clear cut. The superintendent continued to place pressure on the principal; at the same time racial problems were growing in the school, leading to the May outbreak of violence. Some students felt the outbreak forced the faculty and administration to accept the school-in-a-school concept. Staff members, however, pointed out that the program had been approved prior to the racial crisis, citing as evidence the pamphlet *Can You Imagine a School . . . ,* which had been printed and distributed to students before the disturbance. Some believed the main thrust came from the university. "The innovation was very much an empire-building effort for "Weskegan" and the MAT program," a staff member declared. "There was less interest in "Dillington." I don't think it would have come out of "Dillington"; it had to be shoved down its throat."

Certainly, all the details had been sketched out by the planning group by April 1970, and three prospects for funding had been discovered. But no funding was officially applied for until May. No word about the project came through until late June, and that was unofficial, with no money backing it. Not until after school started in September were federal funds made available, followed by the scare of a Nixon cutback. However, during this period, "Dillington" administrators began to support the idea, despite faculty opposition.

In May 1970, students began to get involved. Applications to the school-in-a-school were open to any "Dillington" High student not entering his senior year. There were fifty openings, and one hundred and thirty applied. Fifty were chosen by a lottery arranged to ensure a cross section of abilities, an equal number of boys and girls, and a racial balance similar to the high school.

After the lottery, ten of the fifty were chosen to work with the faculty during the summer to develop the school further. Many of them found the summer job a sham. They did not have a substantial say in the school's development, and meetings were often held without student input. Yet one found it a rewarding experience in which she came to know her teachers.

Nonetheless, during the summer a government system, rules, curricula, and budget were established, despite the uncertainty of funding and the confusion of installing a new principal following his predecessor's resignation. The new principal knew little about the experimental school but felt he could work with it. The superintendent remembers few risks in establishing it; the board saw fit to go along; the public was not antagonistic.

The school-in-a-school is located three houses away from the main school. Students spend their school day here in a six-room, ground floor apartment, with a front and back porch, backyard, and large garage. The decor immediately catches one's eye. The living room has a long cherry table in the center, with high back wooden chairs placed haphazardly around it. One or two strange shapes hanging on the walls turned out to be kites left over from a kite class. A few posters hang beside them. Purses, jackets, and books are scattered around the room. Students can be found seated at the table, standing around in groups, cooking lunch, or sitting on the porches. There is a sense of friendliness and an ease with each other and with the school's five teachers.

Each room has a special touch, and every room is occupied and noisy. Many activities are carried on in the same room at the same time without apparent loss of attention on the part of the students. The whole apartment seems relaxed, yet high-spirited and "raring to go."

Our visit occurred during an inter-phase session, a three-week period in which regular classes are suspended and the time is devoted to special projects, work assignments in the community, independent study, and whole group activities.

When we asked students to tell us what scenes they would choose to capture the school's general atmosphere, we received several responses:

> Advisor meetings should be shown to show reactions of kids to curriculum.

> The Open Forums, so that one could see the new ideas generated.

> Life boat, a group process class.

> Cooking class.

> A little bit of everything.

> I wouldn't show too many classes.

> Candid shots of individual kids working with teachers.

> Students as teachers.

> Kids working independently.

> A comparison of life in and out of school—there is no separation. It's a blending.

Students and teachers alike praised the open relationships they had:

I think it's fantastic. You can't beat it. Everybody's friendly. There's very little hassling with teachers. I mean you really have the feeling of knowing people. It's not like going to "Dillington" High School where the only people you know are people you go to class with. Here, whether a person goes to class with you or not, you know him. (Student)

If you go into "Dillington" and rap with a teacher, "Hey, I saw a good-looking chick the other day," or something like that, the teacher is liable to have a heart attack. Here you can come in and rap with anybody. (Student)

Everything is on a personal basis where you're not afraid to go to someone and say, "Hey, can you readjust this?" or "Can you move this around?" (Student)

I think that the basic idea behind it is that no person, no matter how screwed up he or she might be, is impossible. I don't think if somebody gets in a bind and causes trouble makes a little static, that they are permanently labeled troublemakers. (Student)

It certainly is a very comfortable place to work . . . a lot of activities that look unique, like building kayaks, or parts of trips would be flashy things to make a nice film of. But I think the essence of the program is that there is time to talk. There is just a different kind of understanding as the school begins as to what relationships are going to be—that is relationships between teachers and teachers, students and teachers, and students and students,—the whole gamut. (Teacher)

Student comments about a sense of direction and responsibility, however, varied somewhat:

Here, after eight or nine years of regimentation, you are given a decent responsibility and more or less a word in your education. If you're worried about something or you're really into a hassle about courses, you can talk to the people who put the thing together for you, and it's not just where somebody comes up to you and hands you a book and says, "Okay, this is your book and it's your responsibility to take care of it." Instead you're given . . . your whole credit load . . . and you've gotta make it work. A lot of it is on the part of the student. I think in a way it's more of a confusing situation where you're handed all this responsibility that you're not used to. My personal feeling is that I have a say in my education, and if I don't like what's being done, I can help change it.

As far as I can see everybody's working toward one goal—to get the best education possible. And they're not competing with each other . . . like "I've got 1400 As and you've only got one." It's not that kind of thing. Everybody's striving in the same direction. Of course they're some who don't. . . . They just kind of go their own way like they would in a normal school. But there are others who, and I'd say 95 percent, are all striving for that better education bit and not worrying about I've got this and you've got that.

If you're doing something that's going to affect the general welfare of the whole program, then the chance is they'll put some heat on you. But usually, provided you take care of your own responsibilities, nobody bothers you.

The mood . . . changes according to the phase. You have to be here for the failures to understand the successses. Right now it looks like a great program. It hasn't really been what it started out to be. For awhile a lot of people were really alienated. They weren't getting much out of it.

It tries to fit everyone's needs, but it doesn't reach the kid who needs structure, who doesn't know how to work on his own.

Not surprisingly, since the originators of the program were all involved in a course on affective education at the time of its conception, the primary focus is on interpersonal relations and human development. Although the university's MAT director who helped found the program felt that he was "on the losing end" of many battles concerning the direction of the school, most of the staff and students still concurred with his stated objectives:

The traditional goals that are defined by schools are too narrow, centered on verbal, intellectual, and cognitive school development. This is not to denigrate this, for these are important. Schools can usefully contribute more than this. We try to get wider abilities of human growth than cognitive skills. We have broadened the notion of what should be rewarded.

Many wanted the school to be set up for failure students, but we wanted the richness of mix. . . . Tracking systems have tended to alienate students from each other. We made an attempt to break down the tracking systems to get all types of students involved so we could implement a program that did not have a hierarchical structure.

We are trying to make the school more personal—to break down the kind of personality which permeates schools. By restructuring a high school into schools-within-a-school, you begin to get a structure which

> allows you to build a much more meaningful rela-
> tionship between students and teachers and students
> and students.

Although students on the whole seemed to be in accord
with the general objectives of the school, they became vague
and unsure about its specific goals and even their own. Their
perceptions of the goals varied, sometimes slightly, sometimes
widely:

> It encourges you to challenge the values of the staff
> and the school.

> It tries to get away from the stereotype "student."

> It helps you to become an individual.

> It allows you to voice your opinon. I know this one
> girl at "Dillington" High who never opens her mouth.
> I'm sure that wasn't her to begin with. I mean who
> knows what she might have been like. I don't think
> that there are any truly mousey people.

> It offers me more intense learning about things I
> choose to learn.

> It is more like a college. I'm more independent. I am
> also more sensitive to people.

> Student involvement and responsibility is the key.

REACTIONS AFTER THE FIRST YEAR

Students and staff differed in their reactions to the program
after its first year. Generally, it could be said that the students
would rather be there than at any traditional high school,
even though first-year enthusiasm can be detected:

I'd quit school before I'd go back to "Dillington" High. It's different here. You don't feel closed in . . . you get to smoke. We get out more often, instead of being caged up.

I have never missed a day since I got into the program. I think it saved me; this is the only way I would stay in school to graduate.

Even if I didn't like my class, which I do, I'd want to stay in it because of the opportunities it provides. And I wouldn't have gotten to know half the people I know now . . . and that's important to me. I'm beginning to know what makes them tick.

I wanted it so badly that this girlfriend and me called the White House [when a federal cutback in funds seemed threatened] and left a message with the secretary telling him [Nixon] how great it was and how good we were doing.

Some students had mixed reactions:

I dislike many of the students here—they are superficial and loud. At first I didn't like the program, but gradually I became interested. . . . It gives me a chance to find the real me. . . . I can learn at my own pace. . . . I really like it.

I am generally satisfied, but during the middle of the year I was depressed because of the lack of interest other students showed in the survival of the program. The sense of community deteriorated at that time, but it is beginning to develop again. It is an entity in itself —a place to belong.

Both students and staff members are aware of problems and dissatisfactions:

I still need to find balance between freedom and structure. No one is willing to take the role of disciplinarian. There is a need for consistency in discipline for each individual student on the part of the staff. (Director)

I am satisfied with the direction of the program, but we have not been totally successful. I do worry about the balance between free school values and the personal need people have for structure. It has given me great insight into kids—their needs for clarity, and coercion, as well as affection. (Teacher)

I'm getting very tired of going over the same adolescent problems. They were interesting the first time around and noble the second, but . . . after that I began to feel like a boy scout. I don't dislike it, but I feel there are other things I'd rather be doing. In somewhat a selfish way I'm realizing I'm not that good—a good listener but that's about it. I don't have tools of sympathy for them. That's begun to wear on me this year. I've spent a year teaching kite building, writing, and a whole lot of other things, and what I should be teaching is theater, that's what I want to get back into. If I have to teach anywhere in the high school system, I certainly would want to teach here. (Teacher)

I don't mind some of the things that go on here, but as a black student there are a lot of things that I can't relate to. I like a number of the people around the place, but yet I feel more at home around the kids in my neighborhood. (Student)

I fit more into the atmosphere than any of the other black students . . . because I went to kindergarten with most of the other white students. The other black

> students hardly ever identify with the students here.
> They go back to "Dillington" High. (Student)

After a year's operation, some of the staff had doubts that
the school can work for all people:

> Kids with the least inner structure seem unhappy. The
> radical kid who is insecure often gets depressed and
> needs frequent positive reinforcement. This type stu-
> dent often blames the school for his personal unhappi-
> ness, but his frustration does not lead to despair be-
> cause of staff support and his access to power. There
> are next steps.

> There is another group of students in the program
> who are talking very strongly about going back into
> the regular school next year, the kind of student who
> is very much influenced by the crowd and who feels
> very strongly about fraternities and sororities. That
> kills me, that self-restricting code of behavior that if
> you do this or that, then you're cool. This is the group
> of students who perhaps are least responsive to inde-
> pendent study because that just doesn't have the sup-
> port of the crowd, and I think they are the group that
> the school least helps. I'd say there are at least six stu-
> dents in this group.

> We dreamed almost the impossible, and we've been
> able to do most of the things we wanted to experiment
> with. We have fallen short in how to trap students and
> get them caught up in their own education, and
> maybe we are shortchanging ourselves. Maybe it will
> take kids longer than we think it should. We didn't
> mean it to be a school for everybody, maybe some kids
> would be happier at "Dillington" High.

One student had an instant solution to the problem:

I love the program. The kids who ruin the program
—who don't attend classes or don't do their work—
should simply be kicked out. It's a nice thing, why
ruin it?

COMMUNICATIONS OUTSIDE THE SCHOOL

The communication process, generally adequate within
SIAS itself, broke down in its dealing with the high school
and the larger community. Teachers in the main building did
not seem to show much interest in the experiment. Some were
waiting to "see what happens," others could not have cared
less, still others hoped "it fails." One considered it simply an
inconvenience, because its students who used the high school's
facilities came late to class. Yet she did recognize they came
with a smile and a book in hand.

An influential teacher asserted that SIAS was a lot of
"foolishness." He felt that without the high school, the project would fold. He suspected that the program's founder was
using the project only to win recognition in the academic
community and believed it was quickly moving away from a
school-within-a-school to a school outside the high school: "It
is becoming a private school in a public school system."

Why "private?"

"Because the selection process was more political than a
true lottery. Many youngsters were admitted who had much
to contribute to the high school," he declared, "and their
talents were lost." The project's staff did "not help this situation," and they did "not encourage the students to take part
in the main school either." He was not certain that they were
being prepared properly for college or receiving the kind of

education they should. He believed that they didn't really
know how to handle the freedom that they had. He felt they
no longer respected the high school and that SIAS was building an elite group of youngsters who did not want to have
anything to do with the high school.

Few meetings have been held between the two staffs. The
high school teachers said that project's staff stayed to themselves, rarely attending required faculty meetings. When the
staffs have met together, there has usually been hostility.
Staff members of SIAS admitted their ambivalence:

> Ideally we want to use the school more. . . . It kills me
> to go to staff meetings there. Nothing ever gets done!
> It's very petty.

Yet SIAS's director, partly for public relations and partly
because of personal commitment, was, more than other staff
members, concerned with maintaining a close relationship
with the larger high school. The director was the "straight"
member of the faculty as well as one of the original five
teachers who designed the school with the help of the
university's MAT director. He was highly involved in the
local Democratic Party, was president of the local teachers'
union, a graduate of "Dillington" High, and a member of one
of the town's most influential families. The director commented:

> If the program stops trying to work with "Dillington,"
> I'd leave. We are supposed to be an experimental pro-
> gram to be used by the high school. If we become
> simply another alternative school, I wouldn't want to
> be involved.

The students at SIAS have also broken off much communication with the larger school. They viewed it as the "enemy,"
the evil structure that "trapped them for so many years."

Their need to assert their independence was strong. One high school student related that his only contact was when black students came to the school to play cards.

The lack of communication, the suggestion of elitism, and SIAS's seeming independence has caused the "Dillington" principal's strong support of the project to wane somewhat.

The program has never found it necessary to brief the school board beyond issuing quarterly evaluations to the members. No board member has ever visited the school. There has also been little relationship between the project and the superintendent's office, since the superintendent prefers to avoid any interference in an experimental program.

One of the board members, however, was excited about the project because of its individualized study approach, its new role for students, and its curriculum, which is more relevant to the needs of today's students. Although concerned about lack of attendance, disciplinary problems, and the attitude of the students, she felt that an experimental program was likely to have "growing pains." She has talked to parents who seemed delighted with it yet worried about college acceptance for their children because SIAS does not give grades. (Although none of the students were seniors, the staff contacted popular colleges and universities in the area, informing them of the program.)

SIAS's approach to the community at large has been to ignore it, despite the negative impression it has made:

> We are viewed as flaming radicals to most people in town. They feel we don't have enough structure. They feel there is not enough stress on academic skills. Some feel that it is part and parcel of the whole anarchy of youth. But these people have not become an active force against us. Actually the community has supported us by being tolerant and letting us exist.

GOVERNANCE

Although the governance structures of the school-in-a-school and the main school differed, there were some parallels in the decision-making process. The high school, of course, is traditional. There is a student council to represent student opinion, but the general apathy of the student body made it hard to find students who had knowledge of or interest in student government. Governance could be described as a benevolent dictatorship. Since early 1971, students have been given a social study hall, they are permitted to leave campus during the day, and the dress code has been liberalized, but all these policies were initiated and carried through by the principal. In a sense, issues were resolved before students had any chance to organize around them or advocate their own interests. As the principal acknowledged, "When I hear informal student gripes, I jump on the issue and try to resolve it before it becomes a crisis." Students as well as faculty are invited to his home for informal gatherings.

Faculty reaction to their new principal was mixed but predominantly negative:

> Some faculty think he's too liberal with students, tyrannical with staff.

> I don't like him. I don't approve of the leniency of social study or optional assemblies, but I will cope with it. If he told me that I should give more freedom to my students, I would object very strenuously.

> [He] has enjoyed a certain percentage of success and has expended a great deal of pride in the administration of the school. He made teachers feel threatened at first, but he does take advice very perceptively.

The principal stated his position clearly:

> As far as student government goes, I believe students have rights. I do believe that students should be given the right to determine what the school should be like, as long as it's not injurious to their education as directed by the board of education and specific educational goals set by the faculty. That gives them a lot of leeway.
>
> I'm firmly convinced the board should set the goals of education for the community. I think truly that [it] should be representatives of the parents. Then the expertise should come from the faculty, and the students should be involved in obtaining what their parents really want. If they want to change it, the change should come about by proper established procedures or by parental action on the board to change the view of the board. I really don't believe that the "Dillington" High School or "Dillington" faculty should set the goals of education for this community. They should be set by the board of education.
>
> As far as student government goes, I'd like to see the students . . . responsible enough to accept the responsibility of the actions of the school. If they want to get involved in that, fine. And if they want to make any request of me as an executive of the building, then I should have the right to have a suspended veto. It's like, "Should there be a dress code?" I say "Yes, there should," and if they want it abolished, I should have the right to a suspended veto. Then if I am over-ruled by the student body, their decision should be legislated. But if the student governing body requests something that I feel is in direct opposition to the policies of the board of education, then I should render an absolute veto. They then have the right to go to the super-

intendent or the board of education. But I believe that
in the majority of cases the suspended veto would be
my preferred choice. I can't think of a single incident
when I would use an absolute veto, except those
things that I felt were in direct opposition to board
policy.

If the students wanted to change rules, they have
had the legitimate position to do so in the school since
February, but not a thing has been done. That's why I
don't really know if they are really able to accept responsibility. And I told them that these rules will be
enforced until they're changed, and that if they wish
change, there are channels through which they can be
changed.

The high school's students, however, claimed they had
tried to organize but had been overruled by the principal.
When, for example, the students had petitioned for the right
to wear hats in class, the proposal was vetoed immediately.
In general, most students felt that the principal had great
veto power in every area and used it. "Why give a damn," a
student commented, "he vetoes just about everything." "He
runs the school," another said, "the student council is a farce."

Since its inception, SIAS has wrestled with the problem of
internal governance. At the beginning, a committee of four
students and two faculty members was set up. The students,
picked at random, soon began to feel uncomfortable with
their "unrepresentativeness." The committee actually was to
be used only for crises, and no crisis occurred except for the
issue of the governance process itself. The students hassled
over the process for about two weeks and finally decided
not to accept the committee form. Instead, they proposed a
one-man, one-vote open forum system of decision-making,
which was ultimately instituted after faculty sanction.

The Open Forum operates in part under a majority rule. The faculty each have one vote, and the students each have one vote. But if all the teachers vote against an issue, it is considered a veto. Yet if only one teacher votes with the majority, the issue is passed.

Many students felt that the Open Forum was simply a place for discussion. Issues involving methods of instruction, discipline, trips, and complaints revolving around interpersonal relationships have been raised, but the meetings were seldom attended by a majority of students, so decisions and votes could never be taken. Anyone could call for an Open Forum, but in a four-month period, only three had been called. One student remarked:

> As far as student power . . . it's really not that much. If there's something they desperately want to change or even slightly, all they really need is to go find a faculty member and try to straighten it out there. And if it doesn't work, to go round up students' support. Once you've got student support, you have more of a chance that other people will listen.

A student who attended Open Forums thought the parliamentary procedure hindered its effectiveness. Only a few influential students participated, mainly those who had taught a class within the program. "They assume they are staff members," he said. One "student teacher" referred to herself as a "general" and to other students as "privates."

What success the Open Forum has had was credited to its chairwoman. "She really gets things done," a staff member said, "and I think the majority of kids respect her." Before each meeting, she spoke to every student, requesting his or her attendance and agenda items.

The real governance of the program seemed to take place

in informal staff meetings, to which students were welcome, but only the more influential attended. As one teacher commented:

> I think there is an abstract need for students to feel that their school is their own, and they have not felt the pressure of a restrictive body on the outside that keeps them from doing something they want to do. They haven't felt the necessity to organize in order to achieve. I think there is a very healthy input by students into staff decisions, but that's on the part of six students which I think is par for the course.

Students felt that they have control over how the actual program operates, but they also felt that the faculty *should* have the final say, since it will ultimately be held responsible. Basically the students had a great deal of trust in the faculty, and up until now the faculty had not let the students down.

The "benevolent" governance by the principal of the high school had its parallel in SIAS where students depended on faculty to govern in their interests. The strength of the informal relationships between student and teacher may account for much of this dependence. In both cases, however, there was minimal advocacy by students for themselves.

Also, as in the high school, the black students (they numbered six) in SIAS did not relate to the governance system. One spoke of the "loud-mouth," bossy types who seemed to run things. Since things are white-oriented, she said, blacks stay out of most "stuff."

Within SIAS itself, the director had no more power than any other staff member. The directorship evolved out of a need for public relations and the school system's desire to have one person responsible for the program, particularly for its financial accounts. The director defined his position:

It's a mixed bag. It's a go-between for the regular school system and the program. The staff doesn't care about keeping receipts for accounting. There has been much anger over the lackadaisical approach of certain staff members toward accounting. It's a very political position I enjoy. I got it because I was the staff member most accepted by the community and the faculty at "Dillington."

CURRICULUM, COUNSELING, AND TEACHING METHODS

The SIAS curriculum was completely open-ended. Apparently the only limitation was the availability of teachers, though SIAS could use the university's student teachers or their own students as teachers. Teachers on the staff had taught in fields where they had no expertise, learning at the same time as their students.

In the last six-week period of 1971 the courses planned were:

Myth—Pre-Christian	Reconstruction
Median—Bias and Point of View	Reading
Writing	Meteorology
Judo and Self-defense	Swimming
America the Beautiful:	Study of Cities
Variations on a Theme	Puppets
Orienteering	Multi-Media
Algebra	Botany
Lifeboat	German
How Things Work	Auto Repair
Language Lab	French Reading
French Conversation	Cooking
Art	Dance

Each course was taught according to the teacher's and students' wishes, the possibilities of the subject, and the facilities available, both in and outside the school. A course on Wild Life, for example, was taught in the forest; the class on Law Courts visited local courts, and an auto repair course took students to a repair garage. SIAS was planning to use the community further.

Students have been teaching such courses as America the beautiful, Judo, Dance, Tennis, Eskimo culture, and a class on Group Process. Students enjoyed teaching classes, and most enjoyed taking classes taught by their fellow students.

The number of courses taken per phase was determined by the number of school hours required by state law. Since some courses lasted longer than others, each student may have had a different number of classes, but all spent the same amount of time in school. Any free time could be used as the students wished.

Courses were chosen by the student and his advisor. The staff tried to see that each student had a wide range of courses that would challenge but not swamp him. A slow reader would probably not be scheduled to take five heavy reading courses.

Students were not graded but evaluated. Both students and teachers evaluated themselves and each other in writing and then discussed their evaluations. The evaluations were kept in a file for the students' use and college entrance applications.

The program had a collegiate approach to assignments. Generally there was a long-term project rather than daily assignments, but students were expected to contribute to the daily discussions. The ideal balance between freedom and structure, however, was yet to be established. Originally, the staff believed that all students would become motivated if the material was properly presented. Later, some of the faculty were beginning to believe that some students needed to be pushed and that such coercion might represent concern. They started to require class attendance and more organized studies.

On the whole, students seemed happy with the choices offered and the way curriculum was handled, although there were a few complaints:

> Anyone can get a class started by going to a staff member, and if they couldn't teach it, they would find someone who could.

> There is an amazing breadth of classes. . . . I tutor emotionally handicapped children with reading problems in an elementary school for my how children learn course. This has increased my interest in teaching.

> The stuff I am picking up in school I use outside. . . . It seems 95 percent more useful than when you pick it up outside. . . . Like they had a course called lifeboat. I termed it Social Survival. That's what it was. It taught you how to get along with people and how to get along in certain situations.

> At first I was dissatisfied with the science and math courses, because I thought they had to be structured and rote, but now I can learn scientific concepts and work from there.

> There is a lot of individual attention from the staff. I am taking an independent biology course from [a staff member]. This is the best way to learn—if you have to.

> I asked for a basic grammar class, and I got individual help. I hate independent study; I need more structure; everyone does. We all need guidance.

The students, however, were more satisfied with the curriculum than the staff. To one staff member, the curriculum was too loosely defined and probably the school's weakest point. Another found there were problems with language and basic skills courses because the staff did not review students' records early enough to adjust for their deficiencies: "We should have realized that there were going to be reading problems and brought in reading specialists at the beginning."

SIAS students could take advantage of both their own counseling program and that of the larger high school. Although one high school teacher described the high school's counseling program as a "complete failure," it did provide information on colleges, which the SIAS students needed. At SIAS itself, students had the opportunity to meet regularly in groups of ten with a staff member to discuss any problems or complaints they had about the school. Counseling as such, however, was ill-defined, and most students felt the groups were a waste of time since they already had more effective channels of communication with staff. For example, students met with teachers to discuss course selections and evaluations. Some, who viewed their teachers as friends, brought personal problems to them. Occasionally teachers invited troubled students to talk their problems over with them, which some responded to and others regarded as prying.

The teachers were an atypical group. The university's teachers-in-training were generally full of fresh ideas, along with some inexperience and much idealism. During their six-week tours of duty, they had to learn to motivate a class and gain respect without the traditional methods of student-teacher distance, rules, and discipline.

No new staff members had been added to the original five, and since they were also the program's planners, they had a clear understanding of what they wished to accomplish. They believed that any teacher could work effectively within the program and that it was important to the flow of ideas to vary the staffing. Their own styles of teaching varied widely. A staff member described their different approaches:

It's not just the philosophies, it's the attitudes toward the students. One staff member feels that certain standards should be maintained and worked toward. Another is more interested in the affect of material and long personal contacts with students. Another is more philosophical and abstract than the rest. Still another is more the official-type organizer, and the last staff member is more strongly attached to the good-old-teaching kind of approach. I don't think you would find a person like myself spending much time in the organization of a course. You'd find we'd spend a lot more time with the enthusiasm of whatever it is we are going to do than the others, but less planning. It's just the difference.

Another commented on what it was like to teach at a school such as SIAS:

The teacher works twice as hard as he has to in a structured system. Take someone like [one staffer] who has been teaching for twelve years and had come to the point of doing things mechanically. He has a reputation as a brilliant teacher for his rapport with students, but he was lazy as hell. Now he's had to work and has been a very strong teacher. He's had to work, because it's very hard to duck out on your work when you're doing it with four other people who are depending on you to hold up your end of the contract with the students and the students' parents through the evaluations. You can't dummy grades, you have to make a comment on what they are doing specifically.

You don't have the traditional motivation to rely on. You don't have grades and suspension policy. So what you say is that this stuff is so interesting that you want to do it for its own sake. And kids that have gone through school systems over all these years don't take naturally to this for the first couple of months. Teachers have to work extra hard.

This type of teaching and attitude toward teaching resulted in much positive response from students:

I've never had this kind of thing. . . . The ideal teacher is someone who can get a point across but not have to make you sit there like a robot. Some people, if you're not looking at them every second, really get insecure and start banging around, and you really have a hard time of it. I'd say the ideal teacher is like what we have here. They get the point across to you whether you're going through a little bit of static or not.

[One staff member] is far out. I mean for his age [close to 40] and for a guy in his position, he's fantastic. He'd practically bend over backwards and touch his head to the floor for you. I mean he's really that type of guy. Like he's teaching algebra and he'd lean on you to get it done, but he's still not traditional, which is something which surprises me. He's very far from a traditional type person. I mean . . . when I first met him he hit me as a typical $40,000-a-year type, really square. But he's not, he's kind of . . . he's turned on. He's on the student level. He's not in there batting with the bullshit and typical hangups. He's like one of the guy's. He just fits in.

INTERGROUP RELATIONS

Relationships in SIAS were in many ways unique, but hints of tradition did slip in and out. The idea of a close-knit community was stressed from the beginning. To instill a feeling of camaraderie among students and teachers, community projects were started even before the school year began. Late in the summer, for example, staff and students began building a yurt, a Mongolian hut, to be used for group activities during the fall. Wood and glass were cut, nails driven, carpet laid, and electricity wired in one of the most successful projects undertaken.

Since the yurt, the school has continued to build community spirit with trips, picnics, community lunches and dinners, and outside service projects. One winter the class on Eskimo culture attempted to build an igloo together, smoke fish, and make Eskimo carvings. Yet the sense of community life, one of the school's most important concerns, was difficult to maintain at a high pitch:

> Sense of community has had its ups and downs. When we started, the sense of community was high. We were innovative, new and everything was great! We're back on our way up, and I think that's great. (Staff member)

Relationships between teachers and students ranged from easiness to close personal friendships. While students who found it difficult to break the patterned relationships they had with teachers were not pressured to become more friendly, most began to view their teachers as friends—close friends. Students often stayed hours after school, sitting around talking to the staff:

They're just people. I think it is important to be able to call a teacher by his first name—it's kind of symbolic. Teachers put up with a lot of shit from students. It's really nice to have a teacher for a friend; it's easier to learn from them. Shyness does not exist. Once you pass that shit, you can really learn.

Students and teachers are all basically together because everybody's going in the same direction—looking for the best possible education. A lot of it kind of goes back to the parent "hangup" where the parents want to give the kids what they didn't have. I think the staff, in teaching, want to give the students what they didn't get.

If you told a teacher in the regular school to "go to hell," you'd be suspended. Your parents would be called. You'd be a moral leper. But kids say it here. It is important to call teachers by their first names; it is more comfortable and easier to relate. If this is supposed to be a community, you shouldn't have to call them "Mr." and "Mrs." These teachers are special. They are personal friends.

Although the teachers had diverse styles, interests, and philosophies, they seemed able to work effectively together. Some were teachers-in-training from the university, who taught for one phase (six weeks) or more. Five were permanent staff. Because of their diversity, each teacher had a group of students who felt particularly close to him, and every student had a figure with whom to identify. This had not yet caused any dissension. One teacher attributed it to the ability of the staff to get along:

Any program would only be as strong as the people teaching, the team teaching. I don't think our program is any stronger than what we can do—our own energies, or how much time we can put in, or the very background we have to offer. I think that if you took the same five teachers, in any school, no matter what the structure, it would be about as strong and have the same weaknesses.

It's an interesting staff . . . because I don't think we personally like each other very much. We do work very well together, however. Not that there is any dissension, but we are not the kind of people who would socially gather together, or even whose philosophies would pull us together. I guess we're the only group of people who would be able to sit down and write out a description of things, everybody adding words, that kind of ability.

As envisaged, the SIAS students did represent a cross section of the larger high school. Along with the third- and fourth-generation Yankees were immigrants, blacks, and Jews; along with the rich were the poor; along with the slow student, the average and above average; along with the creative, the mechanical-minded. Thrown together in a six-room apartment, they had somehow developed into a community, with a warmth that could not be ignored.

However, many students, while committed to the community spirit, were independent and individual. One student felt the group as a whole worked together only once and a while and sometimes got lost. Cliques were evident:

The freaks, gearheads, and jocks are all definitely visible. But there's no great class, like you're a freak, you stand on one side of the room, and if you're a jock, you stand on the other side of the room. It's nothing like that. . . . We've got our friends, but everybody meshes together. There's not any actual clique in the sense that they don't mix, like hardhats and hippies don't mix. It's not that kind of a setup.

Both staff and students felt that there was also a small clique of intellectuals:

One of the major goals was to break down the tracking system and the kinds of separation that brought about. I think in a lot of ways that has been very good . . . it is consciously recognized by students. A feeling of equality among the students exists because they recognize different kinds of skills, not necessarily intellectual skills. I think that equality has spread itself out.

There are few people who are thought of as the superiors, of whom you have to be careful or you will appear a fool. Those few seem quite conscientious in trying to listen, trying to share. (Teacher)

I enjoy working with slower kids, but tracking occurs unconsciously. No slow reader wants to take a class in which he must read a book a week. (Student)

The "elitist" students, mostly those who have taught classes, viewed themselves as intellectually superior and readily informed one of it. Yet failure, viewed as natural, was being experienced in small doses by all students, along with success. A mechanics class, for example, posed some difficulty for the intellectually gifted.

On the whole, the program was more successful for white, middle-class students, who could work independent of teacher supervision, than for blacks. The only black teacher on the staff was part-time, and the few black studies courses given were not well received by black students. The operating style of the program was not particularly designed to elicit their response:

They [black students] have not asked for any classes yet, and I don't think they like the courses. Their past experience with the educational system has been totally different than any other kid in [the school]. Their transition is harder. Maybe next year it will be better. I think they'll make the transition; it will just be harder. (White Student)

I think we've been a failure to our black group. I'm not sure the personalities that make up this school are the one's black kids look up to. We certainly get along . . . but I won't chase after people and get them to go to a class. They understand my position, and I understand theirs, but right at the moment it doesn't seem to be working its way around that. It's always left to the minute that they decide not to go to class to get involved, and at that minute it's too far away for me to handle. Afterwards it can be reconciled, but it doesn't make a difference in the next move. (Teacher)

I think that these students, three of them, are the only ones that were not volunteers for this program; they were recruited. It's harder, or less comfortable, for them to feel affected by activities that they don't see as valuable. For instance, the thing they have been most successful at is a course in algebra. Something like the kites course they just couldn't take. The idea of building a kite to learn about physics was just too far removed. And I think it had the stigma of being babyish. (Teacher)

Racial tensions, ironically enough, were increased when black students avoided attending school. White students, for example, said:

They often don't come to classes, and many of our classes depend on all of its members, so other students often get upset and frustrated with the black students and have conflict in class because of it.

We need more discipline. It makes the program look bad when someone is always cutting classes, and it's really depressing for the teachers. I think a student should be made aware of that.

The number of the staff and students at the school had been ideal for the philosophy and operating principles originally envisioned. As it becomes larger (it expanded in the fall of 1971), new probelms relative to size may be created. But it may also create new solutions, making SIAS more relevant to more students. It may even facilitate the larger high school to do the same.

Community High School, Berkeley *By Sue Golden*

Community High School in Berkeley, California, was the first alternative school within the city's public system. Since it was set up in 1969, many more alternative schools have been established within Berkeley's only high school, a large school that encompasses several buildings on two campuses.

This university-centered municipality has its share of factions, but they seem to live in peace. As a student described Berkeley:

> There's a right wing on the hill, a black ghetto in the flats, and the liberal-radicals of the university all living out a tolerant truce—"Do your own thing but keep away from me; if you don't step on my toes, I won't step on yours."

Over the past fifteen years, the Radical Coalition has managed to win several seats on the city council and the school board.

Community High School, in the spring of 1971, had 233 students in grades ten through twelve. As the chart below shows, its population was predominately white, in contrast to the more equitable racial balance in Berkeley High.

	Community High	Berkeley High
Black	19.5%	45%
White	72.5%	43%
Chicanos	3.5%	4%
Orientals	4.5%	8%
	233 Students	3,300 Students

Community High was designed to have the same ethnic balance as Berkeley High, but a large number of its black students have moved to Black House. Black House, which began as a special interest unit or "tribe" within Community High and became autonomous in the fall of 1970, is open to all black students in Berkeley High. Now the cultural majority of Community High consists of white, middle to upper middle-class youngsters with a decided counter-culture orientation.

The school has a staff of ten full-time teachers and one guidance counselor, plus a large number of student teachers. The director, chosen by the students and staff, serves simultaneously as a teacher, a faculty coordinator, and as liaison with Berkeley High School. Most of the faculty are young and share many interests with the students. Their length of teaching experience ranges from nine years to none.

Community High occupies six rooms, connected by sliding partitions, on the second floor of one of Berkeley High's newer buildings. It is surrounded by an air of hostility. Other Berkeley High students who hang out in the area frequently try to extort Community students, who attribute most of the stealing and petty damages to them. Few Berkeley students feel positively about Community High. Those who did moved to newer alternative schools, although some preferred the sure prestige of Berkeley High's reputation for help in getting into good jobs and colleges. Most are not interested in alternative kinds of schooling and simply put down Community High as a "white cop-out," "a rip off," "a mess," or "a waste of time." Such tension at its borders affects the Community students, who usually leave the building immediately after school. "Who would want to stay around that depressing place?" they ask. Some have been campaigning to move the school off the Berkeley High campus, but others fear the school would become insulated by such a move and lose its role as a force for change in Berkeley High.

Students and staff have attempted to make the environment as personal and comfortable as possible. Old rugs, cushions, chairs, and overstuffed sofas proliferate; art work and tie-dyed cloth cover the white ceiling; murals, posters, and cartoons adorn the walls. The overall effect varies day by day, shifting from warmth and comfort to worn and grubby chaos. "My image of Community High," one student said, "is that it's like a ball that goes up and down, never even stopping. It's best when the ball is up and shitty when it's down."

The school seems barren and dull on days when fewer students attend and everyone is off on "their own thing"—teachers might be working individually with students or off by themselves, while students read or lounge in corners. There is no sense of belonging or cohesion—no apparent reason for the school's existence. Other days there is a warm, congenial feeling and a sense of group identity within a "tribe" that might have started the day by eating breakfast together. In one part of a room a class meets for a discussion or lectures initiated either by the students or a teacher. A student reading in the corner looks up occasionally, enters the discussion, and then goes back to his or her book. After class a student might demonstrate some of the physical movements of a Tai Chi meditation. The rest of the day is spent by the groups helping each other, reaching out, and talking about ideas.

Every day is different. The school is anything and everything, changing, always moving. "Freedom is being a yo-yo," a student said, "and feeling the movement back and forth, up and down." But student reaction varied as the following responses, drawn from a class in survival English, show:

> This is a great school, but fuck it, I don't want to be in school.

> Community High, a place of new learning. A place to exchange thoughts and create new thoughts. There is much more freedom to be an individual, to work on projects that really interest me, to find new interests to pursue. I really love this school and if it were ever destroyed, I'd quit going to school at all.

> Shuck, farce, make-believe junkies, make-believe, real people, apathetic to changes in the environment and in general no dependence on each other. Everybody is a separate being, and nobody seems to care about anybody else except perhaps a certain circle of friends. Teachers are still teachers, students are still students; there is no real change in the roles. There is no sense of community in Community High.

> Community High, free and creative, individual. People fuck up but most people dig it.

> For me the essence of the school is joy and happiness. I really love it, no shit.

ORIGINS OF COMMUNITY HIGH

The Community High project began in the spring of 1969 with 110 tenth-grade students. It was an outgrowth of an experimental summer program developed three years earlier by a group of teachers who had attempted to introduce flexible scheduling and interdisciplinary programs in Berkeley High. Discouraged by their minimal impact, three faculty members had set up a summer workshop in 1966 with one hundred students. The goals were: (*1*) to reach a wide range of students; (*2*) to "involve students and teachers in an intensive effort to make public school education personal and coherent"; and (*3*) "to teach a wide range of subject matter utilizing the arts as a vehicle for generating enthusiasm and creativity in the learning situation."

At the project's end the staff issued an evaluation report, which stimulated widespread interest among the high school faculty. Meetings to explore the possibility of developing the summer experience into regular school programs were attended by faculty, administration, and parents. Most of the initial planning for this project was done by the three teachers, and with the help of educational leaders throughout the country, a proposal for the Community High Project was developed and then processed through Berkeley High's curriculum department and the superintendent's office. The program was finally approved in August 1968, for implementation in the spring of 1969.

The program passed with little opposition from the community. Berkeley already had a number of private alternative schools. Other Ways, for example, had been organized by local students and parents with considerable support, and the community was receptive to the idea of similar ventures within the public system. Parents, as well as staff and students, felt that they were participants in an ongoing movement. The main issues were: To what extent should alternative schools be related to or dependent on public schools? What were the gains? What were the problems? What were the costs?

The plan for Community High was to provide a school that would "get students more involved in the planning of their own education so that what they received from the school would be more relevant (or less superficial) than it had been." This was the first goal. The second was to develop an interdisciplinary approach providing students with "a coherent environment," one that would cut across artificial subject areas and "help them to unify the elements of their experience to the relevance of the curriculum." The third aim was to maximize the students' opportunities to change the school environment. The life of the school would emerge from the combined efforts of students and teachers. Fourth, the designers wanted to develop a heterogeneous atmosphere: "The project assumes that students learn most effectively within a dynamic relationship with other students who are not supposedly alike."

The initial planners varied among themselves about the interpretation of the above statements and about the degree of student autonomy that would be functional. While all the staff were committed to the idea of student control, the degree of student involvement was the source of continual conflict during the first school year. Staff opinion ranged between two polarities: either the staff should be accountable to students or the adults should have control of the school—from the Summerhill thesis that teachers extend freedom and then see how far it will go to a posture of "teachers know best." Actually, the staff influenced all decisions because of their greater articulateness, knowledge, and experience.

Some of the original goals were not implemented. The program slipped back into old subject area compartments, and learning experiences were still centered in the classroom, although there was more freedom in the classroom. Yet significant experimentation developed in student-staff relationships. Early on, for example, a pattern was established in which students initiated ideas for classes, and teachers then developed and taught the courses. Since then, students have been urged to become more active in developing and teaching courses as well.

Much time was also devoted in the beginning to building a sense of community within the school and developing a highly personalized working atmosphere. Staff members met together daily and participated in encounter groups. Teachers and students collaborated to test out ideas for creating a new kind of school environment. In the first year, the staff also tried to develop a working relationship with the Berkeley staff, inviting them to all Community High meetings, and also it tried to keep the parents and community informed about what was taking place. The communication flow, however, was one-sided. To the staff's and students' surprise, little interest was shown by the community or the Berkeley staff, once the initial funding was obtained. Few of the Berkeley staff attended the meetings.

RELATIONS WITH BERKELEY HIGH AND BLACK HOUSE

Some interpreted the lack of interest on the part of Berkeley High as deliberate avoidance. Some considered it a form of neutrality, part of the city's ethos of "do your own thing, as long as you stay off my territory." Berkeley High's failure to give active support or to share its resources was seen as neutrality by some and was not entirely condemned. Several students commented:

> You have lots of freedom and tolerance in this town. Nobody really gives a damn here, so you can go ahead and do what you want, as long as you know what that is. People will let you, but they sure won't help.

> People avoid conflict here. A principal at Berkeley High went around the country to look at innovative schools, but he wouldn't even come across the hall to see what we were doing.

Some Community High staff members said they probably had had more freedom than they used. They were in a situation where they could be creative, but they were often unsure about how much power they had or how far they could go in changing the rules. Still, in their negotiations with Berkeley High, they succeeded in introducing new alternatives and a greater degree of freedom to the larger high school. An issue that had to be negotiated during the first year, for example, concerned accreditation. To increase the breadth of the program, the Community faculty had to be able to teach subjects that they were not accredited to teach. At the same time, the other courses they offered had to enable their students to fulfill the basic requirements for Berkeley High credits and diplomas, or else their students would have to continue to attend some classes in Berkeley High as they had been doing. Community staff members spent the early period of the school's life testing and extending the flexibility of Berkeley High's rules.

During the first six months they were also struggling with the challenge of doubling their size while preserving the personalized style of a small community. Expansion, however, entailed more required courses, permitting students to spend less time at Berkeley High and more in the Community school.

As the school increased in size, the staff and students became more sophisticated in negotiating with Berkeley High. The early strategy had been to write proposals, submit them to Berkeley's administration, and wait decision. This often proved unsatisfactory. The administrators frequently met in secret and returned decisions that seemed to be inconsistent with previous understandings. As a result, Community High formed a negotiating committee, composed of an equal number of students and staff, to deal with Berkeley's administration. It insisted they follow the Quaker model of consensus—talking until a consensus is reached. This method of resolving conflict not only kept staff, students, and administrators face to face until a final decision was reached but attempted to humanize the negotiation process by stressing openness and clarity. It allowed continued pressure to be exerted by both sides and may have escalated conflict by bringing into the open issues that might otherwise have been avoided or preemptorily dismissed.

The process worked to the advantage of the Community High team, which knew what it wanted and was tenacious. Some thought it tended to put Berkeley's administrators on the defensive. Both sides found it an exhausting and time-consuming venture.

The former director (1970–71) found it difficult to maintain equal effectiveness in her three roles as teacher, faculty coordinator, and liaison with Berkeley High, although her personal style and articulateness, her clarity of goals, and her sophistication in dealing with Berkeley High and the school district won her considerable allegiance among the students and staff. Struggling to reduce her administrative load, she encouraged students to negotiate with Berkeley High's administration. A consistent advocate of increased student power, she was able to force Berkeley's administration to meet with students immediately about a crisis by making an appointment in her own name, which students then kept. After a year, she took a sabbatical—the role of director of an innovative school is challenging, absorbing, and exhausting.

During periods of intense negotiations, as in the fall of 1970, other work fell by the wayside. The Berkeley principal felt he was diverting the bulk of his time from the affairs of Berkeley High; Community staff negotiators had little time for class preparation; committee work virtually became the student negotiators' curriculum for the term.

The negotiating committee worked its way through several major issues, including relative autonomy from Berkeley High in terms of separate voting and budget and the separation of Black House from Community High.

Interestingly enough, Black House was able to achieve considerably more autonomy than Community High, whose attempt to become accountable to the superintendent or the school board, rather than the principal of Berkeley High, was unsuccessful. Black House, however, was made accountable to the district office and won separate personnel, budget, and curriculum accreditation. Community High members attributed the Black House victory to the superintendent's direct support of it in the open conflict that existed between Black House and the Berkeley principal. The district administration felt that supervision and control would be more effective if the supervisor were black and located in the district office. While escalation of the conflict helped Black House, its success depended on the district administration's responsiveness to community pressure and on the strong commitment of a black administrator in the district to Black House.

At issue was the rationale for developing an alternative school that seemed separatist and counter to a policy of integration. Until 1968, Berkeley's black and white students had had little contact with one another until high school age, when all of a sudden they became part of one large depersonalized high school complex. As a result, students' high school years were filled with racial tensions and unrest. In 1968, however, Berkeley decided to integrate its neighborhood schools by bussing. Many residents have since criticized the development of Black House as being counter to integration. Despite the community's ambivalence, the board and superintendent were fully supportive of the movement toward alternative means of education.

The development of both Community High and Black House were facilitated by their position, sandwiched between the Berkeley High administration, which was resistant to change, and the district administration and board, which were supportive of alternatives in education. Without this support, Community High would probably not have withstood the blockades set up by the Berkeley High administration.

Community High's relation to the larger school centered mainly on the need to share economic and physical resources. At present, Community High has considerable autonomy over its own budget, but it must choose certified staff from the district rolls whose credentials will allow their students to complete the course requirements necessary for graduation. Although the problems of being a part of a larger high school, the inadequacy of physical resources, and the frequently hostile relationship with Berkeley High students have taken their toll on the staff and students, Community High was for many years committed to maintaining its role as a change agent within Berkeley High. This role faded as the numbers of alternative schools increased.

EXPANSION AND CHANGE

As Community High expanded over the first three years, its student body and program changed. In the first semester, tribal units, randomly selected, were formed as heterogeneous groups that attended all classes together. They were intended to foster friendships among those who might otherwise remain strangers. By the third year, however, the tribal structure was based on interest groupings, such as art and media or ecology and social change.

At frequent intervals during the first two years, the total school met for as long as necessary (a half-day to two days) to evaluate their progress. Discussion focused on opinions about how things had been going (what was good, what was bad, analysis of the strategies, tactics, values) and on plans for change. There was always controversy about such large-scale involvement and whether the school should meet as a whole for such discussion or in small groups. Although Berkeley High people were shocked that the Community school changed so drastically from semester to semester, Community members were proud of their flexibility and the open democratic structure that permitted frequent innovations, despite the chaos involved. A Community member explained:

> That we could, however imperfectly, meet like this, as a school, and discuss these questions—What should a school be? What kind of school do we want to be? How do we do that?—was one of the best things I've seen happen in school. It could happen in years one and two, I think, because of the kind of student body we had then—pioneer. Year three this was not possible. Students and staff were worn out, for many reasons, and lacked the energy.

By the third year, the type of students attracted to the school had changed. Initially, the free atmosphere and experimentalism had attracted a large number of responsible, concerned student leaders. But as "leave me alone" became the prevalent attitude, they came under attack for bothering people. By the third year, the school seemed to attract "free loaders."

A study of Community High students their first and second years (written by Dr. Jeanne Block of the University of California's Center for Human Development, on file in the district office) shows the transition. The first year group was ambitious to build an alternative education that expressed humanistic values. The second year group had more personal goals; they wanted to learn what they chose, to have greater freedom, to experience fewer demands, and to escape academic pressures. In general, they seemed to have less initiative and less sense of responsibility. The third year group had even less concern and involvement with the school as an institution. They seemed to take it for granted. They simply wanted an environment where they could do what they wanted to do for their own personal growth. Few spoke of the needs of the school as a whole, of building a sense of community, or of providing as many learning and personal options as possible.

Most had nonspecific goals for themselves such as "I want to learn and feel good about it." The majority stressed personal rather than academic growth.

Dr. Block's study attributes the change to the school's rapid increase in size, which, she believed, resulted in the diffusion of goals and a reduction of communication among students and staff. Certainly by the third year the initial excitement of creating a new learning environment had won off.

Students who came to Community High no longer had to be risk takers or expend energy on formulating new school policies. They were entering a previously defined environment. To some, Community High was a place to "put in time" till they received a high school diploma—a kind of cop-out school. A large number wanted to get out and into "real life" as soon as possible—"This is a good place, these are good people, but this is a school." The majority had little commitment to being in school. Many said they would drop out "without any question" if Community High were to be discontinued. In later years, as the number of alternative schools grew, offering students a wider choice, their motivation improved.

GOVERNANCE AND POWER

Community High's governance structure in 1971 was an Intertribal Council (ITC) with two students, one staff member, and one parent representative from each of the school's five tribes. The school administrator worked for the student body and had no veto. Chaired by rotating student or staff members, the Council had jurisdiction over all school matters, including curriculum and budget. However, Berkeley High administrators did not formally acknowledge the Council's power and held only the Community administrator accountable.

Student governance was not an issue in Community High. School-wide meetings in the past were poorly attended, and few decisions were made. During the first year, students said, the staff that had developed the school made most of the decisions at open staff meetings. Students upset with staff decisions would "scream and yell" to bring up issues for general discussion. A few, who felt this was debilitating, proposed building a student government, but most students saw no need for one.

The impetus for stronger, formal student government came from staff members, a few key students, and a new administrator (1970–71), who was strongly committed to student participation and accountability. She advocated such a council to help students communicate their concerns and to help them assume control over the school environment. Students, on the other hand, pressed for inclusion in the more informal staff planning sessions and on the negotiating committee. Most students, however, felt the Council was an improvement since it allowed them to express their needs formally on the tribal level as well as informally in classes. Decisions made at the Intertribal Council level could be, and frequently were, protested and reversed by the student body.

The student-staff negotiating committee, which had worked intensively on specific issues with Berkeley High's principal during the fall of 1970, became temporarily defunct afterward. Both the student and staff encounter groups were formally discontinued in 1971, although both groups continued to meet, the student group as a course of study and the staff group much less frequently. Since the staff was less unified in 1970–71, the students then had more power.

Student government participation, however, rested on a small nucleus of students for it required an enormous investment of time and energy. The active few were referred to as the "high energy" people. Although active in both formal and informal vehicles for generating change, they were not in close communication with their constituencies' problems and grievances. The staff set the agenda for Council meetings. Members came, often unaware of the agenda, listened, and voted. Back at the tribal level afterward, there was often dis-

sent and a call for revotes. Such crises and reverse communication seemed to be the pattern. Yet students exerted little
pressure on their representatives to gather information from
them before ITC meetings. By 1973 the tribal structure, and
with it any formal student government, had been dropped.
The staff offered no substitute, waiting for student initiative,
which was yet to appear.

Some students thought that representative elected government, as such, was unfair and did not develop leadership
within a group to the fullest extent. Some, who had wanted
to serve on the ITC but were not elected, felt that even if
they were less "popular" or had less political skill, they could
have been valuable. Students who would have liked to share
responsibility with the small group who ran the school had
no defined apparatus to do this on an intermediary level of
governance. Hence what the "high energy" people interpreted as apathy was often due to the lack of channels for
developing potential leadership. The lack perpetuated fragmentation, increased the distances between groups, and
wasted new talent. The activists tended to dismiss inactive
students as turned off or disinterested rather than shy, quiet,
or needing direction. They seldom attempted to discover how
to involve them in a gradual way. One activist said:

> Maybe they are not turned off by the school but just
> infatuated with not having to do anything. It has gone
> to their heads. So they don't [do anything]. They are
> probably enjoying it, and it may not be bad . . . but I
> don't like to see people sitting around.

The *laissez-faire* attitude served to concentrate power in the
same hands.

Indeed, the ethos of tolerance and separateness, the non-
judgmental "do-your-own-thing," helped to further polarize

activist students from the less involved. The activists didn't openly express their resentment of others for not assuming a share of the work, but the buried resentment made it even more difficult, perhaps, for the uninvolved to come forward. Leaders did not get needed support, and everyone was left hurt and angry, feeling nobody cared. Some students described a similar dynamic among the left-wing in the city of Berkeley, where insulated or like-minded groups also carried the burden, not sharing or communicating. Since the demise of a formal governance structure, however, student leadership has decreased, and with it the polarization between active and passive students.

Members of the ITC believed the Council functioned effectively and were encouraged by the fact that students shared responsibility for budgetary matters and school maintenance with the staff. One ITC member said:

> I'm surprised to see that it has worked as well as it has. It works as equally as possible. Some . . . students resent adults saying something and students going along with it, but this is at a minimum.

Although students felt that the staff had more power, by virtue of their greater information, influence, and articulateness, they nevertheless felt they had the "potential of powerfulness," and that, in a crisis, student power could be asserted in the ITC. Some, however, called ITC a sham, because they felt that teachers were really in control of everyday affairs. "Students should fire a teacher," a student said, "to prove their power." Yet many believed students had as much power as they needed or could use, either formally or informally.

Only a handful of decisions were made each year, students believed, which affected the direction of the school, and they said, they would fight such decisions as a body when they considered it necessary. A case in point involved the choice of director for the 1971–72 year. A staff coalition supported a candidate committed to the development of a multiracial school. But the students, for whom a multiracial school was not the highest priority, outvoted them, and the staff's candidate lost. Today, however, when students differ with staff decisions, they respond individually, not as a body.

Most students felt they had as much influence as teachers on the way the school was run and wanted the equality to remain. Teachers, on the other hand, saw a large gap between the two groups; 75 percent thought teachers had great influence; only 25 percent thought students had an equal amount. The staff was often frustrated when students were unclear about what they wanted and did not ask for more responsibility for shaping the school. Only half the teachers wanted great influence; all said that students should have it.

Yet the staff, not the students, were held accountable by the administrators in Berkeley High and in the district office and were dependent on the school system for their jobs. Thus, despite their rhetoric about student responsibility, the staff exerted considerable pressure on behalf of professional positions in its dealings with the district's bureaucracy and the political realities of the community. Staff then had considerably more power, openly acknowledged by both students and staff. In meetings we observed, the most intense arguments occurred between staff members rather than between staff and students, or students and students.

COMMUNICATION

There were both formal and informal means of communication among students. A Communications Tribe put out a biweekly paper called *Sometimes,* which reported school events and reflected student life. Two other tribes published daily news sheets evolved from interviews with students on key issues. The publications were uncensored and conveyed important information and grievances. They also provided a media for creative verbal play and interchange. The news sheets often reflected the fluctuating mood of the school, its daily ups and downs. Yet the school was small enough to allow relevant information to flow informally among the more active cliques, enhancing their hold on power, although no one purposely withheld information. Most people felt they had access to information if they wanted it. The events of meetings drifted back slowly and haphazardly to the tribes, but on hot issues, informal communication was excellent, and everyone knew that was happening.

Communication between tribes, however, was poor, and little effort was made to share resources. For a time, in 1969–70, the unity of the staff helped to counter the separatist trends of the tribes, but afterward cooperation among tribes, too great a task for the director alone, was left to informal, haphazard communication between individuals. Although students and staff were aware of the communication problems between tribes, and between cliques, staff members, and Black House as well, most saw no point in working on such issues at Intertribal Council meetings. At one meeting, "Deterioration of relations" was on the agenda but never reached. Some were afraid of the criticism and anger an open discussion of the problem would bring.

In 1971, the tribes were attempting to build their own consciousness. Identity work of this sort, especially in adolescence, requires some sort of sealing off or separation from outside forces to protect individual growth energies. Nevertheless, the problem remained how and when these groups could come back together. The more ingrown the tribes became, the more entrenched their life style and its priorities became, and the harder it was to reach across tribal lines. It was, in fact, the tribes' fostering of polarization and cliques that caused the students to disband them. Some students were concerned that the developing patterns had implications for the increasingly decentralized Berkeley school system as a whole.

Among the staff, communication was exceedingly poor. As the student body doubled in size, the enlarged staff, which included many student teachers, became more diversified and more factionalized. The daily staff meetings and encounter sessions of the first year disappeared. Instead the demands of running a larger school and responding to more students forced the staff to work out their difficulties periodically in issue-orientated meetings that left little time or energy to resolve personal disputes. Their unresolved tensions, some students felt, helped to fragment the tribes. Students, well aware of the tensions, had difficulty coping with them and frequently became entangled with competing staff members. One committee meeting of staff and students that we witnessed resembled a family fight in which uneasy children are caught up in their parents' quarrel. The meeting was uncharacteristic—but only to a degree. There was also friction between the permanent faculty and the large number of student teachers. Due to conflicting time demands, student teachers often could not attend staff meetings. They were unclear about the nature of their responsibilities, faculty members complained, and yet they had much authority with students.

Communication priorities shifted from year to year. During the first year, external communication with Berkeley High and internal communication among the staff were a high priority; a great deal of paper flowed advising people of the issues and defining goals as the school developed. The second year internal communication continued to be a priority, while external communication declined. By the third year, growing conflict with Berkeley High monopolized the energy of the director, while daily staff meetings, already viewed as a luxury in the enlarged school, were discontinued. As the staff lost interest in trying to talk out their more personal conflicts, so did the students. Group conflicts remained, one tribe against another, or Community High against Berkeley High, but more personal conflicts were avoided rather than resolved. By 1973, when Community High was just one of many alternative schools, its relations with Berkeley High had improved.

CURRICULUM AND GRADING

Curriculum at Community High is designed to meet both personal educational goals and the accreditation necessary for graduation from high school. The required courses (math, chemistry, English, etc.) are taught by people certified in their disciplines, but after the requirements are met, things are pretty flexible. Roughly one hundred courses are offered. Many classes, however, cease to meet on a formal basis once begun, although the pivotal core are well attended. Very small classes are popular, and informal learning takes place in rap sessions, which can occur as a continuation of class or anytime during the day. Occasionally students from Berkeley High audit the core classes.

Courses may be initiated or taught by students as well as teachers or student teachers. Students are encouraged to start new courses, and frequently faculty members attend student-led classes as colearners. The quality of the student-taught classes varied with the student. Some students, trying to emulate their own teachers, became frustrated by the binds students put them in, yet they found teaching a tremendous learning experience. It also made them more appreciative of their own teachers. One said he found it difficult and upsetting at first to be taught by a teacher one period and to teach himself the next, but over a period of time, the role reversal was balanced and became a positive experience.

Another said:

> It became clear that learning and teaching are sharing what needs to be shared, and it doesn't matter who you are as long as you have something to give another person.

Students frequently posted notices of courses they would like to teach. However, if the description did not appeal to other students—that is, if the course was called writing instead of survival English, or novel as opposed to fantasy or science fiction—they did not show up for class. The burden was on the "teacher" to make the course attractive. Frequently the content of a course changed, according to the students' interests, and sometimes it led to independent study.

Students found the curriculum interesting and relevant. They felt they had as much control over their learning as they wanted and needed, and they thought the curriculum helped them develop interpersonal and leadership skills as well as prepare them adequately for jobs and college. Some 72 percent of the students reported that the school was doing a good job of preparing them for the future, in contrast to 41 percent in a sample from traditional schools. It is important to note here, however, that the students who came to

Community High were generally bright and articulate and had already obtained the basic skills to do well on their own.

Most students' specific interests were adequately represented since a student could initiate any course he wanted; if his needs were not met, the onus was on himself. In some classes, students took turns helping to shape the course. In addition, teachers were always asking students what they wanted to study. There was an immense variety in teaching styles, dictated both by subject matter and the relationship between the teacher and students. Teachers tended to see themselves as facilitators; some lectured, others worked individually with students, some gave assignments, others brought in a variety of optional materials for students to work with, and others waited until students brought up questions. Although there were always students in corners quietly pursuing their own interests—reading a book, doing macrame, occasionally writing—there were few quiet places where one could concentrate. Lack of privacy was a problem.

There were two basic sets of rules. One set related to academic requirements for graduation from Berkeley High, mediated by one overworked Community High counselor. The other, a set of behavioral rules, was necessitated mainly by the school's relation to Berkeley High. These restrictions were minimal, however, and aside from these, students could do as they chose and came and went as they pleased. They checked themselves in on attendance sheets that had been posted by each tribe. Sometimes they had friends do it for them and leave school for the day; teachers made some attempt to get in touch with absentees, but it was difficult. By 1971, a few students had dropped out, but none had been asked to leave save one, who was considered seriously disturbed. His expulsion was described as a painful process.

Grades in the beginning were optional. Courses could be

taken as credits earned, rather than grades, and a large number of students took extra credits in order to graduate a term to a year early. By 1973, grades were given, but no Fs. A few students, who had completed the requirements for graduation, stayed on, either because they found it interesting or they did not want to go into college immediately. It was an easygoing learning environment.

The evaluation process was more important than grading. Students and teachers both seemed to be satisfied with the process. Generally the teacher wrote an evaluation of the student, and they talked it over together. The feedback between students and teachers, a mutual affair, was informal and non-institutionalized. Its frequency depended on the student and teacher involved. Most students were comfortable with the process and felt they could candidly discuss reactions to Community High with their teachers.

There have been many attempts to utilize more resources in the community. Students tended to resist moving out, as if the building were a fortress that had immobilized them. Yet a few successful group programs and contacts in the community have evolved: (1) tutoring elementary school children and occasionally bringing them to Community High; (2) setting up and running a cooperative bike shop at the University of California; (3) apprenticeships in the plumbing trade; (4) renovating a local ranch in an ecologically sound manner; (5) developing a farm with a focus on organic gardening; and (6) special events, such as a week devoted to May Day political activities.

Community High has been able to deal with the curriculum requirements imposed by California state (and Berkeley High) and still provide a creative and exciting curriculum. It has, however, been limited in some areas by the requirements for certified teachers. Meeting, or appearing to meet, the state's requirements continues to take considerable time and energy and has created a double image of the school, one for public consumption, the other for insiders. The effect of the discrepancy on students was unclear.

Independent study was highly valued. Teachers have devoted a great deal of time to it, and students felt their relationships with teachers in independent study helped them to adjust to the first term lethargy, to define their interests, and to learn to handle their freedom. In general, students regarded self-motivation as a key to learning, but they experienced self-motivated learning as a nightmare and developed overwhelming feelings of failure, isolation, and helplessness if they were unable to handle Community High's freedom. Some were able to ask for help and be drawn back into activity, and some spontaneously recovered, but still the casualties were many. On the whole, however, students thought the experiment worthwhile, despite the long and painful struggle of working out what they want to learn, as a recent comment in *Sometimes* illustrated:

> Public school which serves the system is the first step in immobilizing people. They are programmed to act and react according to the values of various teachers and to the system that programs them. You [the learner] find that you are taught according to the values of the teacher and not your own. If that is what you call learning, well I call it "imitation of life." A teacher can help teach you what two and two equals or "the basics of English grammar," but you have to learn it *yourself* and what is equally important is making your own decisions from the information a teacher can and should offer. School can be the first step in living your life instead of the system doing it for you.

INTERGROUP RELATIONS

Students and teachers took pleasure in describing their in-school relationships as close, informal, and caring; they frequently spent time together outside of school. Nevertheless, the freedom ascribed to many of the one-to-one relationships didn't fully carry over into the classroom where students still gave teachers the reins. Although students felt free to express anger or criticism of their teachers in one-to-one relationships, they were not likely to be as free in group situations. Rather than risk confrontation or try to change the teacher's approach, students were prone to walk out of class.

Students often played elusive and frustrating games with the staff. Because many of the staff were anti-authoritarian and loathe to set limits, students frequently took advantage of them to test how far they could go, provoking the teachers to anger and then disengagement. Or they frustrated teachers by leaving the room before confrontation could occur. Such provocative games, played as if teachers were parents, made it difficult to enforce limits or even to have openness.

According to students, a cross section of their number included such widely diverse groups as revolutionaries, jocks, ecologists, Tai-Chi freaks, and intellectuals. The tribes were fairly representative of the different groupings, since they were set up by interest areas conceived of as the core curricula. Transfer between tribes, however, was possible, and courses could be taken outside one's tribe.

Most students identified with one or the other of two major tribes. One was Diatribe, described by students as "stimulating, aggressively verbal, facile, debaters and arguers, working politically, but not very, sport fans, not jocks." Its rival, Ferns and Bombs, was ecologically centered, tended to attract students interested in counter-culture, radical politics, building a community, and in subjects like psychology and mysticism. There was considerable competition and aggressive razzing between the two groups.

The other tribes had less group cohesion. The Art Media Tribe, which attracted people who enjoyed working with their hands, did not spend much time as a group talking out issues. Their occasional meetings were described as "everyone talking at once," with little sense of group identity. In contrast, Ferns and Bombs met daily. The Communications Tribe, ironically, seemed to be a nontribe for people who preferred not to be in a group; it seldom met, and the staff assigned to it seemed to be involved with all Community High students. The newest tribe, called The Tribe, was almost invisible—we could never locate any of its members. A tribe then in the planning stage was centered around personal growth, revolutionary self-development, Aikido, Tai Chi, meditation, and consciousness expansion.

Staff members seemed to identify more closely with their own tribe than with the teaching staff or students as a whole. The director, for example, clearly was closest to students of her own tribe. The first two directors, it is interesting to note, had been associated with the strongest tribes; one had been with Ferns and Bombs, the other with Diatribe.

Most students wanted to develop a strong sense of community within their own tribe, to carve out a nest for themselves, "a home in school." Although they were aware of the resulting fragmentation of the total community, they preferred to devote their energies to intratribal cultural and political problems. Each tribe had its own budget, and the tribes did not compete for resources. The trend was toward closed, homogeneous units, and seemed to gratify those who had worked hardest to establish a sense of tribal unity.

Formed around shared interests and life goals, the tribes

were class-oriented rather than race-oriented. The black students who remained after Black House split off, for instance, were middle class in terms of their backgrounds and goals. While they felt Community High met their needs, they claimed it had failed other blacks in Berkeley High, Black House, and other alternative schools later added to the system. Blacks who did not choose the school saw it as unreal and too easy; they feared it would not prepare them for the hard knocks of the world. A black student said:

> We want to get a good education, so we will be able to stand the competition we will face in real life. We see Community High as a white cop-out . . . certainly it does not prepare black people for the black struggle.

Many blacks in Berkeley High, ambitious to get into good colleges, did not want to risk their future in the experimental venture. They wanted a more structured education.

Although the exodus to Black House left Community High a relatively homogeneous, middle-class group, most white students felt that Black House was a "good thing." They believed it was difficult, if not impossible, to meet varied ethnic and cultural needs in one small school community and pointed out that the school clearly did not satisfy the majority of black students its first two years:

> When Black House students come around to Community High now you can really talk to them; you can see they got more together there; that it's really good for them.

Some white students, however, were put off by the insularity Black House had established:

> I'm really curious about what's happening there and wish they wouldn't keep us out.

> I feel Black House is okay, intellectually, but in truth
> it's very alienated. I suppose it's a good thing. I guess
> I have some negative notions. It's nothing I can relate
> to.

Only a minority of white students seemed to feel Community High needed a more heterogeneous population, and particularly more black students: "It's too unreal this way." Although they supported black separatism, they feared separatism would increase alienation and mistrust. They wanted at least to have better communication between Community High and Black House.

Few students expressed any desire to compete with Black House over resources, particularly financial resources. Most were ostensibly nonracist. Yet they had given little thought to white racism. Instead they seemed to feel racism and discrimination were black problems, which they had escaped becoming involved in with the advent of Black House, as if establishment of Black House had removed the problem. A student said:

> The ideal race relations system is not all uptight about
> percentages of blacks and whites in class. We didn't
> get hung up on desegregation. . . . Black House kids
> . . . when they come over now for a class, no longer
> put everyone down or are just angry; we feel better
> about each other now.

Some staff members thought students were able to resolve racial problems more easily than they themselves, of a different generation. Only 25 percent of the students reported that there was frequent tension between students of different economic and racial groups, whereas 75 percent of the teachers reported such tension among teachers. But whether the "better feelings" mentioned above represented true gains in interracial relations or simply an unproductive truce is hard to say. The May 1971, dispute over the choice of a pro integration director showed that the majority of white students were not committed to integration if it interfered with the fulfillment of their needs as a group. They wanted maximum freedom and autonomy in their learning environment, while the majority of blacks sought specific academic and vocational skills. White students, apparently, felt that a more integrated student body would pose a threat to their goals.

Most Community High students seemed to be trying to understand their own identities and culture, focusing on their own internal development (Who am I?) and group relations (Who are we?) rather than white racism.

HOW STUDENTS RATED THE SCHOOL

Students spoke again and again of their satisfaction with the amount of freedom offered them at Community High:

> I have the freedom to do what I want.

> They give me a lot of room to grow here. What more can I ask?

> We have a lot of options for how we spend our time. It's hard to get into things and really start learning, but when you do take hold of yourself finally, even though you may have wasted a lot of time, you really feel good.

They were not in agreement, however, about the effectiveness of the school's reliance on students' self-motivation:

> It was my feeling that the school wanted to develop in all its students a self-motivation urge, or a way that

> they could get things done by themselves, and by encouraging and providing an environment in which they could use this, it would come naturally. Whatever you want, you can get.

> The school works very well for people who already have motivation. You learn about dealing with people. From my experience with Berkeley High, I was very bored. Here . . . if I find something I want to do strongly enough, I can do it. It takes a lot of pulling, shoving, stomping and tugging, but I know I can get it done, if I really want it.

> I don't know what I want to do. I don't care, and I just don't know how to take hold. I guess I just don't want to be in school. There is nothing this school can offer me.

Some students wanted more structure, more direction, and more clarity in terms of realistic expectations by which they could measure themselves and gain a sense of accomplishment and a feeling of competence. They felt they needed guidelines to push them into positive action.

The students who had worked to build a strong sense of community within the school felt they had not succeeded. Worn out and drained, their number unreplenished, they withdrew into themselves. Although most thought Community High should be much smaller, and others felt the school needed a more heterogeneous student population, particularly more blacks, students, in general, saw little need for change otherwise:

> I'm content with Community High School. I feel no one is changing the school because it is still limited by being in the context of a school. People just don't dig that.

> This school is a good place. People and relationships
> are good, but my general disinterest in school has not
> changed by joining this school. I'm still apathetic, and
> I still want to get out. Its biggest asset for me is that
> it makes an unpleasant situation bearable and almost
> pleasant sometimes.

Even those most turned off by Community High, or by
school in general, were the first to say it is not the fault of
the school. A minority were unhappy with school and life in
general, seemed quite depressed, and felt that they were learning nothing. They didn't know what they wanted, felt no
one cared about them or anyone else and just wished someone
would reach out to them. In the face of their apathy and the
magnitude of their difficulties, the staff felt helpless.

In sum, the majority of students were concerned primarily
with personal growth and an environment that facilitated
personal changes rather than academic achievement or tech-
nical skill development. Most wanted the more immediate
satisfaction of engaging in something useful to them now. If
they stressed skill development at all, it was in terms of
enhancing their competence to master their school environment. "I'm not sure what I'm learning here, nothing typical," one student said, "but I like what I'm learning, particularly about myself and other people."

STAFF CONCERNS

By and large, the staff also stressed personal growth,
although they expected the development of a student's personal identity to include his sense of competence and therefore his mastery of skills and academic materials. Most staff

members felt that student apathy was not due to the failure of Community High so much as to student resistance to any curtailment of their freedom. Although students, with few exceptions, wanted a smaller school with a higher staff-student ratio (They discounted student teachers as having a tentative and short-lived commitment to Community High), many teachers felt the desire was idyllic and immature and represented an escape from self-responsibility. Some thought the 1971 size and arrangement was good. Then it was easy for the staff to form small working groups. Money saved from full-time salaries could be put to other uses. The use of volunteers drawn from the community was encouraged. The school had the potential to respond to a wide spectrum of student needs, while removing the pressure on a small staff to be everything to everyone. Some also thought the 1971 student population of between two and three hundred was necessary if the school was to be truly multi-ethnic and that only by remaining fairly large could staff from various racial backgrounds be hired. They felt Community High had abandoned one of its foremost goals—becoming a heterogeneous school whose very diversity is the source of enrichment and learning. The student population has since dropped from 230 to 130 in 1973 because of the increase in alternative schools. The percentage of minority students (27 percent) remained the same.

Far more than the students, the staff was committed to maintaining a heterogeneous school environment and working out the conflicts generated by different racial and ethnic groups. One staff member envisioned "a school that consists of many different groups of people, committed to the school and to learning about themselves—a community." Also, unlike the students, the staff had a strong interest in using the community's resources. It had developed a lengthy file of community and parental resources, but the file was little used by students.

Community teachers felt they could give only what the students asked for. As a result, many believed their professional skills and talents weren't adequately used, either because students didn't know about them or weren't interested enough to ask for them. Some faculty accepted this as the price of working in a student-oriented program, including the prospect that teachers might become expendable as more courses taught by students and community volunteers developed.

In a learning situation that stressed process rather than ends, learning to complete anything was often bypassed; little value was placed on the finished product. Community teachers, as a result, were often frustrated by their lack of clarity about what they had accomplished professionally. More than students, they seemed to feel the need to accomplish, but they found it difficult to evaluate their own effectiveness in such an open-ended environment. They were uncertain about how much direction students needed, how to give direction that would promote growth, and how far to press students to take responsibility for their own learning.

While most students (72 percent) and teachers (75 percent) liked Community High, only 44 percent of the students and 25 percent of the teachers reported that they were excited about their work and fulfilled by it. The marked dissatisfaction among teachers was not perceived by the students; 84 percent of them thought the teachers were excited about their work and enjoyed teaching. While most of the teachers (68 percent) felt students respected their opinions, less than half (42 percent) thought students understood the problems of being a teacher.

Again and again the question was raised—what do people want from this school? Do they want a school that maximizes personal freedom at the risk of educational failure? Does this mean freedom to grow, or to be neglected, without help? Can learning be totally private and noninstitutionalized? Can a "do-your-own-thing" separatism coexist with a strong sense of community? These dilemmas were discussed and reworked each year, as the membership and direction of the school changed.

Sudbury Valley School, Framingham, Mass.

By Dale Crowfoot and Patricia Wilson Graham

Operating since the summer of 1968, Sudbury Valley School is a private day school located in an old mansion approximately 18 miles west of Boston in the town of Framingham, Massachusetts. In 1971, the nongraded school, which enrolls all applicants, had seventy students between the ages of four and forty; all were white. Learning was defined as an individual matter, and students determined their own studies as well as the activities and length of their day.

Tuition for the elementary and secondary levels was $950 a year and $1250 for the college level. Three of the nine full-time and two part-time staff members were certified to teach, but 30 percent of the staff had PhDs and 60 percent had BAs. Ten percent had no degrees. However, the staff was not paid according to tenure, experience, or degree, and each contract was negotiated individually. Although a minimum salary of $10,000 had been agreed to, salaries were actually based on the amount of money the school accrued and were distributed according to need. They were, in fact, very low, and one or two staff members even declined salaries in the 1970–71 year. Both the hiring of staff and the designation of their salaries were handled by students and staff together at the School Meeting, a weekly open forum. Designed to be a "pure democracy," Sudbury Valley School had a highly developed structure in which students and staff shared responsibility for maintaining the school and for monitoring individual and group behavior.

In the fall of 1974, the school will be eligible for accreditation with both the New England Association of Colleges and Secondary Schools and the Independent Schools Association of Massachusetts. The preliminary evaluation of Sudbury, during its third year, was positive, and the result had already forced the accreditation board to rethink its criteria for judging public schools.

Sudbury's general atmosphere varies with the time of year, the weather, the number of people around, and the issues that have surfaced.

The school, an old mansion, is set on ten acres of land, with lawns, streams, fields, and forests; it is isolated from town, with only a few homes nearby. While students must have private transportation to and from school and parents are committed to providing it, few parents are around the school or involved in the program. In warm weather, students are outdoors, playing games, riding bikes, hiking or reading. In winter, they skate on the lake, play in the snow, or spend time indoors.

There are many, many rooms in the house, providing privacy and space for special activities and a sense of largeness and diversity; but they also reduce the ease of communication, making it difficult to know what's going on where and to keep track of people.

On the first floor is a large kitchen, stocked and maintained by the kitchen corporation. Students may cook and bake for a learning experience but not for their regular meals. The kitchen is a gathering place for all, to eat bag lunches and to fool around. Nearby are the children's playroom, the reading rooms, and the art room. The latter, which has a piano as well as paints and a potter's wheel, is another area where cross-age activities occur. The reading rooms have rugs and comfortable chairs; they are quiet places to study. The rule for quiet was set by the students and is observed.

Two well-stocked libraries are upstairs. Like the reading rooms below, they are a vital part of the school and almost always occupied. In one, quiet conversations are allowed. The other, called the fish room (there's an aquarium there), serves as the sewing room as well. Down the hall is the room where the Committee on School Affairs meets each morning, near the printing room, where booklets, minutes, and other publications are printed, and the school office with its typewriter, files, and other equipment. The school office is always busy. At the end of the hall is the smoking room, originally the refuge of uninvolved students. There's also a photolab-darkroom, a small radio room for electronic study, and a music room, where the School Meeting is held each week.

We sensed a feeling of pride in the democracy Sudbury had achieved. Its goals had been spelled out in a brochure about the school:

> One of the overarching goals of the school is to be, structurally, a democratic institution. This goal implies specific objectives, among which are: (a) to involve all those most directly affected by a decision in the decision; (b) to extend the age of responsibility

and accountability down to the age of the youngest students in the school (basically, starting the age of maturity at the age of weaning); (c) to implement the three root ideas of American democracy—individual rights, majority rule, and equal opportunity—in all activities of the school. This goal and its objectives have been constantly at the center of attention in the school and have been active guides in the school's daily affairs.

One staff member thinks the school has reconciled the opposites within democracy:

> In my good moments here, I feel the school has successfully taken the left and the right and fused them —banged them together. And it's incredible. (In my bad moments I think, "What the fuck is this place up to?") Somehow they have taken the good things from the left, about the struggle for freedom, and from the right, the struggle for order and authority. Neither can hang in on its own, because one is chaotic and one is repressive. But somehow we made it work.

The ideal is reflected in the following statements of students and staff:

> It's one institution where children—people—have rights and equal opportunity, and it's a democratic institution.

> I would rather be in a country run democratically with crummy leaders than be in one where the right thing was done everytime.

Believing in the appropriateness of their values and the structure they've developed, the staff hoped the school would eventually become public and as large as any innercity school; in fact, in 1970–71 the program was run as if there were fifteen times as many students enrolled. A larger school, a staff member explained, could better accommodate the variety of individual learning styles and would increase the school's viability as a model for contemporary education as well as ease the financial strain.

HOW THE SCHOOL BEGAN

The school grew out of a young couple's search for a more open learning environment for their children. Unable to find that kind of atmosphere in public schools, the couple began in 1966 to talk to friends about creating a school where their children could learn what they wished, as they wished. Their friends, upper middle-class people in the fields of science, education, art, and business, had both stability and high ideals. They too wanted an educational alternative but not a radical alternative society.

It took about a year and a half for a plan to emerge, and by the spring of 1968, a group of twenty-four people were ready to open Sudbury Valley School for the summer. Some assumed roles as staff members, and twelve, who had jobs elsewhere, became trustees when they incorporated in May. From its inception the operation of the school has involved parents and family friends (though not exclusively), and this is still a unique and important factor. So committed were the original group to their dream that they undertook a heavy financial burden to subsidize the school and were not paid the first year. Yet they were unsure of the outcome and even of what to expect the first day of school. One staff member recalled their preoccupation, prior to the school's opening, with the question, "What do we do if someone hits somebody?"

Before enrolling students, a governance structure and by-laws had been developed. The major legal and operational responsibilities were delegated to the board of trustees, whose twelve members were drawn from the original group, the staff, and the community. However, the board's officers met more frequently than the board as a whole and thus carried more weight. (The officers were elected by the board from among the originators.) In addition, a School Assembly, composed of two dozen staff and community members, was set up to meet several times a year.

The initial summer enrollment, however, included students who wanted only a recreational program and had no intention of enrolling in the fall; about half the potential staff were volunteers, not all of whom were expected to stay.

EARLY CRISES

During the first six months the school went through two crises that, had they occurred simultaneously, could have been fatal. As one school member said, "We had to make a choice between becoming a democratic or a progressive school."

The first crisis erupted over a division within the staff. Two of the staff left the first summer because, a student explained:

> They were more interested in having a community school. They felt our catalog was a waste of time and money. . . . They couldn't have cared less about respectability.

The conflict, apparently, concerned whether the school was within "the system," as fancy catalogs imply, or outside "the system," as inexpensive mimeographs focused on radical content imply. It may seem a trivial issue, but the differences could not be resolved through compromise or coexistence of the two factions.

Those who initiated the school defined it as democratic and maintained control in shaping it. A small group of students helped carry their concept into the fall semester, when a formal weekly School Meeting, open to students and staff, was instituted.

At the same time, the trustees wanted to make their proceedings open to the school community and to encourage broader-based participation. In November 1968, the Assembly, which was the arena for trustee transactions, opened voting to parents of students enrolled for over two months.

At this stage, the School Meeting had very limited power over the daily operation of the school. The role of the staff was to keep the school functioning—making decisions, ordering supplies, and cleaning up the building and grounds. In part, this was due to necessity, in part, to uncertainty about staff and student roles. More changes were yet to come.

The second crisis culminated in the exodus of sixty students. Before that time the student body numbered 140, and to one of the initiators, it was the fall enrollment itself that led to the trouble.

> [It] was caused by attracting every dissatisfied and desperate person in the area. We knew it would happen.

What he seemed to "know" was that among the diversity of people who chose to attend Sudbury (some only to avoid public school), there would be clashes of personalities and ideologies. One of the students, enrolled from the start, saw the problem this way:

> There is a certain group of kids . . . still very much
> involved in distrusting people over thirty or people
> who have short hair—I don't get along with them.

Another original student, confident in his sense of the type
of school Sudbury was slated to be, lamented:

> The hardest thing was getting people to understand
> and believe in what the school was.

The student behavior the staff found intolerable was hard
to determine precisely, its recall distorted by time, emotion,
and victory. One element was drug use. Comments on its extent ranged from "dealing to four-year-olds" and "smoking
marijuana on campus" to "suspicion of marijuana smoking
on campus." Another component was student conduct, perceptions of which ranged from "walking around naked" to
"fucking in the bushes" to "necking in the lounges" to "saun-
tering provocatively." Other counter-culture norms also conflicted with those of the people in power.

Despite these differences, however, there were few confrontations. The conversations and open debates at the regular
School Meetings clarified the issues. Littering, for example,
was one of the initial concerns of the School Meeting, and it
raised disagreements about the necessity of rules. Yet opposition to littering was put "on the book" and became the first
test of the School Meeting's power. Creating rules began the
process of defining the school; participation began the process
of focusing on differences.

However, in the normal routine of the day, people could
easily avoid each other, for each group had its own territory.
If one group used the front rooms, others would enter
through the back. The front lawn was occupied by the less
clothed students, who were suspected of smoking pot. This

image on the front lawn, public and representing the school, aroused the community's disapproval and brought police cars to the area. Since the school's reputation and possibly survival were at stake, those with the greatest investment in the school —staff members and original students—became angry and fearful of the repercussions.

One day in November a notice appeared on the bulletin board announcing there would be a School Meeting in the barn to discuss closing the school. The word spread; everyone was shocked. The impetus for the meeting was explained by one of the original students:

> The crisis came about when the staff really felt the school could not function, there was no way out. There were certain people [students] here whom they just couldn't work with. They [staff] had a choice then; in fact, they were legally able to just throw anyone out they wanted, but if they'd have done that in the first two months of the school, what would that have meant? The whole idea of the school is that kids can take responsibility for their own behavior. But the staff wanted to express how profoundly they felt about these kids, so they said they would resign if the School Meeting didn't solve the problems.

This meeting, called by the staff, was the crisis point. Another student, among those recommended for suspension, remembered vividly:

> The chairman of the staff sat in the middle. On the left side of the room were crowded together all the radicals and long hairs and on the right side of the room were the staff and "junior staff" [students who supported the staff]. Different staff members at the meeting said things about something being wrong but didn't get specific. Then one staff member said, "I

have a list of sixty people who are undesirable and should be out of the school." No one was prepared for this drastic ultimatum; no one questioned it. A procedure was established whereby each student on the list had a hearing and a conference with his parents present.

The hearings started immediately, as the same student recalled:

The first question was, "What did you come to this school to do?" The unanimous answer by all those students was to learn. That wasn't the answer to give, 'cause you can learn on the street. The answer should have been something about democracy.

The School Meeting handled most of the hearings and decided that some students could stay. Because the School Meeting's legal functions were unclear, the trustees were asked to handle the official suspensions and expulsions. They decided to return, in full, the tuition of all who left, even though they had attended for three months. It meant a financial hardship, but no one could say the school kept the money of anyone who did not choose to remain. Twenty students were expelled, and about forty more chose to leave because of the situation and the clarification of Sudbury's goals. One student remembered:

Kids just started to resign. About sixty kids left and started a community school.

Enrollment dropped from 140 to eighty. The remaining students, including some on the initial list of suggested expulsions, had mixed reactions to the exodus:

I wouldn't throw a person out of this school because he thought the school was different than I thought.

Through everything that happened—through that crisis—it occurred to me we were in a democratic school.

A lot of things that shouldn't have, did happen.

One of the founders shared her feelings with us about the emotional cost of such upheavals in starting a school:

It hurts, and you don't want to talk about it. You don't want to discuss the friends you lost and the failures you had. It hurts. Now I think if someone comes to us and says we want to study the school, we would tell them that we had some emotional encounters in the beginning, because you are not going to be able to articulate exactly or picture what you're getting into and people are going to have different interpretations, which are going to flare up emotionally. I think the whole history of this kind of experiment in schools is full of these kinds of things, and I think this is the first thing that someone should tell another who is starting a school.

GOVERNANCE

After the exodus, the school moved on to refine, define, and extend the structure of the school. Morale was low after the sixty students left, but the remaining students and staff shared a firm conviction in the direction to take. In December, "after the blowup," a judiciary Committee on School Affairs (CSA) was established, composed of staff and students, to investigate misconduct, hold hearings, and even trials.

Further development included the election of clerks to tend to certain maintenance tasks and the formation of corporations around various curriculum interests. Thus, through a process of decentralization, the daily mechanics of running the school came to be handled by several semi-autonomous groups of students and staff. With an internally developed set of rules, the founders found it easier to share power.

The shift in control was gradual, however. In December 1970, came "The Reform," and students were enfranchised into the biannual School Assembly, the legal corporation. Shortly thereafter the trustees relinquished much of their power to the weekly School Meeting, including responsibility for the budget and educational policy. The School Assembly, in turn, became little more than the approving and legalizing body for the decisions of the School Meeting. One of the original staff members said that the group knew where it was going in its long-range desire for the School Meeting to have total power. "You know when you're ready to move into a new phase," she said.

These structural alterations enabled students and staff to share greater power and to participate more in the life of the school. When asked who runs the school, people of all ages typically responded, "Everyone does" or "The School Meeting—there are some people who run School Meetings, but no one person."

The School Meeting. The role and format of the current School Meeting is an outgrowth of personal dynamics as well as of the school's philosophical evolution. Every Monday the School Meeting considers business from the corporations, clerks, and the judiciary Committee on School Affairs. An elected chairman presides. Although the official membership includes the entire staff and student body, in practice only the staff and about fifteen to twenty-five students attend. Yet students who are absent for sustained periods, without adequate explanation, may be dropped from the school's rolls. A public, preposted agenda guides each meeting.

One agenda, for example, included:

1. Announcements
     Projects for next year
     Visitors—Educational Change Team [University of Michigan]

2. Report from Committee on School Affairs
     Eleven case investigations, outcomes, and voting on motions

3. Second Readings

4. First readings of motions
     Policy on visitors
     Purchase of new door
     Removal of shrubbery
     Arrears
     Suspension of student for unpaid tuition
     Closing of school during summer
     Purchase of lawn mower
     Amendment to budget categories for art supplies
     Contracts for staff
     Withdrawal of student from CSA eligibility

5. Open agenda

6. No trials scheduled

Straight-backed chairs lined the music room with one chair in the front for the chairman. Students, clustered by age groups in the front, came and left at will. Visitors, interspersed among them, also left at will. On this day staff members were more active than students, although that was said to vary according to the issues. There were few private conversations or friendly exchanges. The tone of the meeting was serious, even strained, partly because of the tension over the biannual Assembly Meeting to follow that very night and the necessity to pass motions for its consideration. The meeting was conducted according to strict parliamentary procedure with votes taken on all matters; it began and ended at the designated times.

At the time Sudbury was undergoing a financial strain. As the treasurer of the School Meeting said:

> The main problem is money, and that's the same problem any business has—trying to avoid any serious problems.

Because money was so scarce, the fair disbursement of it among the staff was a tense and time-consuming issue in the spring of 1971. It raised concern about the privacy of financial needs, guilt at the inequality of previous arrangements, and issues of commitment to the school and staff members. Dealing with the matter was a test of the durability of the democratic structure. There had been many meetings, formal and informal extensions of the weekly School Meeting, to explore all dimensions of the problem. The School Meeting voted on hiring staff members and determined their salaries. An arrears fund, or excess of monies after salaries were paid, provided some hope for attaining the "agreed to" minimum, but the disbursement process had yet to be applied. The low salaries, in contrast to the investment made in the large old mansion and its surrounding acreage, seemed a reflection on the priorities of the founders who purchased the facilities. By 1973, all the staff were part-time, and their salaries prorated to the amount of time they worked. Students elected the staff to be hired by voting on them and putting the amount of time they wanted them for on their ballots. The School Meeting took the results of the voting under advisement.

The Clerks. The clerks elected by the School Meeting were a component of the governance structure. Their responsibilities for the maintenance of the school were defined in the School Meeting's Resolutions and, while the student and staff clerks had autonomy in how they executed their tasks, they had little flexibility in their role as clerks.

A clerk's "business relationship when running the school," a student said, "has nothing to do" with the interpersonal relationships of being a student.

For instance, the clerk elected to open and close the school building at the designated hours had to arrive on time with keys to accomplish the job. When he neglected his responsibility, his offense could be filed with the judiciary. A clerk could delegate some of his responsibility to others, but he was still responsible for his assistant's efficiency.

The job descriptions in the Resolutions were quite detailed, for example:

> The attendance clerk shall maintain a current list of all students enrolled at the school; where necessary, report the fact of enrollment of each student to the Superintendent of Schools in the town in Massachusetts where the student resides; where necessary, within ten days after a student's termination of enrollment or withdrawal report that fact to the Superintendent of Schools in the town in Massachusetts where the student resides; post check-in lists weekly and keep past check-in lists; peruse these lists to ascertain which students are absent for a sustained period; and call such students to the attention of the Committee on School Affairs.

Besides attendance and opening the school, the clerks' responsibilities included: building maintenance, building supplies, student records, diplomas, enrollment, grounds, pond, library, medical supplies, publicity, schools and organizations, office, governmental authorities, cleaning, apprenticeship program, and visitors. That the maintenance of the school was assigned to students and staff within the governance structure made it unique. It gave importance to vital tasks and involved many people in governance activities.

The Corporations. The corporations, eleven in number, focused on various art and skill activities. A corporation consisted of officers, a budget allotted by the School Meeting, and an informal group who shared similar interests and activities. Some corporations appeared to provide support for the clerks, and there might have been some overlap in personnel, for example, the Horticultural Society and the grounds clerk. The corporations, which will be discussed further with curriculum, included: Musical Society, Photolab, Tool Corp., Horticultural Society, Press, Needlework Corp., Sculpture and Pottery Corp., Film Production Corp., Arts and Crafts Supply Corp., Cooking Corp., and the Supply Center.

The Judiciary Committee. The fourth internal component of the governance structure was the judiciary Committee on School Affairs (CSA). Its purposes, as outlined in the School Meeting's Resolutions were:

1. To investigate alleged violations of School Meeting resolutions or reports of misconduct in general.
2. To report to the School Meeting the results of its investigations.
3. To provide evaluations on the performance of each School Meeting official's duties; each office shall be evaluated in turn on a rotating basis.

All rules and procedures were set down in detail and were

available to members of the school and to the public. Each member of the school had the opportunity to serve on the CSA. Names were selected by lottery, with a mechanism to insure a representation of all age groups. The committee met daily at 10:00 A.M., the only mandatory assignment Sudbury recognized. Six to ten members served each month, and no one could serve for two consecutive months.

At the beginning of each month, after an election of chairman and secretary, new members were familiarized with the procedures, and all members reviewed the work of the previous month's committee. Goals were set, responsibilities were determined for each person each day, and progress records were kept. For instance, when a staff member and a student volunteered to evaluate the housekeeping clerk's duties, they divided the labor, arranged interviews with people, set weekly deadlines for themselves, and began filling in flow charts.

Accusations were turned into the CSA for consideration daily. There was usually discussion of whether an incident was appropriate to investigate, a division of labor to interview witnesses, and a report written up for the School Meeting. Where possible, a case was arbitrated; sometimes the accused was brought to trial.

The cases varied in degree and importance, as the following examples indicate:

> Report #435, 4/30/71
> Title: Sharon Lasse vs. S.V.S. Photolab Corporation
> Report: On 3/25/71 the Health Inspector and Capt. Wilson of the Fire Dept. inspected the premises. Capt. Wilson noted the extension cords being used and the thumbtacks which were used to fasten the cord to the wall. He said they should be replaced with insulated staples. Sharon notified Cindy Choules of what he had said on 3/25/71. She made the complaint on 4/23/71

because they were not replaced. Cindy Choules said that she had spoken to Jan Doe about it, and he said he would take care of it. When he didn't, she called a Photolab Corp. meeting. They voted to buy the tacks. She said that she was going to buy them this week. She said this on 4/29/71.

Report #436, 4/29/71
Title: Karen Tuffs vs. Susan Fronim
Report: Karen Tuffs was sitting in a chair, and Susan pushed her and the chair over backwards. Karen said she was hurt. Susan admitted that she did it, and Tom Beels, as a witness, agreed to the incident. Tom did not know why, and Susan forgot.

The functions of the judiciary process were twofold: (1) it was a mechansim to check that daily maintenance was performed and (2) it was also a mechanism for social control, taking the responsibility off bystanders. However, its formality precluded direct and personal intervention in many instances. Sudbury used the process to insure uniformity in dealing with people. A college-age student justified Sudbury's structure and style by saying:

> When you're here the more you realize how easy it would be for an institution like this to fold under, how easy it would be for a conflict to arise between two people or two groups. Then you have to find another way of settling those and that *you can't always assume* that they will find a way of settling that. Because sometimes, when you have to deal with government authorities and parents, with somebody who acts in an irresponsible fashion, you have to have a way to deal with that. It's crucial for the survival of the institution.

That was why the rules were so precise, the judicial process so strict and impersonal; it also explained how the founders, and a few others, maintained control over the school. It was the reason many staff and students initially left. There was no room in Sudbury's democracy for "personal considerations." A few, for example, were given a questionnaire asking: "If a teacher at your school found a group of students smoking pot in an empty classroom, what would he or she most likely do?" Their almost unanimous response was, "Report it to CSA."

The respondents fully supported the school's judiciary process. Several cited the illegality of pot and suggested calling the police. Others would use the CSA to save the school's reputation. Most of them considered the rules to be realistic and fair and, above all, clear. The rules were published in the School Meeting's Resolutions and sections were quoted weekly in the School Meeting agenda. Some were common-sense safety rules, for instance, "Leaning out of windows and using windows as exits are prohibited." Others referred to behavior, for example, "No one may knowingly infringe on another's rights," "knowingly" defined as "having been informed of the infringement, the violator continues it." Still other regulations described contractual and legal obligations as well as powers and duties of School Meeting officials.

A critical issue for the Committee in May 1971, was how to handle people who were selected to work on the Committee but would not attend its meetings. Some members felt overburdened. Standardizing the amount of work was considered as well as penalties for not working or attending.

The School Assembly. The School Assembly, which meets in December and May, was attended in May 1971, by sixty-five to seventy students, staff, parents, and community members.

The music room was crowded, young students walked in and out, and people were dressed up for the occasion, as if it were an important event. The president of the trustees, a community member, ran the meeting by Robert's Rules. Only the staff and a few parent-trustees were active; students and most parents were not. There was relatively little discussion, little emotion expressed, and much voting. Among the items on the agenda were:

Election of trustees
  Debate about number (perhaps a response to
  an unexpected nomination)
  Election of officers of trustees
Consideration of temporary staff
Approval of budget
  Staff salaries
  Use of arrears
Discussion and approval of candidates for graduation
Announcement about parents' meeting

Those attending seemed comfortable with the style and format of the Assembly Meeting. Modeled after the traditional New England town meeting, it was one area where parents could exert influence through discussions, motions, and voting. Several school people, however, felt Sudbury probably exerted more influence on the families than the families did on the school. Many Sudbury students wanted their families managed in a "democratic" manner, a difficult adjustment for parents who had little association with the school.

A Question of Influence. Underlying the formal democratic structure in which students and staff participated was the daily informal life of the school. Each affected the other, and out of this dynamic relationship came the real power and control of the school. To what degree was the individual's power as equal as the structure recommended? To what extent had the original group truly divested its ownership and control?

Certain natural factors, of course, stood in the way. As a staff member commented:

> There are influential people here and noninfluential people. There are people who radiate a lot of energy and those who don't radiate much.

The staff questioned felt that both students and teachers had a great deal of influence. Students agreed they shared equal power, but among themselves disagreed on how much power was actually involved and even whether much should be. For some, the ways to gain influence were clear:

> The ways of getting influence are clerkship, going to School Meetings, or talking at School Meetings.

But not many students took advantage of them. About sixteen students and nine of the staff who as clerks or corporate chairmen, did the bulk of the work to maintain the school. In addition, there were a dozen more students whose involvement fluctuated. Students explained:

> As long as the school is running smoothly, kids don't come. But you can bet if the staff were in there trying to make a rule that everyone had to take English— everyone would be there.

> The school is fine the way it is. I have no real hassles with it. I just can't get into it.

> People have a right to vote on things or not to vote. A small group of people can change the course of history. Look at how . . . [few] work in the School Meeting.

The formal structure allowed for fluctuations in participation, enabling people to engage and disengage. Looking at the effects of the school's methods of decision-making and administration, almost all the students and staff questioned in a small sampling believed that students learned leadership and political skills, had more control over what they are learning, were more excited and interested in school, and were able to relate to the staff as equals.

The question of influence, however, was complicated by the school's early history. One couple, for example, loaned the school corporation a disproportionately large sum of money for the land and buildings. Understandably, the original group had feelings of deep commitment and ownership, and their sense of proprietorship has been respected by others. At meetings during the first summer of 1968, for instance, it was considered a dilemma whether to elect a chairman or give the gavel to someone with feelings of ownership. Again, at an early School Meeting when the elected chairman was absent, the meeting was turned over to his wife. Such expectations had to be overcome, but the balance between ownership and leadership remained to be worked out. The influence of the founders could still outweigh the democratic structure. As a staff member said of one of the original group:

> He is probably the strongest. People accept it. What can I say? He's not in a strong position, but he is a strong person. He's in the same position as everyone else is. He came up with or formulated most of the school's principles and philosophies. So, yes, he is more influential, but that's because he had the energy to be, so it is just a chain of events. He is strong and when he speaks in the School Meeting, a lot of people listen. Some even blindly accept what he says.

CURRICULUM

In contrast to the governance structure, which was clearly organized and operated in strict adherence to expectations and rules, was the flexibility of the curriculum process. There was no predetermined curriculum at Sudbury Valley; it was all individually defined. There were no classes; there was no suggested program of study; there were no requirements or credits; there was no evaluation process. *What* an individual learned was up to him or her. *How* an individual learned was also a personal matter. Students had absolute control of their time at school and how they spent it. Because of the wide range of ages and interests, learning had many forms, and each had several levels. A pamphlet, *About the Sudbury Valley School*, stated some of the basic educational tenets, the outline of which follows:

> Learning through self-motivation and self-regulation.
> Equal status to all pursuits.
> Evaluation through self-criticism.
> Teaching based on interests.
> Spontaneous formation of learning groups, centered on common interests.
> All can learn and all can teach.

One student, referring to a lively and engaging volleyball game on the front lawn with ten to fourteen players, suggested it as a good example of a class. She elaborated on the personal and educational value of such spontaneous activities and the legitimacy of any interest. Each person's choices were trusted, for she or he was the only one who questioned or evaluated his pursuits.

Staff members had a responsibility to be around the school,

and their activities attracted students to join in and participate. The staff member in charge of the outdoor grounds, for example, was often assisted by several students as he went about this work. Another staff member (or a teenage student) began baking bread in the kitchen and ended up sharing the task with several others. An artist on the staff turned from her professional work to help others develop their skills. An older student, painting a landscape, came in to find out, from another student, how to best preserve an animal carcass she was using in the foreground of the picture.

Nutrition, chemistry, the news, or a particular book were topics for frequent informal conversations; more formal individual tutoring also occurred regularly. Students could obtain equipment, books, or supplies necessary for their studies through a ten dollar discretionary fund accessible to each person. (At the beginning, the fund was replenished each time it was used up; later replenishment was financially unfeasible.)

The best way to describe the curriculum is through a glimpse of the activities students and staff were engaged in during one late spring week:

1. A staff member had posted a notice to meet and discuss Shakespeare, an interest of his. The seven or eight people who came decided to meet on a regular basis.

2. Many students and staff of all ages went to the art room to paint, draw, or work with clay.

3. Several girls, aged eight to eleven, gathered in the sewing room or outdoors to sew costumes for the puppets they had made. They planned on presenting puppet plays of their own creation.

4. A yoga class disbanded because of the irregular attendance of the group's leader.

5. People attending a film workshop planned a TV film about the school, and edited other footage.

6. Several practiced on musical instruments. A young man who played his French horn for hours alone occasionally joined others in duets. Another spent his days playing drums in the barn.

7. Many students were outside, playing basketball, volleyball, climbing trees, or riding bikes.

8. Several staff members went to a nearby town for individual instruction in yoga and drawing.

The corporations, previously mentioned, provided the core activities. Formed by students and staff members who shared a common interest, they were legal entities with autonomy over their activities and finances. Some provided and maintained supplies, such as the Tool Corp., the Needlework Corp., the Sculpture and Pottery Corp., the Arts and Crafts Supply Corp., the Cooking Corp., and the Supply Center, which maintained supplies for the School Meeting. Others were organized more around an activity itself, such as Musical and Horticultural Societies, the Photolab and the Film Production Corp., and the Press Corp., which publishes materials—articles, books, and a newsletter for assembly members—but not a newspaper. Anyone could organize a group and request incorporation from the School Meeting. One student expressed an interest in having a school paper but had not tried to form a corporation for it.

The school also supported activities taking place in nearby towns. In fact, it had evolved into a *base* for learning rather than a center where all learning took place. Many adults had volunteered as resources to come to the school and work with students, but as the school became a decentralized learning base, the need for such volunteers diminished. Few were active. A teaching staff was still considered necessary, however. As one staff member remarked, "We never intended it to be an empty base."

There were apprenticeships based on students' interests. Some were set up by an apprenticeship clerk, but many of these learning experiences happened informally. As a staff member related:

> People just go off and do things. Like two boys are interested in radio so they work at a radio station. The only way I knew is I heard them talking.

These two boys had their own morning radio program in Boston. One student had a job in a law office as clerk. As an expert in parlimentary procedure, she was also the law clerk at the school and reviewed the development of Sudbury's rules over its first three years of operation. Another, planning to go into premed, had a job at a nearby hospital. He had studied with one of the staff who had a PhD in biochemistry and is a resource for other students interested in chemistry and medicine.

Although the cross-age and multi-degree program had many strengths, it required tremendous energy from the participants and the availability of many resources within or outside of the school. A student was expected to arrange his own learning situations with the staff member or student from whom he wanted help.

Students' progress depended on their commitment. Teenagers arranged to graduate when they felt they had gained as much as possible from Sudbury and were ready to pursue their studies at another institution or to assume independent employment. The process usually began with students choosing a staff sponsor and writing a thesis explaining why they felt ready to assume full responsibility for themselves in the community at large. The sponsors often assisted the students with their theses of explication and self-evaluation. When ready, a two-hour "defense" was scheduled at which the theses were open to the questions and challenges of students, staff, and Assembly members.

The defenses in the spring of 1971 were reportedly tedious and difficult. Although the process could occur any time during the year, candidates for graduation were also voted on by the School Assembly in December or May. Whether the Assembly vote represented a serious evaluation, however, or merely a rubber stamp of the School Meeting's opinion was argued at its May 1971 session. Assembly members who had not heard a candidate's defense were eligible to vote. Criteria for a graduate's "readiness" had never been agreed on by Assembly members.

In a short questionnaire administered randomly to a small sample of students and staff, most thought the school did a good to very good job in developing political and social skills and in preparing students for jobs. Fewer thought the school did well in preparing students for college. Curiously enough, as many rated the school "very good" in developing interpersonal skills as rated it "very poor."

INTERGROUP RELATIONS

Students seemed to be able to ask each other for help easily. Most responded readily to younger students' requests for support, helping them, playing with them, or caring for them. One teenager said he felt that he was more important to the youngsters' education than they were to his, although he enjoyed them. Other teenagers, however, felt the viewpoints and abilities of the young offered some learning experiences as well as pleasure, supporting the belief that "Everyone learns, and everyone teaches."

Many of the school rules that protected the youngsters from accidents freed the older students and staff from having to baby-sit or take great responsibility for the younger children. Since everyone knew the rules, each person took responsibility for himself. The heavy emphasis on rules and rigidity was seen as a framework that provided freedom. Because everyone participated in creating the rules, everyone knew the reasons behind them; having well-defined and enforced parameters allowed more energy to be directed to constructive activities rather than testing, daring, or other counter-dependent behavior. One staff member attributed the low accident rate at Sudbury Valley School to an absence of hostility:

> The thing that kept impressing me and impressing me is the absence of what I saw in other private schools, the number of so-called "accidents"—people getting hurt—broken legs, bloody noses. The infirmary was always loaded. Here kids do a lot more active and dangerous things. Like last year, they were into "chicken fights" with old tricycles, but no one got hurt. Yet at other schools people would have been hurt. In trying to figure it out, I realized that in the other schools it was hostility redirected against each other; here no one is trying to hurt anyone else.

When people entered Sudbury, either as staff or student, they were faced with problems of adjusting. For some, the personal changes required to adapt to the school's educational assumptions and lack of structure were a struggle. A staff member described it:

> I'm talking about getting yourself together so that you
> can change yourself from a person who has been
> taught all his life that he was incapable of making his
> own decisions regarding his own behavior.

At Sudbury, no one made decisions for another person.
Each person could be independent, with no questions asked
and could regulate his experience at school as he chose. It
was assumed that people would be responsible in the ways
they handled their freedom—responsible to themselves, to
others, and to Sudbury.

Each student and staff member learned to deal with his
own time and to respect the rights of others to theirs. Often
this meant adjusting one's expectations of others, particularly
of the staff. The staff expected the same rights and responsibilities that students had; and to avoid being leaned on, as
well as to avoid appearing authoritative, the staff stood back
and waited for students to decide what they wanted to pursue.
Adapting to new roles and ways of relating was difficult.
In most cases, students visited the school for a week and
made the decision to attend Sudbury themselves. Yet it still
took weeks or months for a new student to begin knowing
what he wanted to do and to set his own personal and academic goals. For some, it was an awkward time, and there
was no standard procedure or ritual to help. During this crucial period the student was left alone to test whether he could
get himself together. Those who stayed have proved they
can take responsibility for themselves. The staff had begun
giving a week to the beginning student to help him get in the
swing of things, and a staff member said, "My hunch is that
it takes less time now because the place is more settled, and
we have the week which we give." Most students were able
to accept responsibility for themselves, whatever the pain of
adjustment.

Respondents agreed that teachers treated students as responsible, and that students treated teachers with respect. Further, they believed that the staff listened to students' opinions but were not so sure that students listened to teachers' opinions.

A Matter of Style. From the staff point of view, the learning process depended on an "unstructured" personal relationship:

> You can't afford to structure personal relationships for learning because you usually go for advice from a person who has authority over you. You know, your parents, your guidance counselor, your teachers, your professor; it's always somebody who in the end is going to evaluate you, so you don't even want to hear what he's going to say because he'll catch you with your pants down. Now here this doesn't happen. You're going to let each person choose whatever he needs, to make his own mixture. It's important when this rugged individual can ask a lot of questions. Nobody can force him to take the advice that he gets, and that's why he finally goes around and asks questions.

Each staff member had the prerogative to deal with requests as he chose, and there were probably as many teaching styles as there were staff members and students. Since there was no preparation or teacher training programs to draw on, all depended on the kind of interaction that occurred between staff member and student. A staff member who taught French gave an example of the process:

> A girl came to me and asked for a course, so we met three or four times. I arranged it so I was never a

prompter. I don't like to teach French when I have to
tell you what to learn or give assignments. That's got
nothing to do with abstract ideas of education. I'm not
opposed to a person, on some subjects, telling me what
to learn, teaching whatever way he has to teach, but
I set up the course that way because that's the way I
wanted to teach it. I wanted to be like a consultant or
advisor. She'd meet with me and ask questions on
where she was stuck, and that was fine for her. She
worked on her own. I don't know if she is still working on it or not.

A student might or might not be satisfied with a staff member's style. But should bias, for instance, crop up, a student
said, it was not a problem:

People here arrange their own studies which may or
may not involve "courses." The staff here are from
diverse backgrounds. If one does take courses and/or
works closely with them, one uncovers bias just as one
does in himself. But we have the opportunity to work
with outsiders, to plan the course ourselves, and so the
question [of bias] doesn't seem applicable. *We* control
what we learn, and so the amout of bias is something
we can counteract.

Yet a student might not always be able to exert control. He
or she then had the choice of compromising or establishing a
new learning relationship with someone else.

Reactions to New People.   The emphasis on student responsibility in establishing relationships was clear. As noted, the
staff stood back and waited for others to decide what they
wanted—friendship, help, or tutoring. Not all the staff found
this easy or natural to do:

> When someone new comes in, I hold myself back
> from pouncing because I like to make relationships, I
> like to talk to people.

Striking a balance between barging in on a new person and
holding back was considered advantageous, however:

> What I call barging in is when a person is forced into
> a position of having to say "get lost." Now why not
> wait, and this is what I think is smart, why not wait
> until that person has had enough time to get himself
> oriented and knows what you look like and you know
> what he looks like and you have a feeling for when
> the guy has a little time. Then you say "Hi, do you
> want a coke?" (Student)

> Especially since they come in so awed, especially of
> the staff. They feel immediately put on the spot by
> somebody. (Student)

> One of the reasons why it is so hard to stand back and
> just let it happen is because we have to believe that
> human nature is such that it will happen. You have to
> believe that people are basically warm. Now if you
> don't believe that, you better structure it real tight so
> that everyone is nice to each other. But if you believe
> that, you can relax and let go and let it happen. (Staff
> member)

For the students who could reach out, the freedom to
initiate relationships on their own was valuable. For those
who couldn't, the struggle was painful and occasionally resulted in withdrawal from the school. The rationale, stated
by staff members, sounded harsh:

> What we're saying seems paradoxical but it isn't the
> worst thing you can do when these kids come here

and obviously are starved for love, so clearly starved
for real friendship they go around like puppies with
their tongues hanging out, it's pathetic, and what you
say to those people is almost "BOO! We can't guar-
antee a thing. . . . We will not offer you the slightest
hope that you will have a single friend, much less any
love in the school." Now that's a hard thing to say.
But that's exactly what the school says because that's
the only way that you'll ever get any love and friendship.

Yet a natural reaching out to new people by staff and students, not institutionalized or advertised, was present. The
Sudbury philosophy was not a rejection of relationships or
fear of personal involvements. Behind the rhetoric was a
great deal of concern for personal relationships, as a staff
member attested:

First of all, we are not into the interpersonal thing. . . .
We do not believe that to institutionalize ideas into the
personal thing is a healthy thing at all. And we think
that you cannot possibly force personal commitment,
you cannot institutionalize it . . . it has failed in those
places where they tried. Now what we're saying is
that this place makes it fertile ground for it to happen
in the most natural, organic way. And it's not going to
be interfered with. Now the kind of positive advertis-
ing or trying to create the situation is damaging to the
organic growth of this kind of thing; it is very self-
defeating. Because I don't think that you can teach
a person, in any formal way, how to be responsible to
another person until something happens. And that's
why we are so careful with it.

And so, in an effort to make a place where "real" relationships can develop and "shit grins don't survive," time was provided for "something to happen." But often this time, this stretch of freedom from obligation or expectation, resembled distance between people. To an outsider, personal relationships at Sudbury appeared cool, even stoic. But a staff member brushed such observations aside as superficial:

> There's a big place for being all soft and warm and sensitive and all the things that you seem to expect to be on the surface, or you seem to want to look for right away. This is something that you can't summon up for examination. Like I go around being the rugged individual, the way we all do . . . you try to do this all yourself. And you drop the ball and you really screw up, then you find out that there are people around that care that you screwed up. What happens to you when that happens is what I'm trying to get at. It's not like you're in prison. There's *no obligation* for people to even say boo to you if you drop the ball. None! They do something because they're humane and they care . . . that really gives you the message fast . . . you just can't be one of those automatons that go by a formula. Okay, now in the public schools, they say, "Well we have to teach these children to be more human," and they really concentrate on interpersonal relationships. It's all very noble, but it didn't look to us like it worked. So we decided to immediately take all pressure away. Because you're not going to force personal things.

Another attributed the cool tone to lack of experience in finding the proper balance between supporting a person and pressuring him. Not wanting to barge in, some rarely reached out, leaving too much distance:

One mistake is some of us lean over backwards to be very cool and not put any pressure, not interfere with peoples' lives, though we are ready to help, whenever they want. As we gain confidence and learn to handle these things, the school gets better, and we continue to expand our educational philosophy.

Vis-à-Vis Visitors. At Sudbury there was a compelling zeal to "sell" the idea of the school to others, and a great sense of mission. The school was wide open to visitors, but their number had to be limited to twelve a day, not counting those who came for an extended stay. Students and professors from nearby colleges or schools, community people, researchers— all were welcome. The visitors' clerk greeted them on arrival, gave out reading materials, and answered questions. Then the visitors were on their own, to explore and learn.

Students and staff were willing to talk about Sudbury, but the responsibility for asking questions was left to the visitors. When visitors were unable to do this, they lost out. Often disappointed, they blamed the school. Sudbury people were critical of superficial attempts to understand the school and this, too, put visitors on edge. Often they felt intrusive or out of place; sometimes they asked questions that turned people off; some who disagreed with the philosophy could find no one to argue with about it. A phenomenon, common to free schools, occurs, where visitors stand around talking to other visitors.

Though the principle of being open for visitors was accepted, the reactions to visitors were mixed. Some considered them a priority; others far less:

The school is not set up to be a real school; it is set up to be a prototype for what we would like to see education be.

> People in this school have learned not to talk about
> their feelings with visitors because so many of the visi-
> tors challenge or deny those feelings.

Self-protection from visitors was often interpreted as cold-
ness or aloofness. Yet staff members emphasized that it was
self-protection rather than protection of the school that was
involved. A protective shield, which students and staff felt
they had to create, prevented them from responding freely to
visitors and may account, in part, for the difficulty they sensed
in getting the message of Sudbury across:

> This gap exists between what we know about the
> school and what brief visitors frequently go away say-
> ing about this school. We know it's not true, but we've
> never had a handle on how to get it across.

The School Meeting once considered formulating a visitors'
policy that would request more information about the purpose of the visit. Other alternatives were suggested at an informal meeting:

> You're saying we should be more extroverted. That's
> one appproach, and another approach might be to
> have visitors only three or two times a week.

> Do you have any kind of an idea of how to make a
> day's visit more effective? Do you think we should
> give a tour or a lecture?

AS A MODEL SCHOOL

Sudbury Valley was committed to changing and improving
education; it wanted to be a model for other schools to consider and adapt. Publications described the philosophy of the

school; the staff and students spoke at other schools and community meetings. A college-age student, as publicity clerk, handled requests and arrangements, and volunteers assisted.

It was hoped that more publicity would attract more students. Larger enrollment would ease the financial strain and move forward the goal of being large and public. By 1973 the student population had risen a little, from seventy in 1971, to eighty or eighty-five.

Although Sudbury claimed to be a diversified group, it was limited to a white middle-class population. Its tuition charges and its isolated location, requiring transportation, meant that many could not afford to attend. The all-white staff was another block to attracting people of minority groups. No specific ways to remedy the situation were voiced during our visit, beyond vague references to "scholarship funds" next year. The 1973 student population was still "mostly" white.

Consistent with the school setting, few students were studying or working in the areas of race, poverty, or contemporary social issues. This is a rather grave note on which to conclude. Institutional racism was an issue for Sudbury, as it is for many alternative schools. How schools are dealing with racial identity and autonomy, whether in the context of an all-white or multi-ethnic setting, is a criterion in evaluating innovative schools. As a model, Sudbury's curriculum process and governance structure would have to be adjusted to deal with race and racial issues. Certainly, there are valuable things to be learned from the Sudbury experience, and although not all of them are positive, much of its structure and style would be exciting to try in different settings.

Milwaukee Independent School, Milwaukee

By Dale Crowfoot

Milwaukee Independent School (MIS) is a private high school completely defined and controlled by students. It opened in February 1970, with about forty students who had dropped out of public school to join the experiment. The first students were chosen by lottery, but later student applicants, as well as staff, were selected after interviews by a student committee.

The student population is 100 percent white and primarily middle class. In the spring of 1971, it still numbered about forty, while the staff had risen to ten, bringing the teacher-student ratio to one–four or one–five. All the staff members had BAs, and a majority had MAs as well. Three had state teaching certification. By 1973, the student population was down to twenty-five, and the staff numbered four or five.

Students established the length of their days, their curriculum and classes, and took an active part in the staff evaluations of their progress. Although there were no graduations, students were primarily college oriented and 80 percent of those leaving MIS went on to college. A number of colleges and universities that were queried, also all white, expressed support of the Milwaukee Independent School. They assured students that they would not be penalized for attending an unaccredited alternative school, and some considered it an attribute. The school will not be eligible for accreditation until 1975, when it will have been in operation for five years. In any event, accreditation was not a priority for MIS. According to a founder, "Existence is *de facto* accreditation."

Students had to get jobs to earn their tuition of $300 a year, paid monthly. In 1971, their monthly payments, which totaled about a thousand dollars in all, covered the $225 a month rent, the phone bill, and the staff's subsistence salaries. Three of the staff were not paid at all, and several had part-time jobs elsewhere. Parents' contributions and fund-raising events supplemented the school's income.

The school was located in a cluster of rooms on the fourth floor of an office building in downtown Milwaukee. It had several prior locations—an old house, which students and staff renovated, several rooms in an innercity elementary school, and the second floor of a grocery store. The present central location is relatively convenient for students who hitchhike to school, work, or other activities.

The school was the people. It was small enough and unstructured enough to permit individual personalities to set the tone of the place. People at MIS were pretty relaxed, and so was the school. Each day was different—depending on what classes were scheduled, who was around, the season, the weather, the city's cultural calendar, and people's moods. In the spring of 1971, for instance, people's spirits were high. The weather was warming up, hitchhiking to school and around the city was easier, people were meeting, eating, and playing outdoors, the windows in the lounge were constantly open. After the hassle of January and February and the resting period of March, there was a new urgency to do things and tackle problems. Public school vacations provided comrades in adventure for MIS students. The city was also waking up after the winter, offering concerts in the park, a hunger walk campaign, and community clean-up projects. The building was a base where students gathered, made plans, and went off in pursuit of action. A student would ask a group sitting around the lounge if anyone wanted to go to an exhibit or event at a nearby high school. Or someone would announce that theater tickets were available for a dress rehearsal or matinee. Sometimes people would go, sometimes not.

As each day proceeded, students flowed through the cluster of rooms. Some came for classes, some to see other students or staff, some just wanted a place, a group, something to do. Some only dropped in between outside activities. Many students worked and studied away from the building, at home, in the library, at day care centers, and in preschool programs. For others, the school was their main activity. Because the fourth floor setting was small, seven rooms in all, the flow was apparent, communication was easy. By 1973, the space was reduced to three rooms.

Students usually arrived first, around 9:30 to 10:30 A.M., and gathered in the lounge. When members of a class were present, they moved into another room to begin class. A few students might stretch out and read in the lounge; others preferred the library, usually a quiet place. Many of MIS's books had been donated, and they were cataloged by the student who coordinated the use of the library. A small room with a sink served as an art room; another, with two desks, as a language room. The office, with two desks, some files, and a table, was another place to congregate.

Students and staff members were friendly and open with each other and with visitors. They took time to explain the school they had created, not with missionary zeal, but with honest, personal responses. Often, when asked questions, students replied, "It's good you are asking me these questions so I'll think about them."

Since the purpose or definition of education was an individual matter at MIS, there was no right or wrong way to learn. There were style differences and a variety of needs, which sometimes conflicted, but there was freedom to operate, to disagree, and to establish one's own pattern. Yet the open structure, the stress on individual fulfillment and the variety of extramural activities made it difficult for students to share their academic interests. Because they were relatively unaware of what others were doing, there was a gap in the learning process; goal setting, already an individual matter, was not stimulated by others within a contest of diverse possibilities. Learning from each other was limited. Even sharing complaints about school as such, as students in traditional school are accustomed to do, might have proved threatening, since the school was controlled by students and the choice of subjects (academic and nonacademic) as well as progress and satisfactions were the students' responsibility.

Yet, openness, honesty in relating to others, and sharing feelings and perceptions was emphasized. In general meetings quite a bit of time was spent "processing" the dynamics of the group. Still, some said there were issues just below the surface that were not dealt with openly. Women's rights was one; whether there should be graduation was another.

The general atmosphere was often highly colored by the students' efforts to support "the revolution." The exact focus of the revolution was difficult to discover, and there had been several versions. In the fall of 1971, the revolution seemed to center on community development until it was learned that community development could not be forced in the abstract. Then it was gay liberation, for which MIS became the city-wide headquarters for a time, and gay libbers hung arond the building. Most MIS students either accepted them as doing their own thing or ignored them—until the MIS student publication, *Doughnut*, became involved. When its January 1972, edition featured cartoons and comments about gay liberation, many felt it was inappropriate for a publication representing the school, and some considered it pornographic. The result was acknowledgement that gay liberation was not the revolution for MIS to support.

Supporting alternative life styles and education, however, it was agreed, did further the revolution. This was done through guerilla theater productions at public schools, city-wide meetings and informal gatherings, speaking engagements in classes and clubs, and personal contacts. Alternative ways of life were pursued through work and apprenticeship programs. Many of the white, middle-class students viewed the learning experience derived from a job as crucial, and, hence, the requirement of earning their tuition instead of receiving it from their parents developed. The ninth graders, of course, were limited in the kinds of jobs they could get—baby-sitting, yard work—but otherwise most of the work experiences students chose were associated with counter-culture, white revolution, and peace activities that would prepare them for another society. They worked in day care centers, Planned Parenthood offices, draft counseling centers, and neighborhood offices. These were ways an alternative school prepared people for an alternative life style.

The kind of future these activities prepared students for was unclear. Students had a sense of what they don't want to do in the future, but their positive goals were harder to determine. Testing out various jobs and roles may be temporarily satisfactory, but one staff member had argued for more structure and content in the academic program to "protect" students from meaningless jobs such as working in a fish market. Students, however, resented both his evaluation of such jobs and his suggested standardization of their learning. They resisted his criteria for success and any need "to protect themselves" and strove to retain their alternatives. At the same time, the backgrounds and life styles of some of the staff provided alternative models. Two or three lived in community houses, sharing with other families or single people. One woman was associated with the Women's Center in Milwaukee; another had arranged day care for her daughter in order to teach.

FROM IDEA TO REALITY

A school started and run by students was a novel idea and a guiding principle of MIS almost from the start. The beginning itself, however, was surprisingly modest.

In the summer of 1969, several Marquette High School students got together to discuss the formation of a student union and other innovations that might be developed within the Jesuit school for boys. The principal was not receptive to the idea of changing many classes, and the students looked elsewhere for adult support. As other students became involved, the original idea of a political base or student union gave way to the idea of starting a school.

Two of the group contacted community people to ascertain potential support, and an employee of the Center for Civic Initiative made his offices and supplies available to them. To comply with the legal regulations of incorporation, the students selected an advisory board of directors, composed of both students and adults, with adults in the majority.

During the first phase of planning, the support of adults who helped the students create the school was vital. In addition to giving advice, they drew support from the institutions where they worked or were known, such as the University of Wisconsin's School of Education in Milwaukee, the Center for Civic Initiative, the United Community Service, the Jewish Vocational Center, and the State Department of Health and Social Service. For example, although the School of Education could offer neither financial aid or space, it did finance and supervise student teachers at MIS.

Most of the media were favorable toward MIS: The *Milwaukee Journal and Sentinel* and the local TV station gave it coverage. The Milwaukee "underground" and local grapevine endorsed and spread the word about it. Later the school attracted reporters from the *New York Times*, the *Boston Globe, Chicago Mirror*, and the *New Schools Exchange*, to name a few. Although the founders were unsuccessful at obtaining funding, the press support, crucial for an alternative school, lent them prestige and led to potential funding and contact with individuals interested in being involved in some capacity.

Despite the widespread approval, however, Milwaukee school board members opposed MIS; they weren't sure it was a school.

The Board of Directors' Role. Shortly after the MIS board began meeting, a split developed between some members when one or two students wanted to ask another student to leave, and the board supported their recommendation. Some saw the decision as an example of student control; others noted that it was an adult who forbade the student access to the board's office. Again, when the students dropped out of regular school in the fall to establish their own school, there was disagreement about the amount of structure and requirements the new school should have and the amount of power the board should have.

Some adult members seemed to want to be part of the student body, to sit on the floor with the kids. Others wanted a more advisory role as "enablers" who facilitated student interests when asked. One felt that some had "hidden agendas" for being on the board—seeking prestige or a feeling of youth.

As a whole, however, board members saw themselves mainly as protectors of the school's philosophy and were concerned not to overstep their role as advisors. At meetings they regularly offered progress reports (on site selection or fundraising, for example) and tried not to make any policy decision that hadn't been sent to the students for approval. From the start the students approved personnel decisions, such as having graduate teaching fellows and a volunteer secretary. Students admitted for the first semester were chosen by lottery among those applying.

As the date set for the school's opening, February 2, 1970, drew near, the possibility of a legal case on truancy raised more questions about truancy, conditions of legality, and accreditation. The public school board, responsible for all students up to age eighteen, was worried about the difficulty of transferring students from MIS back to the public schools should the need arise. It wanted the status of MIS clarified by the State Department of Public Instruction but promised that no truancy actions against MIS students would be taken until a reply from the state has been received. Later, there was clear support by the Department of Public Instruction, but the attendance policy remained unclear as public schools marked MIS students absent throughout the spring of 1970.

Meanwhile during the previous fall, the MIS board felt a full-time, paid director was needed to coordinate the program and the staff. Two people were considered. One was an educator from Vancouver; the other, suggested by a board member, was director of student teaching at the University's School of Education. When the latter met with a group of the students, they were impressed. The student's newsletter reported:

> At the prospect of becoming our project director both he and all of the students with whom he has met are very excited. Already he has spent a great deal of time working with us on MIS's needs. We hope that anyone who hasn't met him has an opportunity Friday night or Saturday.

However, when he presented some of his ideas in a twelve-page paper to the board in December, board members were not impressed. They felt he would direct too much and not be responsive to student control. When the students hired him anyway, against the reservations of the board, one adult member resigned. The decision to hire was seen as a major test and proof of student control. Two more adults left the board shortly after, to be replaced by one adult. The board then numbered five adults and four students.

Problems with the First Director. As the year progressed, personal antagonisms with the director developed. He began his job fresh from an academic career, unsure of how he fitted into the new scene and confused about his role. He had

enjoyed great popularity with university students, had a substantial following, and, it was said, "expected MIS students
to follow him as others had." Many students did, responding
favorably to his way of relating, his teaching style, and his
goals.

He was a planner "big on public-mindedness" and developed many contacts important to the school's survival. The
son of a minister, he was described as having "the righteous-
ness and enthusiasm of a YMCA director" and as a "gatherer
of souls." Early in the year he defined his role in broad
terms as coordinator, teacher-group leader, PR representative,
and primary fund-raiser. Not until May did he decide to con-
fine his activities to the last two aspects.

Three criticisms of the director were: (*1*) his overdirec-
tiveness, which the board had predicted; (*2*) his insistence
on keeping the dilapidated house on Resevoir Street as the
school site and renovating it as a method of building cohesion among students and staff, even though the students were
sick of it and wanted to move elsewhere; and (*3*) his salary
of $16,500 in the midst of the school's financial struggles to
survive. Although he had requested his salary on the basis of
need (he had a chronically ill wife and several children),
students felt discouraged and resentful after a successful
fund-raising venture when all the profits went for the coordinator's salary instead of equipment. For several months, when
students could not raise enough, his salary was secretly paid
by a staff member.

Personal conflicts developed over the semester between the
director and staff members and between the director and the
chairman of the board, who had opposed hiring him and
continued to oppose him. The director held the chairman
responsible for the board's noncooperation, and as the conflict

continued, some of his original supporters changed their position and opposed him on many matters.

Because the director did not call staff meetings or collaborate with the staff, issues were taken instead to the board meetings, which were frequent. They became an open forum where staff, students, board members, parents, and the director could disagree. Often when all parties, sometimes numbering fifty, were present, the emotional level was high.

Uusally, after an issue was raised and discussed, the board made a recommendation and sent it to the students' meeting for final approval. Although the board made primary decisions, student governance did prevail in the end. Still, a number of students, staff members, and adults who supported student control and a more open, unstructured environment formed a coalition to give more leverage to the students' position. They, too, often found themselves in opposition, direct or indirect, subtle or argumentative, to the director's positions. General meetings of the school were called when necessary to handle smaller matters. No records were kept of the issues or decisions. One student described them as "crisis oriented," and since crises were numerous that first semester, so were the meetings. So frequent and so wearing were they that students and staff often wondered whether all the hassling was worth it. Yet, a student explained, there was not much fighting during the early period because the initiators and director "made most of the decisions." That was acceptable since it took many students time to understand what was going on. Students were quite unprepared for dealing with as many things as they were expected to—self-motivation in learning and lack of structure, interpersonal relationships in a more intense setting, and maintenance of an educational institution on a day-to-day basis.

Several felt the school had started too soon. A staff member called it "premature" because the majority of students had no experience or planning abilities. A board member felt the school's formation went too fast and that the "board members hadn't gotten to know each other well enough." One of the original students said, "In the beginning few kids knew what it was all about. I didn't either . . . not for four months." Inexperienced in the processes of effective student control, students had not included a form for governance in their original seven-page description of goals and practices.

During the first semester, the majority of students were either too individualistic, too alienated, or too little prepared to participate strongly in matters of governance. The promise of independence and an individually created learning experience—to say nothing of escape—attracted students. One initiating student described the dynamics of the situation as "a group of alienated students coming together in an interdependent way of learning to work through their feelings." Another said the school attracted "turned-off kids who turned off at MIS also and never came around."

Confrontation and Resignations.   That factions existed among students and adults was clear; usually they met away from school to gripe and, with the exception of the board meetings, there was little open, general sharing of feelings. One of the original students thought the problem was the "separation" between the director and "the rest of the staff; he wasn't ready for our school."

A staff member believed the director had tried to gain consensus:

> But no one had a good idea of what the school was going to be, and he was unable to. I think he made the staff more passive in the beginning of the year,

though it's not that simple. He came at a hard time, with a hard role, and he was caught in the middle. He didn't want to take over, but he felt compelled to do something. If he'd been as strong as he felt, it might have been easier for others to clarify their own positions.

By April, a leveling out period, some had lowered their expectations and accepted whatever occurred, but others were ready to confront those with whom they differed. By May, a confrontation with the director was at hand.

The minutes from the board of director's meeting for May 14 show that second thoughts about both the director (here called "the coordinator") and his role were being openly discussed. The minutes first summarized the director's comments and then the ensuing discussion:

> There was resistance from students to his or the staff's leading or organizing. He felt that he could not function in his most effective way. He feels that it was a mistake for him to meet classes eight hours a week at the expense of one-one contacts between students and himself. Consequently *he will now leave these classes.* He feels that we should be able to ask students to commit themselves to continue classes they have chosen. He asks that all students rethink what a coordinator should do and then see if he fulfills this role. But also rethink what the coordinator has said about structure and freedom for him to direct the school in the direction he sees as right.

> Effort made to direct discussion away from the present director.

> Question raised as to whether we can afford a coordinator. Effort made to make discussion of coordinator separate from our question of finances.

Focus: What things do we want and need in a coordinator? Staff and students need leadership at times. Need a person perceptive as to when not to, and how to lead.

Before the meeting concluded, the board recommended "that we continue the coordinator for ninety days (May 15-August 15) at which time a decision will be made."

More trouble loomed ahead. All the staff but one had decided to leave. At the following meeting on June 3, two student initiators unexpectedly presented a letter they had written to the board that was highly critical of the school's direction generically and of the director specifically. The opening paragraph read:

After four months of MISs operation, we are very concerned with its present direction particularly in two areas: the overall lack of sensitive response to student concerns and role and function of staff and board in the school.

An atmosphere of "defensiveness and indecisiveness," it continued, diverted people from focusing on students' needs and left most students in a vacuum. The kind of leadership the students wanted was missing. Both the staff and the board were in part to blame:

What the students require, the structure alone cannot provide. Such requirements include an awareness of feelings and the reasons for them, a sense of direction to deal with them, and the responsibility for their decisions. All this is called for. The staff needs to be in touch with their own feelings to be capable of empathizing with the feelings of students and to be asking themselves and students significant questions. This has evidently not been seen as a priority. Various staff members have made insufficient attempts to raise questions, but no one has been able to help in exploring these feelings. Board members might have been more perceptive in recognizing and responding to these problems. They might have been more supportive of staff initiative, and provided more leadership themselves.

Still it was the director who was primarily responsible for the "education and functioning of the staff." Yet the director had optimistically diverted their feelings and questions into task-oriented channels rather than helping to clarify them. After proposing an $8,000 ceiling on the director's salary, the letter concluded:

> We don't think MIS has incorporated an alternative in life styles, enhanced interpersonal relationships, or enabled ways to solve problems. We do not see the staff as functioning under a process of open communication, critical thinking, and conscious responsibility.
> We urge an open dialectic on all the questions this statement has posed around the general direction of the school and specifically concerning the coordinator. Students must be able to honestly raise these and other concerns without being made to feel guilty or threatened in doing so.

The next day the director resigned and sent the students, staff, board members, and parents a long letter criticizing the school and listing the difficulties he had had:

> The Milwaukee Independent School is failing, if it hasn't already done so. It is failing because many aspects of the dream which led to its creation have no basis in reality and because *some of those who dreamed the dream have refused to bend or compro-*

mise. . . . Unwilling or unable to accept the fact that maybe something was wrong with the dream, they have chosen to find in me the cause for its failure. . . .

I will not accept sole, or even most of the responsibility for the situation in which we now find ourselves. . . . And most of all, I regret the need to sever my relationships with the student body . . . because I did love them, I tried to "do" for them, and it is because of that "doing" that they find it difficult to return my love and respect. For me, then, it is over, and over, I fear, for MIS.

Since the very begining, I have had no ground upon which to stand. I was hired with the knowledge that several board members had serious reservations as to qualifications. I was informed . . . that my willingness to take initiative, my creativity . . . were liabilities which had the potential for thwarting the emergence of student initiative. . . . I was constantly challenged every time I took initiative and equally so when I did not. . . . I have now been called upon to accept major responsibility for the present state of MIS, despite the fact that I was given no authority or autonomy with which I might have been able to prevent it.

The director left for a new job in an innovative community school. The events surrounding his departure roused the anxiety of parents, who had read in his letter about students' "promiscuity, use of drugs, stealing, lying, deceitfulness," the concern of board members about their role, and the apprehension of students, excited and ambivalent about the challenge ahead.

A New Start. The June 11 board meeting, attended by three adult members, six students, two parents, and a member of the community, was called to reevaluate the role of the board. Students suggested it act more in the role of consultants and attend to legal matters and that students initiate proposals for the board's approval, rather than the other way around, as it had been. When the suggestions were adopted, it was also decided there was no need to select another adult member to the board or even for it "to meet regularly." By 1973, the board no longer existed.

Before the meeting adjourned, however, plans were reviewed for the summer, including staff recruitment and fund raising. The students' proposal that parents also provide $300 tuition, in addition to the $300 earned by each student, was accepted to ensure funding, with a stipulation that arrangements be made for those who could not pay. To recruit a new staff, "Let's just all go forward—bring people to the attention of students." The lone returning staff member was selected to provide liaison for all parties.

After the director-coordinator resigned, "the people coordinated." There were long meetings focused on commitment and on what MIS and students could expect from each other. Interaction with others was considered a priority, and, as such, required, at the very least, attendance at general and small meetings, taking two classes (one with community involvement), and weekly evaluations with the staff. This burst of intense involvement, as people moved toward consensus, strengthened the students' hopes for their school.

Work continued through the summer. A handful of students met daily and continued the discussions of coordination, minimal requirements, and student and staff roles. MIS was not dead. The administrative work went on—letters were written, and colleges and community people were contacted. Twenty new students were interviewed and accepted over the summer, and eight new staff members (two part-time) were chosen. The interviews were handled by five students and the remaining staff member. No new director or coordinator was hired. The role was divided instead between two of the staff—one was assigned responsibility for financial coordination, and the other for supplies, building repairs, and the like.

Few of the new staff knew each other, and few of the new students did. School reopened in September 1970 with a retreat, aimed primarily at getting to know people.

Some students wondered if the incoming students shouldn't be screened more closely for leadership qualities and willingness to work for the school, "at least for the next year or so while the school is still settling its foundations." From the beginning, even under the lottery system, those who had emotional problems or couldn't read were "deemed completely unacceptable." Now, with the fate of the school largely in student hands, more positive qualities seemed required.

GOVERNANCE

Students did control Milwaukee Independent School. Not only did they hire the staff, select the students, and support the school financially, but they governed its day-to-day affairs in an open weekly meeting. They controlled their studies and how they managed their time. Although control by students was inherent from the school's inception, these responsibilities have developed over time.

Acknowledging the dimensions of responsibility was a continuing process at MIS. Although the fact was accepted that governance and maintenance depended on participation by a majority of students, student involvement ranged from active to passive, from committee membership to absenteeism, from pursuit of relationships to withdrawal and isolation. The structure of the school allowed for such diversity, but the necessity of school management ran parallel. Students elicited each others' time and energy for that shared purpose. The norm was to leave people space but to ask for help when necessary.

General Meetings. Probably more than three-fourths of the students and staff attended the weekly General Meetings. As the only total-group function, attendance was considered one of the "minimum expectations." The agenda was determined beforehand in an informal open meeting, usually chaired by a student and usually attended only by those interested in current issues. Students sometimes raised topics for the agenda, but the staff were often left with the task. Only those who attended knew the agenda beforehand or the things that had been dealt with as they arose.

The atmosphere of the General Meetings was also informal. People walked freely in and out. Conversations, questions, and laughter were shared by students and staff, each cutting off the other at times. Anger was openly expressed. Some students seemed particularly aware of the "process," as they tried to move the meeting along or make a decision. Decisions were made by consensus, or a vote could be called requiring the consent of three-fourths of those present to pass. Sometimes no decisions were made.

For example, after disposing of minor announcements, a meeting in April 1971 reviewed the problems of a crafts and rummage store that had opened to provide tuition money for students who worked there. Was it working out as planned? Or was it being used as a hangout and competing with the school for student energies? Then graduation, as an issue, was discussed. Would it help legitimize MIS to the community? What would it mean in the area of expectations and evaluations?

The meeting continued as long as people wanted to talk, about three hours. No decisions were made. A board member who attended, said, "It could have been the first meeting," criticizing the "interminable discussion."

Students felt that the school's educational philosophy would "never be completed; it'll always be changing." The emphasis on the "development of the individual," complicated the governance process. Rules or decisions, it was felt, could not be made if they conflicted with individual desires. After the list of "minimum expectations" had been drawn up, for example, a sentence was added making the requirements optional. By 1973, there were no minimum expectations. Diplomas, too, it was suggested, might be offered as a matter of individual choice, "a personal thing between student and the staff member. . . . It wouldn't have to be the same for everyone."

As a result, there were few rules. As one student said:

> There's nothing punishable here except what's punishable by law, and then you're punished by the laws not the school.

There were standards about drug usage and sex and about attendance at weekly meetings and classes. But there is one rule, adopted in February 1971, after a year of operation—pay tuition or be expelled. It was adopted during a weekend "summit meeting" after an unpaid staff member was forced to pressure students to take responsibility for seeing that tuition was paid. At the same time, a board of appeals (four students and a staff member) was elected to review cases of students in arrears. By late spring, the board had heard six appeals, granting two and denying four. Students accepted the tuition rule and the board's role:

> It gets people to think about it, to prevent something rather than to punish them for what they did.

The Staff's Role. Whenever governance was discussed, questions about the role of the staff were raised:

> If students do so much in terms of governance, what do staff do?
> Who determines staff responsibilities?
> How do staff members feel about this?

The labor of running the school was divided among students and staff at the General Meetings. Students took turns working in a variety of areas, from administration and student selection to the visitors' committee. Short-term committees were formed by volunteers spontaneously when a need arose, but because they were volunteers, there was unequal sharing of the tasks and often a problem with follow-through. As a result, staff members had been assigned the job of coordinating activities in: office administration work, finances and books, experimental curriculum and resource people, fundamental curriculum and SAT preparation, housing and repairs, and board and legal matters.

Although the staff were perceived as learners, their function differed from that of the students. They were expected to be around the school and available to students—to offer courses, counsel a small group of students weekly, and provide a setting for regular evaluations—as well as coordinate the areas mentioned above and work on ad hoc committees. The staff was active in the informal learning activities, too—trips, concerts, and conversations. Two staff members edited a publication concerning the school's progress and activities. Others worked on *MIScelany,* a public relations news sheet that was sent to colleges and universities, businesses, funding agencies, community members, and parents.

How teachers could be trained to assume a role in an independent school like MIS was a consideration. One staff member felt that such teacher training was "nonexistent" and "impossible." Few could say specifically how they learned to be at such a challenging school.

In general, the style of the under-thirty staff members was a person-to-person, almost peer relationship to students. They were committed to student control. Most reached out to students and sometimes to each other, showing concern. They seemed confident that they could help without creating dependence.

The staff's relationship to the students colored its relationship to their parents. One staff member told parents he was not a substitute parent or anything like that, but instead the students' "friend on the street." He referred their questions about their child's drug usage to the student, telling parents it was between them and their child. Like other staff members, however, he wanted parents to function as an interest group, with full participation.

Strangers to each other when hired, the staff rarely saw each other outside of school. At the beginning of the year, they met three times a week, later only once a week. Though not as factionalized as the original staff, it was still "terribly difficult," a staff member said, to reach a consensus among themselves.

The staff's contact with resource people was limited, often less than that of the students. Meetings had been held for staff and resource volunteers to become acquainted, but further contact depended on a staff member being interested in a volunteer's course offering. The resource people were separate from each other as well as from the school.

As the staff got to know each other better, some came closer together and others farther apart. But the differences had not caused conflicts, a student explained, because, the staff, like the students, had a do-your-own-thing approach. The approach created inconsistent expectations of other staff members, and sometimes a stance of expecting nothing, from either staff or students. Yet there was a pull toward sharing. Several of the staff, for example, in discussing where to draw the lines in their relation to students and the dilemma of sexual attraction, found they had common standards:

> Most of us deal with it by sticking to a code of words and accepting the mores of an adult role relative to a student's role and by a little distance, exaggerated in public high schools. Most of us tend to be people of custom and manner.

In some areas, such as firing, the staff had little control. Most accepted this as part of working in a student-controlled school, but it remained a threat. One staff member, who had had a bitter argument with a student, later received an anonymous phone call saying someone wanted to fire him. Whether this aspect of student control inhibited the staff was hard to say, but certainly the students did not want that dynamic to occur.

At first staff members did not have a vote at the General Meetings; later they did. Though committed to student control, the staff found that its role in governance increased when students were passive:

> This last semester the staff has taken a much more active role because of a void, a lack of leadership. (Staff member)

> The staff at the beginning of the year tried to let students go on and orginate ideas for themselves, but, I guess, around the middle of the year, February, the staff were initiating all the new ideas and pretty much taking responsibility for everything. Then we had a couple of meetings . . . a weekend, and we really talked it out. It went good. I think students have been taking more administrative roles, initiating ideas. (Student)

There was some question, however, about what student control actually meant. It "doesn't necessarily mean student-initiated and student-implemented," a staff member said. "The students have policy control." The staff, another member said, made proposals about curriculum and so on, and the students said yes or no. Before the tuition rule was passed, he noted, the staff had made several financial proposals, none of which were approved by students.

Some students expected more of the staff role than their peers. One commented:

> The staff person is forced to be a little bit more responsible than the students are. Students don't really have to do anything. Staff is expected to be at general meetings and take part in conferences with the students he advises.

The staff's responsibilities were determined at staff meetings as well as the General Meetings. On occasion, the staff meetings were not open to students, leading to the following kind of complaint and countercomplaint witnessed at a weekly meeting:

> Staff: I think that the staff has been kind of working by itself in the last couple of weeks.

Student: It was because we can't get into a staff meeting.

Student: I keep asking you, and you keep saying that maybe sometime it will be okay, but not for now.

Student: I sat in on a staff meeting three months ago.

Student: That's why most of us haven't been around to help out or to try to be a part of what's going on.

Staff: But that was a long time ago when you asked that, I think.

Student: Because you told me that when we do decide that kids can come, okay, then we'll let you know; like nothing has ever been brought up in a General Meeting.

Staff: I would submit that your slowness in following up might be part of what we're talking about.

Student: I get to feel when I keep asking questions that I'm hounding.

Staff: So what? I think that's part of life.

Student: I don't feel guilty; I just feel the longer I keep hounding, the less honest response I'm going to get.

Closed staff meetings, some students thought, were a threat to student control. When, for example, the staff began planning a comprehensive skill program with team teaching, without letting students in on the plan from the beginning, it drew the following criticisms at a weekly meeting.

Student: I don't think it [curriculum changes] should be something that comes from staff members. I hate to use the term, but it's going to have

> to come from the broad community of the
> school. It's not going to be the General Meet-
> ing format, but it is going to be meetings
> concerning this topic which are open to every-
> body.

Staff: But, therefore the staff assigned to this function or whoever, won't do anything. You
know what I mean? What you're saying is
you want to see some of the students involved
in this, too.

Student: What I actually feel is that if the students
aren't involved in it, the staff is going to blow
it. Because your conception of what you want
the students to do may be a little off.

Staff: I intended to bring it up at a General Meeting.

Student: It could have been brought up at the General
Meeting first of all. Why was it brought up
at the staff meeting first?

Staff: Because I wanted to get it refined. If I had a
small group, maybe I would have brought it
up.

Student: Why didn't you bring it up with a small
group of students? Because we don't have
that mechanism, don't you see.

Student: That's right, and I'm saying we should get
the mechanism.

To some students, the staff meeting itself, open or closed,
had begun to look like a mechanism for influence. Yet at
least one student admitted that when there were needs to be
met:

> If it isn't going to come from the students entirely,
> then it'll have to come from the staff. I don't mind if

> the staff gets the glory, 'cause they probably will end
> up doing it in many respects.

"They'll end up doing it" raised the question of who had the most commitment to the school. Some students acknowledged that the staff might be more stable than the students, who moved on, that the school was the staff's career, and that, while students concentrated on classes, the staff was concerned with the day-to-day maintenance of the school. Students also recognized that a divided staff, with different goals and styles, presented less a threat to student autonomy than a united bloc:

> If there were no division, I'd have my doubts. As a
> bloc they'd have significantly more influence in the
> school than they do.

Student Influence.   Students also felt there was no influential group or bloc among students. They said everyone had influence on decisions. One staff member believed students were fleeing the cliquishness of public schools. Among students, of course, there were recognizable groups of friends or people who held similar opinions, but the groups overlapped. They did not remain constant or polarized. There could be differences of opinions or arguments at meetings without affecting personal relationships. Following an angry exchange between two students at a meeting, for example, the two came together afterward to check how each was feeling. The groupings seemed to follow the traditional lines of rich and poor and age and sex, as well as "revolutionaries," and "busy people." An adult, however, divided the student body into thirds: "a third really with it, a third wanting to be with it, and a third misfits."

Although groups of MIS students did social things together

on weekends, there was not much dating among students. Still, the relationships between students were more open, students said, than they would be in public school, where dating takes on a possessive or experimental nature or may be motivated by status-seeking.

Some of the original students were still perceived, in 1971, to have a special sense of what MIS was about; they had been continually active in various groups and committees related to the school's operation. The first year, two students who were primary initiators and who sat on the board and had roles as staff members as well, had a great deal of influence. By the second year, however, a dozen students were seen as the "most influential," a third of them newcomers. "People who have been here longest don't have more influence," a student from the original group said, "it's equal." Influence, she explained, came from learning to communicate, and new students could have that skill as well as old students. The influential students, a staff member remarked, are simply "those taking the most responsibility."

There was little talk of status-seeking or power plays. One student attributed her more active role in the school, after a year of uninvolvement, to her decision that since nobody was taking responsibility, she would. Committee participation and work in the office, she said, "gives you something to back up what you say, so that you're actually capable of working out decisions." However, she added, since becoming more active, she found she had become more impatient with other students and defensive about the school.

To obtain maximum student participation in school affairs, small counseling groups, of five to seven students selected at random and one or two staff members, were created. They were designed to help students determine which of many study approaches best meet their needs and to establish close working relationships between students and staff. At their weekly meetings, however, they also discussed matters raised at the general school-wide meetings. Sometimes the matters were referred to them for discussion; sometimes they brought issues to the General Meeting. It was a counseling group, for example, that suggested a retreat in the spring of 1971 to evaluate the year. The General Meeting accepted the idea and asked the counseling group to coordinate it.

The counseling groups, however, were not a strong governance mechanism for students. They were not based on students' relationships with their peers. The five to seven students assigned to work with a staff member had differing commitments to the group, as the following student comments indicate:

> Small group is a time for everyone to talk since the General Meeting is so big. Sometimes issues are brought back to the small group, which is usually like sending them back to a committee at Congress . . . sort of fade out in the process. We maybe help each student and staff member with problems they're having.

> People aren't willing to commit themselves that much or there just isn't enough time in small group or not the right atmosphere.

> No one's there when we're supposed to start.

> No one likes the surroundings; it's really depressing, so we all sit there.

Sometimes groups were cancelled or changed locations; sometimes other activities were planned rather than discussions, such as listening to music or going to a park, a movie, or a trip to a lake. One group sponsored a successful rummage sale to raise tuition money for members who couldn't pay. Another planned a day to clean up the school, but no one showed up, not even the student who suggested it. Another did not meet frequently; when they did meet however, the focus was on *doing* things.

The Role of Parents and the Board. Parents, at the students' invitation, started meeting together in January 1970, before MIS opened. The minutes of an early board meeting indicates the concern of students to help parents understand what they were trying to do:

> Linda reported that the Pit will be available for the parents' meeting . . . chairs will be picked up . . . refreshments will be provided. George suggested that parents be given a proposal and press release booklet. The problem of how communications can be established between the board, students, and parents was discussed. Tom suggested that students make formal evaluations of Milwaukee Independent School to be delivered to the parents. George suggested that the board present in some way a supplement for the students' statements. The need seems to be to break down the old stereotypes of "school" and still enable parents to be reassured. Bill suggested that we be sure to listen to parents to find out in what ways we can be helpful in enabling them to understand Milwaukee Independent School.

Later in the first year, parents attended board meetings and had a representative on the board. They served on committees as well. But parents had little influence, as one parent reported:

Parent meetings are held once a month, first to deal with current business, often financial crises, which are constant. Other matters have been whether the school literary magazine should be censored, individual family problems.

Since, in the final analysis and in theory at least, this is a student-run school, the discussions are often academic and the parents are frequently frustrated.

However, the meetings, I think, serve an important purpose in acting as an airing ground and a meeting place. Out of them has grown an additional parent group—about fifteen parents meet every two weeks on another night with a psychologist for the state, who was on the board last year, and who volunteered to be a sort of discussion leader for parents while they tried to come to grips with the idea of independent schools, free schools, alternative education, counter-culture, etc. I think these meetings have helped a lot in relieving tensions and developing insights.

The psychologist leading the additional parent group, however, noted several reasons for its formation:

The request arose partly out of the [parents] own expressed need but largely because the MIS staff felt that such a program would help to get the parents off their backs and, of course, to bring in tuition from resistant parents.

By the spring of 1971, the board itself had little influence on the school and, as noted, no longer existed by 1973. A parent on the board described the situation:

Throughout the year, and until this month, the board has been short three adult members. This situation was, I am sure, not at all distasteful to the students.

A parent once asked at a parents' meeting—"What do the students do if they disagree with a decision of the board?"

A student answered, "We try to change their minds."

"What if you cannot change their minds?"

"Then we elect a new board."

Mostly, the board serves as a link with the community and as a group of people to sign checks when money is available.

CURRICULUM

MIS students had sole responsibility for their learning and freedom to take initiative in many areas of curriculum. They controlled both curriculum components—content, the subjects, and range of courses they take—and process—the orientation, methods, and arrangements of the teaching-learning experience. The control, however, was exercised more as an individual matter than as a group.

Anything a person chose to study was considered legitimate. The staff offered courses in subjects of their strength or interest; resource people from the community did the same. The topics offered in *Impressions*, the course booklet, included:

Art	Latin
Audio workshop	Herman Hesse
Auto mechanics	Institutions
Ballet	Karate
Black history	Love + Sex = Romance
Carpentry	Modern dance
China	Musician's workshop
Classics	Nonmusician's workshop

Consumer economics
Contemporary literature
Drama
Education
Filmmaking
Fundamental stuff (Programmed
    learning in several subjects)
Trig and calculus
Russian
German

Norman O. Brown
On becoming
Photography
Psychology
Reading plays
Science fiction
Speaking on the run
Story writing
Wandering
World literature

Students also pursued other interests in relation to their jobs. For example, a young man who worked half-time in a day care center related:

> Most learning this past semester is nonacademic. I've learned an awful lot about myself and how I related to people, and I've learned a lot about friendships, relationships that I never realized before. Now I'm trying to get into academic things because I'm going to take the SAT's this fall [for college].

He was reading *Between Parent and Child* (Haim Ginott, Macmillan, 1965) to understand how parents affect what children do and talking to students about their parents' affects on them.

Students influenced the process of a course through one-to-one or group discussions with their course leader. Class norms, format, attendance, and expectations were negotiated with relative degrees of openness and success.

Class size ranged from one to seven. The small size was regarded as a disadvantage by some because of the few people to share ideas with and an advantage by others because everyone could participate in depth. In 1971, no students were teaching, though some had during the previous year. The reason was unclear. One student said students didn't want the hassle; another said it was because there were more tensions between students and staff than expected. Because students thought of themselves as the "lesser of two equals," a third said they let the staff offer what they wanted to and accepted the courses. Some staff members thought the students regarded the school as a "protective mama from public schools," or a temporary way station on the journey through school to college.

Several students and two staff members mentioned their concern about students who do not have basic skills. "Kids who come here without basic skills are going to be lost," a student commented. Algebra, geometry, and basic English, he continued, were the problems. The curriculum was deficient in the basics necessary for college, a staff member concurred. Two notions of basics—reading-writing skills and college requirements—were referred to. More staff members to teach math and science were sought, though the subsistence salary of MIS staff could not compete with public school salaries. At the time, staff members were thinking of broadening their courses, where possible, to include history, mathematics, and science.

The curriculum was broadened each semester by about two dozen resource people in the community who described the courses they could offer. Students were free to pursue those that interested them. In some cases, a resource person came to the school to teach a group; in others, one or more students met in the home or office building of the volunteer—an adaptation of a school-without-walls. As noted, however, the resource volunteers had little ongoing relationship with the school. Some had difficulties with students who didn't come on time, or sought attention, or expected their friendship. Some had difficulty defining their role with students to their mutual satisfaction.

Whose responsibility was it to familiarize a resource person with the standards of the school and the expectations of the students? One student suggested "some kind of program" was needed to "draw them in . . . maybe they should sit in on a General Meeting." Others expected staff members to provide the necessary orientation:

> It's really very simple. There're two steps involved: find a resource person, and be able to talk openly enough with your staff members, so that your resource person and you can get together and find out what's best.

Staff members were sympathetic to some of the difficulties volunteers faced. As one explained:

> In my own course as far as expectations go, I expect when I give my assignment that the student will do it. We had a small group of people, four people, that had a rare opportunity with a professor from the finest film school in the world. I gave one assignment, I remember, to write out a script; the only person who did it was a person who doesn't even go to this school. . . . When I'm going to spend my time Sunday night finding the materials to give them on Monday morning, *I expect some participation.* . . . And I'm a staff member; I'm supposed to have understanding. What if I'm a person who works all day like Mark, an insurance actuary, who gives up about two or three of his nights to teach trigonometry?

Despite the difficulties, a number of the volunteers found their work highly satisfying:

My work as resource person has been one of the most satisfying experiences of twenty-five years in theatre. . . . Classes are made up of students who, at that particular moment in time, wished to come to drama class rather than do anything else. Hence there is no wasted time, no problem with motivation, full participation. After several months of workshops twice a week, the students organized a street theatre in which they created their own pieces, mostly concerned with critiques of education, parent-child relationships, the "establishment," etc. They have performed several times for university classes in sociology, education, psychology, for high school groups, etc.

The staff was concerned about how much responsibility it had for the students' learning. Some students, for example, felt the staff should place "more demands on them." The problem was discussed at a General Meeting:

Student: The student can do what he wants, and the staff kind of sits there and facilitates what the student comes up with. I think the official role of the staff member should be shifted so that . . . more emphasis [is] placed on the staff's directions.

Staff: I feel the same way. . . . There has to be a fair amount of leadership even if it's somewhat nondirective. . . . I mean if I want to learn carpentry, I would expect the teacher on carpentry to take a fairly active role and to tell me what to do and things like that. We've always conceived of the staff as not a teaching staff. Even though everybody taught, the teacher role in the school kind of gets watered down. . . . The staff at least could get themselves together as a group and form

> a core curriculum of some sort . . . a series of
> courses that would be constantly evaluated.
> If a student wanted to, he could relate mainly
> to that core [or] entirely dismiss it and go
> his own way. But the student that wants to
> could get a certain set number of courses or
> some kind of proficiency in basics.

In part, the curriculum was seen as a process of finding a new student role. In the first semester, a student recalled, the method of developing a new learning environment was to reject everything, even the word "class"; they became "learning experiences" or "joint learnings." Yet the process, "How to push yourself to do it," another said, "needs to be worked out." Some students did absolutely nothing at MIS, it was noted, not even attend a class.

Most students wanted to learn. They had an idea about how to learn, but what to learn was a harder question. Establishing goals usually took several months and some trial and error. One student felt that her difficulty adjusting was due to the fact that, "Everything depends on you; you have your education and must take responsibility for it." Knowing this and not being able to put things together were frustrating.

Some students did not complete their courses. In the first semester, a student said, all the classes fell apart. Later, students dropped courses for a variety of reasons; they lost interest or weren't very serious to begin with or the class was terminated by mutual agreement. Some staff members felt students needed to complete things to gain a sense of accomplishment. Some encouraged students to clear the air by being more outspoken about their expectations of and commitments to classes. Some suggested reshaping the curriculum. Others suggested shortening courses to six-week periods so that involvement could be maintained.

Biweekly evaluations were developed to enable staff and students to take stock and give feedback to each other. The evaluations, which students were expected to ask for, were causal progress checks with comments written in students' folders. (Counseling was a more personal, not necessarily academic, procedure, sometimes involving a reciprocal sharing of problems.) However, people did not regularly participate in evaluations, and many students' folders were empty.

A few students felt that some standards or guidelines would help. Others strongly disagreed:

> When we wrote up the minimal expectations last year, we couldn't really get on to a consensus. Nobody, not everybody, agreed with the fact that people should have to do this and that, academically, evaluation-wise or whatever. . . . I don't want any minimal expectations.

Some staff members argued for basic expectations:

> I think the staff is trying to create an atmosphere of something to do, and minimal expectations to me are just a blueprint of what is expected of you, what has your commitment been. And if they don't fit, it can be adjusted, and that explanation can be written right into your folder. What I'm saying is that there's no blueprint, so people come in and they don't know what to do; they don't know what's expected of them. I don't want this to be a two- or three-year period of vegetation before you decide to go out into society. Some people who are graduating in June are staying on an extra year. So there still are some expectations.

To this a student responded:

> The basic problem isn't that we don't expect people to do things. The basic problem is that the things to do

are not available enough. Or maybe . . . available [but] structured wrong.

In the discussion of curriculum, then, several opposing principles came into play:

minimum expectations	vs.	student autonomy
standardarization and control	vs.	an individualized, do-your-own-thing approach
sometimes even, staff	vs.	students

Staff: The whole thing is, your point of view, is don't run this school, that's what it's come down to. The do-your-own-thing approach has won over in this school.

Student: Is that bad or good?

Staff: That's all right if you want to. I think it's a question of value and attitude, and you don't sit down with another person and argue about it. But I do have a proposal. . . to develop a comprehensive program in the different skills, skill areas, and everybody that comes into this school would feel a pressure to respond one way or the other to those basic values. Because those are the values that exist out in society, unless you want to work in a fish market all your life.

Student: Why doesn't a person who wants expectations go to a staff member and say, "Hey man, can you get *on* my back for a while?"

The debate went on. Both "do your own thing" and "hey, man, get on my back" rely on student responsibility and initiative. Minimum expectations and core curriculum were seen to compromise initiative, since a framework would be established, and counseling would tend to evaluate how a student was measuring up to established, rather than personal, goals.

Control of governance and curriculum were linked. If students could not determine their own programs, could they be said to control a school? Student control at MIS was difficult for students who were not used to being independent and relying on themselves for motivation and direction and for staff members who wrestled with developing a new and meaningful role. But many were able to adapt to a school where students had control.

HOW WELL IS MIS DOING?

In general, people expressed satisfaction with the school and its style. When the question of MIS's success in "educating people for their later life," was raised at a General Meeting in 1971, as the ensuing dialogue shows, student responses were for the most part favorable.

> I feel we've had successes and we've had failures. For me it's enough; I'm very satisfied with MIS. I'm not saying that we shouldn't have plans; it's always changing.
>
> Do you think it's enough for everybody.
>
> Is anything ever enough?
>
> I feel that the school is in an evolutionary process, and I feel excited about the possibilities.
>
> I don't feel that MIS is successful in terms of [preparing] people for later in a number of respects. One is in terms of relating to the other people around them. Also you have to show them some roads or at

least be actively searching for some roads leading to vocations. And I don't think we have been doing that.

I've always seen a school as a place where I would come to educate myself. That's what I wanted to do, and if I come to MIS and I really want to learn, I can.

We have a problem with that because first of all, if that's it, you can probably operate just as well at home.

Not legally.

Well, all right. I felt essentially the same way. But in of just judging the effectiveness, just take any particular classroom learning experience. My only valuable class this year comes from such a setup where the class is taught in that fashion. . . . This whole ambiguous process of getting our heads together.

For me, I've gone through all kinds of phases. I get to one point and I think, well, I'm really together now. Then I turn around, and I realize that I am really fucked up. And I find something else. I've been through that about ten times. But I think they've all been important.

Academically I decided that the goal that I previously had set up was too big, and I learned that I just had to start out with smaller things for myself. And now I've set out on smaller things, and I've achieved smaller steps within those smaller things. That was what I wanted to do, and the only real way for me to learn about how to do that was just to do it myself.

I've been through lots of things that nobody could have told me about or experienced for me and told me about.

There's no success like failure.

A number of students have been accepted at college;
that's training.

In a questionnaire answered by a small sample of MIS students and staff, most agreed that MIS was doing a "good" to
"very good" job in developing political, social, and interpersonal skills and in training both teachers and students for new
educational roles. They reported only moderate success in
preparing students for college, however, and even less success
in preparing students for jobs.

More racial diversity was said to be a goal. A black student
was in on the initial planning but dropped out along the
way. When choices about location were made, the goal was
mentioned again. But neither students nor staff could see, in
their life style or the kind of school they had created, the
racism inherent. Nor did they have any kind of program to
raise their consciousness of racism. Since MIS was an alternative only for middle-class whites, the University's School of
Education later withdrew its financial support. But in a
school such as MIS, survival became the priority, and many
important goals remained unrealized.

PART TWO

Analyses and
Comparisons

The Process
of Innovation

By Joan Chesler

Despite their differences, each of the six innovative schools (for convenience arranged in comparative charts (on pages 231, 247, and 256-7) was alike in many respects. Each program —no matter how unique—had to go through the same stages; determining goals, designing a structure to reflect these goals, selecting students and staff, pilot-testing the innovation, and building a sense of unity to ensure its continuation.

The leaders of each innovation, whether teachers, students, or parents, had to confront the impact of their own influence and ultimately share their leadership or surrender it to others.

And each program, whether public or private, had to deal with outside agencies, such as public school administrations, universities, businesses, or communities, to gain support, legitimacy, advice, and funding, often with considerable struggle.

So striking are the similarities that one might almost say

there are natural laws of innovation regarding leadership, initial development, and external relations. We enumerate them here in hopes they will serve future innovators as rough rules of thumb.

LEADERSHIP

The most consistent, and critical, phenomenon is that the initiators of a program usually become the most influential group in the program's first year or phase.

In the case of Metro High School, for example, the three consultants from the Urban Research Corporation found themselves more influential than they had anticipated; even when they wanted to transfer leadership completely to the principal, teachers continued to bring problems to them instead. At Sudbury Valley School it took three years for the original parent-trustee group to feel comfortable enough to shift power and ownership from itself to students and other staff members. At Franklin High School, many of the students and teachers in the planning group became Senate representatives the first year. "Next year, when it's really on its way, we'll move out," they explained.

At Community High, students were invited to share in the planning only at the end, three days before the program started, and the initiating teachers maintained dominance over the program's first phase. Similarly, at "Dillington" the teachers' group had been working together for half a year before students joined in the planning during a summer, and the following year the teachers still carried far more weight than students. It was students, on the other hand, who initiated the Milwaukee Independent School, and student control, three semesters later, had increased.

THE SIX SCHOOLS RANKED BY DEGREE OF STUDENT CONTROL

	Name	Date Innovation Began	Prime Initiators	Number and Ethnic Makeup of Students	Governance Structure 1971
	Public Schools				
Lowest	Franklin High Seattle	Nov. '70	Teachers	1,550 47% White	Senate of teachers, other staff members, students, and parents
Low	Metro High Chicago	Feb. '70	Urban Research Consultants	350 50% White	8-member Policy Board (staff, students, parents, and participating organizations) and informal faculty meetings
Low	"Dillington" School-in-a-School New England	Sept. '70	Teachers and university consultants	50 92% White	Open Forum and informal staff meetings
Low	Community High Berkeley	Spring '69	Teachers	233 73% White	An Intertribal Council of students, staff, and parents
	Private Schools				
High	Sudbury Valley Massachusetts	Summer '68	Parents	70 100% White	All-school Meetings
Highest	Milwaukee Independent School	Feb. '70	Students	40 100% White	All-school Meetings

   *High personal investment seems to increase the feeling of
ownership and the desire to control.*

   Intense participation brings rewards and exacts costs. Sudbury Valley School is a prime example. The parents and core
faculty at Sudbury made great personal and financial sacri-
fices to establish their school. (Two bought the estate on
which the school is located.) Not wanting their educational
model distorted before there had been time to test it out, they
exercised tight control over the school's goals and direction,
the staff, and the students. Rather than change direction,
they permitted an exodus of students the first year when
some were suspended and others left in protest. Of course,
all initiators feel some degree of ownership in their program,
all experience some difficulty in sharing control, and all, in
time, have to overcome these feelings. But at Sudbury Valley
an unusually high personal risk and investment generated an
unusually difficult struggle.

   *After three to four years of intense participation, initiators
of a program are increasingly able to give up control and pass
on leadership to another group.*

   At Community High and at Franklin the initiating teachers became "burned out," weary of the planning and leadership tasks they had performed in addition to their normal
teaching duties. After three years they wanted to return to
teaching full-time or take a sabbatical, as an administrator at
Community High did. Even at Sudbury Valley, after three
years, the original trustees had relinquished some control,
although a core group remained on the staff. Elsewhere, in
the case of student leaders, many had to surrender control in
two or three years automatically when they graduated.

   *Generally the group to whom initiators pass on leadership
share similar, but not exact, goals.*

   For example, the second year's leaders at student-run Milwaukee Independent School revised the original goals somewhat when they drew up an optional set of "minimum" rules or requirements and reduced the power of the already weak board of directors further.

At Community High the second year's faculty—including two teachers from the original staff—shared the rhetoric of the program's goals but were divided over which parts to emphasize. The original goal had been to provide a humanistic education, with as much emphasis on the process (humanistic) as the outcome (education). The second year, as the emphasis shifted back and forth between the process (How much freedom and responsibility students should have?) and the outcome (What kind of education?), the teachers split. One group supported the student movement away from academic goals; the other group continued to favor more traditional educational goals. By the end of the year, the split had produced two sets of leaders among the teachers.

At Metro, when the Urban Research Corporation's consultants, who had designed the program, left after a year and a half, the principal and staff modified (and continued to modify) the original design of the governance body and counseling groups.

INITIAL PHASES OF DEVELOPMENT

The impetus for starting an innovation is similar in most cases: the initiators are experiencing pain in their current school settings.

To bring about change, they set goals, design strategies to meet them, and then proceed through a series of trial-and-error steps. In some cases, evaluation of the new structure follows.

At Franklin there was racial unrest and polarization. To deal with it, strategies were selected to increase communication between all groups and to share power more equally. After several governance modifications, a structure (the Senate) was devised through which greater communication and power-sharing could be channeled.

At Community High and "Dillington" teachers pointed to failings in the school setting: isolation and separation of teachers and students; rigid, unsuccessful curricula; and cold, emotionally flat schools. The strategy chosen was to break away from the parent school. At Community High this same strategy was developed after the initiators saw how difficult it was to innovate flexible scheduling and interdisciplinary staffing in the larger high school. The "Dillington" initiators opted for separation immediately.

Similarly the Milwaukee students were prevented from making changes in the Jesuit high school they attended, encountering too much resistance from the principal and too little support from the majority of students. As a result, their strategy, too, was to draw up plans for a small separate school, only this time it would be a student-run school of their own.

The parents who initiated Sudbury Valley School were highly dissatisfied with public schools. They wanted learning to be more open, mutual, and individualized and schools to be more democratic, offering more choice in curriculum and more opportunity for those affected by decisions to be involved in the decision-making process. Since their school was to serve as a model for public schools, however, their design may have been influenced by its applicability to public education.

When we compared certain goals to the structural outcomes, several findings were evident. For example, it is well known that stated goals can lead to behavior modification. The six schools studied here all had power-sharing as a goal, to a greater or lesser degree. When the teacher-initiators at Community High remembered this goal, they scrapped their plans in order to include students in the planning process. Similarly, because more equal power was a goal at Franklin, the Senate was structured accordingly: half the members were students, and each standing Senate committee had a student cochairman.

Where power-sharing is pursued, it grows.

In each school the governance body was preceded by a less broadly participatory policy-making body. The Senate at Franklin, for example, was an outgrowth of the Principal's Cabinet, which had been expanded to include not only students, teachers, and administrators but also noncertificated personnel and community members. At Metro, "Dillington," and Community High the original places for policy-making were staff meetings that allowed student participation. But student involvement was advisory, occasional, and sporadic, and in each case staff meetings were replaced by more representative structures. Metro designed a Policy Board to include teachers, students, parents, and business representatives. Community High established its Intertribal Council, which represented students and teachers from each tribe and, later, parents as well. "Dillington" set up an Open Forum, on a one-man, one-vote basis, to use at times of major importance. At both private schools (Sudbury and Milwaukee), the board of directors' role was modified to give students more power and control of key policies. At Sudbury, the School Meeting replaced the Assembly, which had not included students, and the board became primarily advisory. At Milwaukee, adults originally had outnumbered students on the board, but later, student members joined adults in equal number, and power was shifted to the student-dominated, weekly all-school meeting.

Where power-sharing is not adequately provided, it fades, and the concept itself falls into disrepute.

We visited several schools whose power-sharing experiments had failed, and the opportunity to try again had been lost as well. All had reverted to traditional authoritarian styles of policy-making. Either shared power had not been a stated goal, or the structures designed to achieve it were defective. Most of the teachers and students became convinced that power-sharing was a poor philosophy, that it was doomed to failure in educational institutions, and that students and teachers were ill-suited to make policy decisions for themselves. They blamed the idea; they did not examine or blame the structures that made its success impossible; they did not think about ways to restructure the program.

In general, they did not recognize that members of a shared-power structure need to spend a great deal of time and energy helping each other learn how to participate skillfully, to represent special interest groups, and to share information effectively. Nor did they recognize that the structure must allow adequate time to accomplish such things. As a goal, then, shared power needs to be more than stated—it needs to be made a priority, too.

Certain goals—combatting institutional racism or establishing a pluralistic school—need to be given top priority to succeed.

The patterns of institutional racism in American schools run all too deep. If initiators of new schools include anti-racism or pluralism as basic goals, they must have priority over other goals so that *all* decisions—student and staff selection, curriculum, governance structure, and the ranking of other goals—will be made in relation to it.

The Franklin, "Dillington," and Community High innovators all wanted and expected to have a heterogeneous and pluralistic program. The student populations were multiracial, but minority students soon felt the new programs weren't working for them. At Franklin black and Oriental students had more difficulty with the rules than whites and felt that Senate's style and choice of issues were white-dominated; minority groups were represented but not accommodated. At "Dillington" the school-in-a-school started with a larger percentage of black students than the high school, but only half the blacks planned to return after the first year. They were turned off by the counter-culture approach to teaching and learning, they did not value the affective emphasis of the curriculum, they were separated from their friends, and, in general, they felt isolated and estranged in a white-oriented program. In Berkeley Black House split away from Community High. In each of these cases, the innovative programs started with diverse interest and ethnic groups but they failed in their attempts to provide a pluralistic educational innovation because they operated with a cultural style that was white.

Like goals, staff selection can also be crucial.

If staff and students are inappropriately matched, a great deal of energy is diverted from the innovative program itself. The most successful programs involve teachers who work well with students and each other, despite differing philosophies of education. This was not the case in two schools. At Milwaukee, the original director's values and goals conflicted with those of the students; after a period of strain and bitterness, he resigned. At Franklin, philosophical differences among faculty members, as well as racial imbalance, slowed the rate of desired change. Conservative teachers were said to impede the Senate's progress, and minority students wanted more black and Oriental teachers to support and relate to them.

Staff selection, it seems, is best done early, during the planning or pilot-testing stages, when mutual adjustments are possible, before teachers are locked into new roles or contracts, and while pressures are lower.

Student enrollment is basically self-selected.

Berkeley students, if they choose to be well enough informed can now select among several alternatives offered by Berkeley High—Community High Schools I and II, Model A, and Black House—the one they feel best matches their interests. Students applying to the student-run Milwaukee school knew the type of setting they had selected, were willing to attend a nonaccredited school, had command of basic skills, and could earn the $300 of tuition. Students at Sudbury Valley, or rather their families, could afford $1000 for tuition, and even though some were rejected by the staff, the student exodus that followed was also self-selected. Students attending Metro and "Dillington" similarly chose to participate in those programs and were further selected by lottery.

Summer is a good time to test aspects of a program before it begins.

By running a summer work-study program utilizing various businesses and industries around Chicago, the designers of Metro demonstrated to the school board that business and industry could indeed be involved in the curriculum of a school and that such a program was valuable. As a result, the school board hired them to organize Metro as a pilot program to begin that winter.

The success with a summer project at Berkeley legitimized the proposal for a separate school within the high school. The three teachers who ran the project widely circulated an evaluation report in the fall, creating further interest among the faculty. Although the summer curriculum was not a forerunner of the final program, it paved the way for a semi-autonomous school within the high school.

Similarly, the content of a summer program at Sudbury Valley did not influence the growth of the school's curriculum, but it was important in developing staff unity as well as loyalty among students on the "junior staff." Of the fifty potential staff members on hand during the summer months, some left voluntarily and others were not hired. By fall the staff selected felt they shared common goals and values.

At Franklin and "Dillington" the initiators met regularly with students during the summer months to plan and develop —but not test out—their programs. (At "Dillington," the ten student participants were paid.)

During the first year, the processes of defining and organizing the programs, defending them, and fighting together for survival tended to unify students and faculty. Students and teachers at Metro found great satisfaction struggling for the school's existence during the first year. Similarly, at Milwaukee, "Dillington," and Community High, students were excited by the sense of interdependence and community that initially developed. Some, however, lost their newly formed sense of unity as conflicts could not be resolved to their satisfaction.

One of the pitfalls to success is increasing a program's size before participants have really learned how best to benefit from their new school experience.

Thus, at Metro and Community High the large increases in student population in the second year seriously damaged the cohesion and sense of community developed during the first year.

EXTERNAL RELATIONS

*Powerful administrative support is needed to establish an
innovative program within the public school systems.*

At Metro, Community High and "Dillington," the superintendents' *active* and visible support was needed before
those programs could be set up to function independently. It
was the superintendent who helped convince the Berkeley
and "Dillington" high school principals and teachers that
mini-schools were viable and necessary.

The Franklin principal needed the superintendent's
approval, if not his active help, since he already had the support of some of his staff as well as community members.

The cost of the programs to the public schools was not an
issue. Either they were financed at low cost or funded in
part externally (at "Dillington" and Metro). Had the costs
been higher, the superintendents' support probably would
have been much harder to obtain.

Universities can often provide vital services.

The University of Wisconsin at Milwaukee provided financial aid, supervised the placement of student teachers, and
gave consultant help to enable the Milwaukee school to "get
off the ground" its first year. "Dillington" received similar
help from a nearby university. Faculty members from various
universities helped develop the original proposal for Community High, and the University of California at Berkeley
provided student teachers. Finally, consultants from the
University of Michigan staffed the initial workshops at which
the plans for power-sharing at Franklin were developed.

Proximity to a supportive community is a distinct advantage.

Community High and Milwaukee had already demonstrated support for alternative schools. Herbert Kohl's semi-
public Other Ways had been in existence in the city of

Berkeley since 1965, and numerous free schools had been established before Community High began. Milwaukee had had several community-based private schools for black, Indian, Spanish-speaking, and low-income white students. Both cities also had a number of liberal civic organizations. Members of Milwaukee's organizations gave office space and advice to the students initiating the Milwaukee school. Berkeley parents supported Community High from the start and are now represented in its governing body. Metro reached beyond Chicago to draw on the experience of Philadelphia's Parkway project, using Parkway's success to influence Chicago's superintendent, school board, and business community to consider a similar program in their city.

Not having local support usually meant trouble. In Chicago, the manipulations of middle-level school personnel against Metro constantly threatened its well-being, if not its survival. In Seattle Franklin's tired and discouraged innovators had no similar schools to turn to for comparisons or help. In "Dillington," the school-in-a-school was surrounded by a hostile community, particularly the high school faculty, which increased its isolation and reduced its ability to influence similar changes in the high school's program.

Support of other innovative schools, if there are any in the area, is always worth seeking. By establishing a network of communication, ideas can be exchanged, common problems discussed, and issues explored. As we have shown, there are enough similarities in the process of innovation to make such sharing feasible and productive.

Student Power

By Dale Crowfoot, Glorianne Wittes
and Joan Chesler

That many students consider their schools have failed them has been amply documented. Masses of young people in secondary schools now are forcing society to reconsider and reevaluate the educational system as they question the current mode of education, try to define their own modes, and attempt to exert some control over their own learning. As powerful adults deny students such control, this search for redefinition is developing into a movement for student power.

In the schools we studied, students were encouraged to exert more influence than is usual in traditional schools. How much influence students were able to exert depended on each school's governance structure: the tone, quality, purpose, and extent of communication in youth-adult interactions and the extent to which students were organized as a group. Thus it becomes necessary to examine informal as well as formal governance processes to see how decisions are actually made, to recognize the affect of school size on student involvement, to weigh the relationship between curriculum and student power, and to analyze student attitudes toward participation as well. We begin, however, by defining student power.

WHAT STUDENT POWER MEANS

All students have power. They can, for instance, be said to have *expert power* because, of all school members, students know best and more directly what their needs, interests, and learning styles are, although they may not be able to articulate them with adults' precision. They also have *coercive power* because the school depends on their attendance and cooperation, and they may choose not to attend or to be disruptive. But when students have significant influence as members of a governing council or body whose decisions affect their lives at school, they are said to have *legitimate power* or *student power*.

In traditional schools students often have *individual power* to make decisions that affect their school careers, for example, which of the subjects offered they may study, when, how, and with whom. And students, as a group, may be in charge of student social activities and clubs. But rarely are students able, as a group, to share in the policy or curriculum decisions that affect the fundamental nature of the institution itself. Compared to teachers and administrators, students have very little power. Thus if students are to realize any real control of their lives at school, they must gain significant influence over key institutional decisions.

To gain overt *collective power*, students must first perceive their group interests as separate from those of their teachers and administrators and organize to articulate their needs.

Generally students' interests are different from those of teachers and administrators. Students, for example, may want to evaluate their teachers' performances, while teachers would resist feedback that might affect their salaries, promotion schedules, or careers. If the process is agreed to, there are still differences about the criteria to be used. Teachers might rate themselves according to how well they present course content, how much they cover, and how effectively they control the class, and students according to how fair the teacher is, how likeable, approachable, and interesting.

Following the development of interest groups, a policy-making structure would have to be designed to represent all concerned groups adequately. Each group represented would constitute a meaningful segment of the school population from which its power derives.

Such a structure, termed shared-power governance, involves joint decision-making by students, teachers, administrators, and, sometimes, by parents, other community members, and noncertified school personnel. In shared-power governance, all members have access to power—both as individuals and as members of various interest groups. Further, no one individual or group is so powerful that it can dominate the decision-making process. Ideally, all groups have approximately equal access to information and power.

The power shared would have to be real, involving the key policy decisions concerning curriculum, rules and regulations, budget, financing, teacher hiring and firing, principal hiring and firing, student population, student activities, and special programs. Student representatives, like the representatives of teachers, administrators, and other separate interest groups (racial, philosophical, ethnic, political), are free to vote on various issues as a bloc or as individuals.

We believe that student power and participation in school governance could benefit all members of the school community, but only:

■ If students and other oppressed groups (e.g., blacks, Indians, and Chicanos) are able to make the school policies and programs more directly responsive to them—the clients— rather than to powerful white educators' ideas of what their needs are.

■ If students, teachers, and administrators become mutually contractable to one another—not unilaterally students to teachers and teachers to administrators, as it has been demonstrated is usually the case.

■ If students gain experience in independent and self-assertive styles of thought and action and increase their self-esteem and sense of potency.

■ If the participants deal openly with conflict and accommodate different needs and styles in a pluralistically operated school system.

■ If all members of the school learn how to make the institution more humane.

■ If youth, blacks, Chicanos, and others are able to participate meaningfully.

The extent to which students and members of oppressed minorities are able to participate in shared power determines the degree to which the above considerations will be met. If students control only student activities, if blacks determine only the curricula of black studies programs, then they will realize only limited benefits from their limited power and participation. If, however, students also help determine hiring policies, curriculum, and evaluation procedures, their influence will be broader and more significant.

FORMAL AND INFORMAL STRUCTURES COMPARED

Each of the six programs studied started with a commitment to involve students in the decision-making. But at least half did not provide initially for students' formal participation. At Community High, "Dillington," and Milwaukee, and to some extent Metro, student power was expected to be the natural outgrowth of an informal, unstructured environment. It was hoped the open atmosphere would generate active student participation in all phases of school decision-making and planning. Ad hoc gatherings of the total school body were to be convened when issues arose and vital decisions had to be made. The initiators believed people, not necessarily structures, directed an active democracy. They assumed that in a free environment students would naturally and spontaneously develop the motivation and drive to determine the scope of their own institutions. Further, they believed that the daily informal processes of communication and collaboration between youth and adults would be a sufficient base for students' extended participation in the active governance of their school. However, most students did not spontaneously participate in school governance. Their socialization had fostered dependence on adult authorities. As youngsters, they had been taught to trust and to be subservient to adult control. Further, on the basis of past experience they distrusted student councils and collaboration with teachers. Some students distrusted all forms of government. Finally, students were neither skilled in the political processes nor taught political skills. Thus, students usually needed a formal structure to engage their participation in decision-making and make it less threatening and frightening to be involved.

THE SIX SCHOOLS RANKED BY DEGREE
OF FORMAL GOVERNANCE

School	Original	In 1971
Most Formal		
Sudbury Valley Massachusetts	All-school meeting (powerful Board of Trustees and adult-dominated School Assembly)	All-school meeting, formalized with committee structure (Board and Assembly much less powerful)
Franklin High Seattle	Senate, with 16 students, 9 teachers, and administrators, 1 noncertified staff member, and 5 parent representatives	Senate: no change after six months
Community High Berkeley	All-school meeting	Intertribal Council with two students, one staff, and one parent representative from each "tribe," tribes meet regularly for their own decisions
Metro High Chicago	All-school meeting	Open faculty meetings with increasing student participation and Policy Board, with student representatives
Least Formal		
"Dillington'" School-in-a-School New England	All-school meeting	Faculty meetings, occasional all-school open Forums
Milwaukee Independent School	All-school meeting (board of directors quite powerful)	Weekly all-school meetings; one-man, one-vote (Board much less powerful)

At all schools but Franklin, the first formal structure tried was the all-school meeting. (Franklin, with 1,500 students, turned instead to a Senate.) All found the form, without modification, unsuccessful. The all-school meeting tends to be diffuse, confusing, and endlessly long, with no effective process for making decisions or insuring their implementation. As a governance structure, it lacks form and is frustrating to adults and more so to students, who often respond with apathy or withdrawal.

The essence of a formal governance structure is that it clearly lays out procedures for participation. Students can test the extent of their influence through the available mechanisms, rather than through interaction or guesswork, and determine whether in fact they have real power. But in informal structures it is not easily recognized how much—or little—power students have.

In informal settings, power is a delicate matter, depending on personal influence and interaction and who has access to information. If information and communication can be controlled by one group, that group will hold the power. In traditional schools, informal systems of governance assure that information and communication will be one way—from adults to students at the adults' discretion—and that interaction will be limited and determined by adults. In such settings, student power is minimal, whether or not formal governance structures exist.

A formal setting alone, even if governance processes are clearly delineated and understood, is not enough. Informal communication between youth and adults also has to be open and honest, and information freely shared. In addition, students also need to be organized as a collectivity, despite their separate interests. Indeed, these factors can be more important than a formal setting—students at the least formally organized school (Milwaukee) had the greatest power.

Most schools found it necessary to modify the all-school meeting. Sudbury Valley added a committee system, making its government the most formally structured of the six, outranking even Franklin's Senate in formality. Community High substituted an Intertribal Council, and Metro added a Policy Board. "Dillington" and Milwaukee remained the most informal.

Sudbury Valley School. Sudbury's elaborate formal structure depended on the all-school meeting and numerous committees to carry out its legislative functioning. The committees, made up of students and staff elected by the School Meeting, were responsible for various aspects of school affairs, such as attendance, student records, building maintenance and supplies, and publicity. In addition, a number of corporations with autonomy over their own budgets and activities were engaged in various curriculum areas, such as music, photography, horticulture, and arts and crafts supplies. The school was managed by this network of committees and corporations, while the policy-making and judicial activities took place at the all-school meeting. The formal structure was clear. Even the elementary students understood it.

Informal communication at Sudbury was open, honest, and trusting. Resources as well as information and ideas were shared. While students had a great deal of *personal* power, participating in school governance or directing their individual curricula, they seemed to have less collective power, because there were so many small committees and because the curriculum was so highly individualized. Students did not organize as a group; rather they tended to focus separately on their different interests. In contrast, the faculty seemed more "together," more powerful, and more influential than the students. Yet the school did operate openly and democratically, with a relatively high degree of student power.

Franklin High. At Franklin, most students felt they had more freedom than at other public schools, and the staff generally favored student participation in school life. However, participation is not power, and the Senate apparatus at Franklin was designed more to achieve participation than shared power. The Senate was a large council with a set ratio of students and staff representatives. It had four committees (executive, curriculum, student-staff relations, and due process and hearings), which made recommendations for the Senate's decision.

Although its formal structure was clearly delineated, not many students understood how the Senate operated or how it might benefit them. They had elected representatives, but few students, including their representatives, could articulate what the important issues were. Students had access to power but did not know how to use it.

The system, by its very structure, discouraged student organization. The Senate was not part of the school's regular schedule but met after school hours. Informal means of sharing information were underdeveloped. Student representatives did not seek their constituency's advice in policy-making or even know which sector of their constituency, if any, they were supposed to represent. They represented their own opinions, not the interests of a larger group. Although they numbered half of the Senate's voting members, they never once voted as a bloc nor even grouped to caucus. Nor had the blacks or Orientals among them caucused to clarify their concerns or plan strategy.

The staff, on the other hand, communicated more openly and regularly with each other during lunch and teaching breaks. As adults with influence and expertise, they dominated the Senate, just as teachers they dominated the classrooms. Students and teachers were unaccustomed to feeling parity, and participating as equals in the Senate was difficult.

Further, the administration controlled most of the information by determining which items to refer to the Senate and which problems to handle administratively. Finally, the principal retained a veto over Senate decisions, which, used or not, posed a threat that inhibited some. However, in May 1971, the Senate was only one semester old, the school population was over 1,500, and changes slowly but surely were being effected.

Differences between Sudbury Valley and Franklin were striking. The Franklin Senate was created, following racial disturbances, to extend communication between groups, to increase student participation in decision-making, and to improve the school itself through diversified representation. Nonetheless, the new Senate operated within a traditional context, and real power was still lodged in the school's administration and faculty committees. In contrast, Sudbury was developed as an experiment in "applied democracy." Its all-school meeting was not an appendage like the Senate, tacked onto a traditional framework mitigating against its power. Rather the all-school meeting, along with the committees and corporations, formed a total gestalt of formal democracy.

Despite its formal system, Sudbury concentrated on creating an open, flexible, and informal environment in which students had the maximum opportunity to decide their own school careers. Each student had the right "to choose his own way of spending time and to judge how profitably this time has been spent." Thus, the power to direct their school careers extended to all seventy-five students, whether they participated in committees, corporations, or the all-school meetings. The traditional structure at Franklin did not allow such flexibility and decision-making. There were still course requirements, scheduled classes, obligatory attendance, and regulated activities. Its 1,500 students had far less freedom to determine either institutional policies or individual curricula. A sense of power or influence was enjoyed, not by the masses of students, but only by the few who participated in the Senate.

Milwaukee Independent School. At Milwaukee, governance relied heavily on informal interaction. The emphasis on individualism discouraged much use of the formal structure, while the do-your-own-thing ethos mitigated against any rules other than the tuition stipulation. A requirement that students attend the weekly all-school meetings, for instance, was suggested but made optional. Nonetheless, most students did attend, and many were active on committees. Others, however, fought successfully for the right to be uninvolved. Their success reduced some of the staff's potential influence over which students had power and on which issues; teachers found it more difficult to urge only the "good" students to participate. Generally students moved in and out of active governance participation, depending on their schedules, interests, and the agenda up for discussion. However, when issues became crucial, governance took priority and frequently became the curriculum for all students.

In its communication structure, Milwaukee combined both formal and informal processes. There was a good deal of informal communication about issues before decisions were formally made at the all-school meeting.

Of the six schools, the greatest amount of student power existed at Milwaukee. Students had started and maintained control of the school. Information was shared among them and not withheld. And because they intended to maintain control, they were very conscious of the need to protect themselves as a group from co-optation by adults. On several occasions they acted as a bloc to retain their control. They wanted to make their own decisions and not permit teachers or parents to do the thinking for them. They allowed no one to advocate for them, nor did they give adults more power than students. Instead, the number of adults on the Board of Trustees was reduced, and the students forced the school's first adult director to resign.

On the whole, students were verbal, articulate, and comfortable with the dialogues that governance activities required. Beyond this, they had a humanistic orientation, a political view gained from their experience as innovators, and an understanding of how new roles could allow people to develop control over what happens to them. Thus they wholly entered into their new roles as administrators, teachers, and policy-makers. Most of them were active in all-school meetings in order to give personal direction to the programmatic thrust of the school.

Metro and "Dillington." In comparison, student power in governance was low at Metro and "Dillington." Here key decisions were made at informal faculty meetings, and though they were open to students, few attended. Metro students often failed to show up at important meetings, because they did not know the agenda in advance. "We don't know our agenda ourselves, before our meetings," a teacher explained. But the failure to post agendas suggested that teachers didn't really want students involved in governance—or that information discussed in faculty meetings was of a different order, perhaps more secret, than information shared between students and staff informally.

However, students at Metro and "Dillington" were informally involved in school governance through group counseling sessions and "raps." School governance was treated as a legitimate educational activity, almost part of the curriculum. But as long as students depended on informal contacts to make their interests known, the staffs' response was a benevolent form of paternalism.

Community High. At Community High the formal governing body was an Intertribal Council that kept in close touch with its constituent tribes. The formal structure was clear, and the informal lines of communication open and accessible. Some students and even tribes chose not to participate, and, as at Milwaukee, nonparticipation was permitted. But, unlike Milwaukee, student leadership did not shift frequently; power was lodged with only a few students, and the leaders resented their peers' apathy or inactivity. Yet in 1971 student power was real and available at Community High, though it depended on student initiative and the staff's willingness to share information. Generally the staff was open and communication exchanges were frequent. All this changed by 1973. As the number of alternative schools increased in Berkeley Community High I lost almost half its student body. The tribal structure was then considered cliquish and abandoned. Formal student governance no longer existed.

In sum, students in May 1971, had the most power in schools where governance was basic to the school's functioning and philosophy. At Milwaukee and Sudbury, decision-making was continual, integral, and a valued part of the schools' program, and there, we believe, students had the most power. Community High students, then organized in tribes, were close behind. Metro and "Dillington" students had far less power and were drawn into decision-making only periodically, at times of crisis or evaluation. Franklin students had the least power. There, policy-making was a feature added on to the curriculum and available only to a few. Our data convincingly indicate that if students are to function meaningfully in the daily operation of their schools, then governance must be built into the school's ongoing basic curricular organization and philosophy.

HOW DECISIONS WERE MADE

The way decisions were made or agreed to varied widely among the schools. Milwaukee's all-school meetings operated primarily by consensus. Some decisions were passed with a three-fourths majority vote, but crucial decisions were made through consensus, a long and arduous process, which allowed students and staff to share their viewpoints, advocate them and convince others, and gave maximum weight to minority opinions. The informality of the all-school meetings provided opportunities for open and honest confrontations and for full, spontaneous participation, both indispensable to genuine consensus. Much time was spent by staff and students outside of meetings "checking each other out" on issues. Although consensus was difficult when polarization occurred, it remained the favored mode for making crucial decisions.

Few of the other schools utilized the consensus process. Voting was the format at Sudbury Valley, whose all-school meeting and biannual School Assembly were run much like traditional New England town meetings. Students, young

VARIATIONS IN TYPES OF DECISION-MAKING

School	Maintenance Decision (e.g., buying a typewriter)	Policy Decisions	Emergency Decisions
Public Schools			
Franklin High Seattle	Decided by the administration.	(E.g., policy on prohibiting undercover agents in school.) Drafted by Senate subcommittee, voted by the Senate.	None yet. Unclear whether Senate committee or principal would decide.
Metro High Chicago	Decided by the group at open faculty meetings.	(E.g., attendance policy.) Discussed in small counseling groups; then brought by staff to open faculty meeting where students had strong influence.	(E.g., eviction crisis.) All-school meetings, with parents and community people, handled this crisis.
"Dillington" School-in-a-School New England	Decided by the faculty at open staff meeting	(E.g., scheduling and vacation policy.) Decided at open faculty meeting where students had strong influence.	(E.g., replacing representational structure with Open Forum where everyone has a vote.) Decision made by all participants after several all-school meetings.

Public Schools			
Community High Berkeley	Decided informally by the director and a few students or staff who may then ask the Intertribal Council for money.	(E.g., financial autonomy from Berkeley High School.) Negotiated by committee of students and staff working with the BHS principal.	(E.g., selecting a new director.) The Intertribal Council considered two candidates, then held an election. The students' choice won out over the staff's.
Private Schools			
Sudbury Valley School Massachusetts	Decided by the all-school meeting after the office clerk puts the item on the agenda.	(E.g., visitors policy.) Voted on by all-school meeting after visitors committee puts item on agenda.	(E.g., funding salaries.) Criteria voted on by all-school meeting and later made part of the budget.
Milwaukee Independent School	Decided by the staff member responsible for maintenance and several students, who then buy it. They may request money at the weekly all-school meeting.	(E.g., policy of minimum requirements.) Discussed at all-school meetings, then approved on the condition they be optional.	(E.g., financial crisis.) After the staff's financial proposals had been rejected at the all-school meeting, a staff ultimatum led to a weekend of meetings where it was decided by consensus that students must pay their tuition or leave.

and old, behaved as responsible voters, abstaining when necessary rather than voting naively. Consensus would have been
difficult since the openness and sensitivity found at Milwaukee
was not emphasized at Sudbury.

Community High had also utilized a voting format, with
majority rule, in its Intertribal Council meetings. However,
the tribes represented had each sought consensus by discussing issues before they were voted on in the Council, and their
representatives to the Council had to reflect their wishes. The
process, while it lasted, combined consensus within like-
minded groups, and majority rule within a Council of heterogeneous groups.

Franklin's procedures of voting and majority rule did not
adversely affect students, since they composed half the Senate's membership. Yet the absence of organized constituencies, such as those promoted by the Community High structure, minimized student input into the Senate's decisions.

Metro and "Dillington" also relied on voting and majority
rule. There, however, majority rule worked against students,
since few generally attended the decision-making meetings
where the majority was the faculty. However, students did
not appear disturbed by that since they trusted the faculty to
protect their interests. Only in emergency situations, when all-
school meetings were held, did students converge en masse
and become a majority voice.

Within each school decision-making also varied, depending
on the type of decision being made. A simple maintenance
decision took one form, general policy another, and an emergency a third, as the preceding chart illustrates.

In some cases, student influence was achieved through a
formal governance structure, in others, through the more
informal means of discussion in counseling or special interest
groups. Student participation in maintenance and emergency

decisions is valuable. However, its greatest importance lies at the level of policy decisions. It is here that students can exert power at the most fundamental and continuous levels.

THE EFFECT OF SCHOOL SIZE

It is probably no coincidence that student power was greatest in the smallest school, Milwaukee. The smaller the program, the more opportunity there is for students to participate actively. Similarly, the smaller the program, the more dependent it is on students to maintain it. A smaller unit allows its participants to feel more responsible for its growth and more easily fosters a sense of cohesion and group effort. Furthermore, in a smaller unit, participants are likely to have more information about what is going on, what various needs are, whom to contact, and how to influence other members. Thus, in a smaller setting, members can more easily influence one another and feel comfortable in joint decision-making. Many we interviewed felt that for these reasons fifty to one hundred people was a good size for a school or program unit. It permits diversity yet community and allows for a variety of influence and decision-making modes.

The smaller schools—Milwaukee, "Dillington", and Sudbury Valley, whose students numbered forty, fifty and seventy respectively—used all-school meetings where students and staff arrived at decisions by consensus or by voting (one-man, one-vote). In the larger schools, whose populations ranged from 230 to 1,500, governance generally was on a representative basis, and voting predominated. At the smaller schools there was direct and widespread informal sharing of individual opinions and needs; the larger schools were too big. Voting was the only efficient means of resolving conflict. Consensus would have been too difficult, and widespread informal communication on an individual basis impossible.

The public or private status of the school—regardless of its size—may have had an effect on the extent of student participation. Student power was greatest at the two private schools, Milwaukee and Sudbury, greater than at Community High, which encouraged student participation, and far greater than at "Dillington," which was smaller than Sudbury. The difference seemed to be that the public school students took their school's existence or survival for granted, whereas the private school students did not. When a public school's innovative program was in jeopardy, as it was at Community High and Metro at times, the crisis elicited student participation, but following the crisis, participation dropped off.

Primarily, however, students at the two private schools and Community High had more power than their peers at "Dillington," despite the latter's small size, because the staff and students at the three schools were committed to student self-government as a goal, whereas the "Dillington" teachers acted as advocates for students and thereby prevented student self-determination. A small program, then, tends to encourage student participation and power, but only when the entire population is committed to power-sharing.

STUDENT POWER AND CURRICULUM

If students are to have some control over their school lives, they must have some control over the instructional process. The instructional process includes the range of curricula offerings and extramural opportunities, teachers' pedagogical styles and methods, and teaching-learning materials and resources. Student power here involves the freedom of students to pursue their individual interests, using the school's or outside resources. It involves teachers structuring their classroom interactions to support students' self-determination and responsibility for their own learning, helping them in a way that does not overwhelm them with adult expertise or authority. The instructional process includes continuous evaluation of curriculum offerings, classroom interactions, and governance processes—all data being shared with students and teachers alike. It includes teaching students political skills, such as how to organize, how to change courses, how to be a representative, and so on.

Only when students' power extends over the broad range of instructional processes will they have significant power. At Milwaukee, for example, students had free choice of what, when, how, and from whom they wanted to learn. Evaluations were a matter of mutual feedback in conversations between students and staff, and the two groups enjoyed more or less equal power in managing the instructional processes of the school.

In contrast, students at Sudbury Valley enjoyed a highly individualized, open curriculum, but informal teacher-student relationships supported deference to adult authority and expertise. In governance meetings, for example, few students spoke. Furthermore, the highly individualized learning settings were dominated by adult norms, expectations and expertise; peer learning in groups was rare. Even though students there were encouraged to be active and influential in governance and curriculum planning, in reality the learning setting was adult-dominated.

Obviously, student power is strengthened when students are able to influence their course requirements. Milwaukee students determined their own list of minimum requirements (the list was optional), while Franklin's were set by the public school system. Metro adhered to course requirements for accreditation yet offered a diversity of orthodox and unorthodox selections—but not teaching styles—by which students could fulfill the requirements. "Dillington" and Community High also offered considerable choice, along with certain requirements. However, students being offered a choice of staff-developed options is very different from students having power to decide and implement their personal and collective concerns.

To enable students to determine their own learning styles and directions, teachers need to offer an appropriate amount of help. They should not withdraw entirely. In several schools with open curriculum choices, teachers were reluctant to offer guidance or direction to help students make sound decisions, fearing it might infringe on students' power or diminish their self-responsibility. Such an analysis, however, represents an abdication of responsibility through a misunderstanding of what student power is all about. Certainly an open curriculum, defined by students and teachers collectively, must exist in a school with real student power. But it does not mean that a student will necessarily be dominated by a teacher who works with him to develop his curriculum choices. Individual students can make unwise choices for themselves, and their power is not diminished when someone of equal power, but perhaps more educational expertise, helps them to consider more appropriate choices.

It is a question of balance. Help and direction must not be transformed into faculty control. It was unfortunate, for example, when some of the Milwaukee staff took it upon themselves to plan, without student input, a core curriculum, with hints of course requirements, and were ready to recommend it. That the staff had moved so far in this planning process without student participation was a governance control issue.

The implications are distressing since they suggest a strengthened staff role, a weakened, subordinated student role, and an imbalance in power relations that could have resulted in a move away from student control at Milwaukee.

THE NEED FOR FEEDBACK AND POLITICAL SKILLS

Student power is developed and supported when evaluation data are shared with students as well as with teachers. Evaluation procedures can provide feedback about students' performances, teachers' performances, and the over-all school program. For example, when Metro offered courses to meet black students' interests and needs, evaluation feedback from black students (and some white) indicated their satisfaction with the content range but their dissatisfaction with their teachers' pedagogical styles. Such information can help students and their teachers design courses more appropriate to various learning styles.

Further, where students are involved in school policy-making and curriculum development, evaluation data allow them the influence that comes with well informed judgments. However, even if they believe in sharing power with students, most school administrators do not give this kind of evaluation data to students and thereby deny them the power that comes from having such information. Metro was an exception. Besides evaluating its program through a long-term comparison of 110 Metro students with 110 students at other schools, it has incorporated procedures to produce ongoing feedback about issues of immediate interest, both to clarify issues and to generate students' interest in participating in upcoming decisions. Metro's evaluation of individual students also encourages their taking responsibility for their own learning.

Finally, to develop and enhance student power, students need to learn political skills so that they can participate effectively. Through workshops, such as those held at Franklin and experiences such as those encountered by the students and adults who helped to establish Milwaukee, students can be taught political skills: how to organize, how to clarify and state issues, how to be a representative, the various styles of influence and decision-making, and so on. Adults cannot assume that, if given the opportunity, students will naturally know how to take responsibility for their own learning. At Community High, for example, after the demise of the tribes, the staff was still waiting in 1973 for students to initiate a formal goverance structure.

Despite the structural supports for students' self-determination that existed in schools such as Metro and Franklin, few students understood how to change policies or curricula they didn't like, nor did they have the sophistication to attempt the procedures required. Even in the more innovative schools, bureaucratic processes existed that tended to favor adults and thus prevent students from sharing power equally. Despite faculty commitment to student participation, no structure or courses existed to help students share in the structural control of the curriculum and governance of their schools.

STUDENT ATTITUDES TOWARD PARTICIPATION

Besides the institutional, systemic, and social hindrances to student participation in decision-making, student attitudes form a barrier too. On the whole, student participation is sporadic. They distrust government with adults, because adults always dominate. They distrust student government too. As noted, many students lack communication, problem-solving, and political skills. In addition, the broad disparity of student interests often prevents effective coalition.

For a long time, and in most schools, student councils were fashionable as a training ground for citizenship in democracy. But these councils had limited power and effectiveness. Often they were a farce or a front for the administration. Most students have learned to distrust such ventures and are cynical about them. At Franklin and Community High, as at most public schools, the majority no longer believes that student government can be effective or real. Students are either apathetic or anarchic. The apathetic students are resigned to the anticipated failure of self-government. The anarchic do not believe in government at all. They want total autonomy to "do their own thing" and will not join a body engaged in making any rules that restrict a student's freedom. Adults may influence some students to believe their rhetoric—that they do want students to join in policy-making—but most students have a "wait and see" attitude. Only if an experiment proves successful will the others participate. "Wait and see" was the dominant feeling at Franklin.

Distrust of student government also leads students to let adults advocate for them. Reasoning that youth have little power while adults have much, many students—such as those at "Dillington" and Metro—allowed, and perhaps even encouraged, teachers to speak for them.

That students have not been taught effective communication, problem-solving, and political skills are serious barriers to their effective participation. All too often, adults believe their work is done once they have built a structure in which young people can be involved. This abdication of their teaching roles is one reason many forms of student government fail. All participants in a system that relies on participation need to learn the skills of organizing, caucusing, defining issues, planning strategy, negotiating, collaborating, and compromising. When, without training, unskilled and inexperienced students participate ineffectively, adults blame them for it instead of realizing their co-responsibility. Of course, if students had political skills, adults might find themselves outmaneuvered and outvoted by student coalitions, which may account for the "hands off" attitude of some administrators.

As it is, student coalitions are uncommon, except in times of crisis. The wide variety of their interests, styles, and needs often precludes the kind of çoalition that would enable them to gain more power as a group. This was the case at Sudbury Valley School, where students' collective power was much lower than their individual power. Furthermore, adults can and do use student diversity to divide and rule.

Thus, many students distrust working with adults in a collaborative governance and are cynical and pessimistic about the benefits of such collaboration when they see adults continually dominating meetings. Students at Franklin pointed with dismay to the first issue the Senate had settled—separation of the teachers' lounges for smokers and nonsmokers— while students still had no place to smoke.

It is entirely possible that student participation in formal school governance is a middle-class ideal, favoring a cultural style that stresses verbalization, debate, and procedure, and neglects those who do not value or lack these skills. Such a style is becoming more and more unpalatable to lower-class black students, who have never valued it, and to many middle-class students, who have grown weary of its shortcomings.

Student involvement is greatest at times of crisis and survival and lowest when an ongoing program only needs to be maintained. Routine management seems slow, boring, and unglamorous compared to policy-making during an initial or crisis period, and students aren't eager to spend more time in school in yet another dull activity. Furthermore, their interests change. Many adults have been unwilling to involve students in school governance because of their sporadic participation. They claim students' interest in the school's life is limited, narrow, and transient. However, our data suggest this is not the case; rather, students' interest and involvement waxes and wanes with specific issues. If the program really depends on their participation, then students will be involved; if their influence is limited and narrow, then they will participate only sporadically.

The question is, what *new* forms of decision-making can be developed that will allow individuals to feel that they have significant control over their lives in an institution. How can a shared power structure function economically, yet not consume the energies of the institution's members? Metro, for example, has evolved an informal structure for shared power that is based on trust, confidence, cooperation, and enthusiasm. But is it adequate to engage students fully, or will decision-making continue to rest largely in the hands of Metro's adults? How can governance structures be extended or reinforced to enable students to play more active roles within them? These are provocative questions, and there are no easy answers.

Autonomy vs. Community

By Sue Golden and Joan Chesler

In all school settings, students and staff members are pulled by opposing pressures both to work alone and together. Traditionally school authorities decide whether classes will be large or small, whether independent study will be offered, and whether the learning style will be cooperative or competitive. In our six schools, students and teachers struggled with the inherent conflict between autonomy and community, between "doing your own thing" and "building a community." Autonomy was encouraged by providing interpersonal and structural supports to individuals to pursue their own interests and to work at their own pace. A sense of community was fostered by school-wide projects and governance meetings that represented the range of shared values and concerns. Students and teachers in each school experienced considerable autonomy as well as a sense of group identity, although the extent and balance varied. Fully satisfying the two conflicting goals was impossible.

268

THE PULL TOWARD AUTONOMY

Each school was committed to experimenting with open learning settings where students could develop their personal definitions of learning and be responsible for their own successes and failures. To varying degrees, teachers and students supported independent courses of study as well as the freedom of movement and spirit to "do your own thing."

Each school found ways to individualize the curriculum. All offered independent study in certain areas and free time, although this was hard to arrange in the large public schools. "Too much red tape, too much hassle," complained a student at Franklin, where independent study was the exception rather than the rule. At small Sudbury Valley, on the other hand, individual study predominated.

Several schools (Milwaukee, Community High "Dillington," and Sudbury Valley) offered apprenticeship programs and even allowed students to have semester-long projects in which they were totally independent, except for periodically checking in with the school. A "Dillington" student, for example, spent a term as an apprentice teacher in an elementary school, and a Community High student spent a term restoring a farm to an ecologically sound basis.

Individualizing the curriculum meant orienting classes toward student interests and learning styles. The administrators of Metro and Franklin made their course offerings as wide and varied as possible. Elsewhere students were able to choose among courses geared to their expressed interests (Community High and "Dillington"), or organize classes themselves (Milwaukee), or make individual arrangements with their teachers (Sudbury).

Absenteeism was a problem in each school but its treatment varied greatly. Some teachers at Community High did not object to absences caused by students' involvement in community affairs or students' inability to "get it together"; they were willing to wait until students could profit from class. Some teachers at Milwaukee brought up absenteeism only as a way to help clarify students' goals. But at Franklin, the most traditional school, students were penalized for excessive absenteeism, and their grades were lowered. Although students were offered the opportunity, through the Senate's Curriculum Committee, to express their curricular interests and possibly change course offerings, few did so. In general, they were expected to adapt to what was offered and were penalized if they did not.

A special problem at Sudbury, Metro, and Milwaukee was the often poor attendance at classes conducted by resource volunteers. Resource teachers resented volunteering their time and energy only to be rejected, and students resented the obligation to attend a class whose teacher might not be stimulating or interesting. At Milwaukee the problem was acknowledged, but the solution was unclear. Whose responsibility was it to inform resource teachers of student norms and goals—the students' or the staff's? Who was to change—the students or the resource teachers? By May 1971, no solution had been found; absent students were simply reminded to attend class. At Metro, a resource teacher whose class was ill-attended often dropped the course the following semester.

Each school offered students some degree of freedom, but how much depended on the program and the ability of each student to use the freedom offered. Students at Milwaukee seemed to enjoy the most autonomy, since there were so few restrictions on them. They were free to come and go as they pleased, and they met the school's "minimum expectations" only if they chose to. At all the other schools, the requirements were more structured and systematized, and students were expected to meet them in order to graduate. The requirements either offered a broad range of options (Franklin and Metro) or could be satisfied in a broad variety of ways (Sudbury Valley and Community High).

Regardless of how much freedom a school offered, each student exercised only as much as she or he was able. It was up to students to define their interests and explore ways to develop them. If they could not move ahead, they were forced to examine what was preventing them from developing interests. Some schools regarded students' freedom to learn from their own inaction as the major learning experience it could provide.

While most schools shared the rhetoric of student autonomy, teachers varied greatly in their approach to helping students gain the ability to use independence. Some felt they fostered independence by helping students make appropriate choices; others took the laissez-faire attitude of "do your own thing and learn from your own mistakes," or maintained a hands-off policy that communicated, "I have faith you'll do it in your own time," combining a sense of high expectations and low pressure.

This latter stance proved difficult for many students and teachers. To students, the laissez-faire attitude at Sudbury Valley, for example, seemed cool and distant as the staff waited to be invited into a relationship by students. Staff members generally seemed to be acutely aware of their students' conflicting needs for freedom and help at the right time. Yet helping students to acknowledge their need for help, and even assessing their need for help, was difficult in settings that placed a high value on autonomous and self-motivated learning.

The issue is particularly poignant in a free school setting which, by its very freeness and openness, often frightens and sometimes paralyzes teachers and students accustomed to a more authoritarian and confining structure. Take, for example, the freedom to learn wherever may be most appropriate. Although such freedom was extended in most of the schools, the majority of students and teachers restricted themselves to the school building, limited not by rules and regulations but by their socialization, expectations, and imagination. Becoming liberated from the repressive and confining aspects of traditional schooling could not be done overnight. Students had to decide what to learn, how to learn it, with who and what their criteria were for a job well done. Teachers had to decide how active and directive to be and what to teach, how, to whom, and when.

Learning to use a great deal of freedom and autonomy was exhilarating but often painful and always difficult. Asking for help is difficult for people of all ages, but particularly so for adolescents who are loathe to express dependency but are seeking boundaries or limitations within which to define their growing sense of identity. While students found their new autonomy exciting and challenging, ("I want an education that will match the true me, and this program offers enough room to do that"), many spoke of their difficulty adjusting at first. Paralyzed by inner confusion about what they wanted to do, to learn, and to be, they generally took at least a term to pull themselves together:

> We have a lot of options for how we spend our time. It's hard to get into things and really start learning, but when you take hold of yourself finally, even though you have wasted a lot of time, you really feel good.

Some found their new freedom a lonely thing. Socialized by traditional schools to conform, they were overwhelmed by the stress on individuality and the encouragement of individual pursuits. Teachers, it seemed, had no clear authoritative expectations of students; perhaps they didn't care enough. The difficulty of asking for help and of sorting out ways to explore individual interests were all the harder in a setting that offered little sense of community direction or support. In this sense, do your own thing sometimes became a prison that enclosed individuals in their loneliness.

THE PULL TOWARD COMMUNITY

Many students and teachers, especially in the smaller programs, hoped to be part of a learning "community." While this had various meanings, ranging from a central gathering place to a warm, supportive environment where feelings, activities, and resources were shared freely, in general, the students and teachers meant a community based on interdependence, caring, participation in governance, and some unity of purpose.

Why did they desire community in an institution that traditionally has been experienced as closed and repressive? Students and teachers, by and large, were not rejecting schooling *per se*. They were, however, rejecting the traditional forms of schooling that have come to mean depersonalization of students in large, conforming classes, alienation of students from their peers through competition for grades and honors, fragmentation of schooling through courses in separate disciplines that are taught as though they were unrelated, fragmentation of their lives into "school" and "after school," and exclusion from policy decisions affecting their education. Instead, teachers and students wanted to bring "life" and "school" closer together by learning in a group that shared common values or respected disparate ones, by eliminating competition for grades, by interdisciplinary courses, by personalizing learning in smaller, more cohesive groups, and by participating in decision-making relevant to their lives at school.

Several schools considered the development of such community spirit a critical matter and a primary goal. Community High, for example, defined "a learning environment" in both academic and social terms. The director of "Dillington" spoke of building "a much more meaningful relationship between students and teachers and students and students."

Many educators are critical of such goals. They feel that talk of community is merely giving students' social needs and interpersonal skills an unwarranted place in the curriculum. Other critics feel that a realistic community cannot be generated in any school setting, free or otherwise, and would move beyond free schools to the outside community. Many students would agree. Black students seeking community, for example, have turned to work in the ghettos. White students have joined together to work in rural or mountain areas or to live in urban collectives. Such students do not want to center their lives around school.

However, the six schools studied here operated in the belief that real community could be achieved within the school setting. All six attempted to foster a sense of community in a variety of ways: interpersonal, political, and academic.

The interpersonal aspect meant building strong supportive ties among members. Feelings of comradeship were achieved in a number of ways: by addressing teachers on a first-name basis and by encouraging students and staff to share time outside of school hours going to plays, baking bread on Sundays, taking trips to the country, and so on. All these served to strengthen personal ties, making it easier to ask for help, to share expertise, and to foster caring and trust.

Sometimes, however, the emphasis on loving support and concern boomeranged. Many innovative schools concentrating on supportive ties failed to recognize the value of creative confrontation to the detriment of community development. Take, for example, the first three years of Community High: its members were so concerned with building a place that was warm and open that it became difficult to express angry, negative feelings. The repression of anger, which often is a driving force for change, fueled the school's insidious enemy, apathy. Apathy led to noninvolvement and noninvolvement, in turn, to the demise of warm, open ties and feelings of community.

The political aspect of community involves the development of shared values and political activities. It could mean working together to bring about change in the institutional structure of education, as Milwaukee students did by visiting local high schools and nearby universities to share their experiences. It could mean the unifying experience of participatory democracy at Sudbury Valley, where feelings of community were developed during the Assembly meetings. Franklin's Senate served a similar purpose, at least for the active few.

Academic pursuits could also foster a sense of community. For example, small-group learning projects, such as building the yurt at "Dillington," produced feelings of cohesion and community for those working on the project. Frequently, however, the sense of community developed through a task-oriented activity was as short-lived as the task itself.

A sense of community can also develop in response to crisis. Each school faced threats to its survival. The series of crises at Metro, for example, brought students and staff together to protect the program. Once the program seemed secure, students and teachers again divided into varying interest groups. But such crises forced members to share their values and goals as they jointly decided the fate of the programs, and often, after the crises passed, goals and programs were more congruent. At Sudbury Valley, for instance, the change in focus that led to the exodus of a large group of students and some staff members, left those who remained more in agreement with the basic approach of the school.

It may be that the most powerful factor in community formation, aside from shared values, was the relation of the community to outsiders. Frequently these relations were hostile or, at best, distrustful. Such opposition kept the new community together and motivated the resolution of internal conflicts to produce a facade of strength. The process is similar to adolescent identity formation on an institutional level. Perhaps Milwaukee was the most "mature" of the six schools since it didn't rely on hostile external relations to define itself as a community. On the other hand, Milwaukee was already fairly well defined as a white, middle-class community and as a private school and was under little public pressure to become more heterogeneous. In contrast, there was considerable pressure upon Community High to become heterogeneous, partly in terms of racial balance. Because it experienced more value conflicts within the school community, it had to rely on pressures from outside to develop cohesiveness and community. It is worth noting that since our study Community High has changed its name to Genesis, which might mean a shift in emphasis from community cohesion to diverse and explosive regeneration.

Members of the innovative schools did not all want to experience community to the same degree. Some wanted to feel a great affinity with their colleagues during much of their schooltime; others felt such closeness was oppressive. They wanted a sense of cohesion but also space for individual autonomy. Still, the sense of community achieved through collaboration and sharing helped provide a base to those who wanted to work in groups and gave strength to the program when it was threatened by external forces.

THE EFFECT OF SCHOOL SIZE

Just as student power was greater in the smaller schools, so was student investment in community life. In larger schools, such as Franklin, students had feelings of warmth and sharing, but those in the smaller schools ("Dillington," Milwaukee, and Sudbury Valley) spoke of the schools' rapid response to their changing needs in ways they had not experienced in any previous school. These students had the greatest feeling of fulfillment of personal needs and seemed willing to invest more energy to maintain and develop their schools.

In each school, there was a core group of ten to twenty student leaders. However, there was a different feeling about participation and sense of potency when the ten to twenty leaders came from a student body of 1,500 as opposed to 100. In the smaller schools, leaders felt less discouraged by the lack of student participation in governance. There, as already noted, governance was based on direct participation in all-school meetings where everybody had the opportunity to participate and to feel involved, important and useful. In the larger schools using a representative form of governance, student and teacher representatives had to work hard to be in close touch with their constituencies, and the benefits of direct involvement were limited to fewer members.

The smaller the program, the more personal it was, and

the more it encouraged warm ties. Members knew one another; relationships were informal, casual, and easy. When a school expanded suddenly, as Metro and Community High did, something of this easy relationship was lost. A Metro student contrasted his experience during his first and second years there:

> Last year I had no personal fears. I could walk up to anybody at Metro, a kid, a teacher, anyone and say come on, let's go to lunch, but now, this year, it's different. I have to go searching for a particular person I know to go to lunch with.

In the smaller settings of fifty to one hundred students there was less tendency toward exclusivity in cliques. Where cliques existed, there were overlapping memberships. At Milwaukee, for example, there were distinct interest groups, but as students' interests shifted, so did their allegiance to various groups. Friendships shifted and were not exclusive.

Where it was difficult to develop close, caring relationships with hundreds of students, many cliques developed. This did not bother those who found comfort and support with others most like themselves, but a minority of students committed to working out difficulties within a heterogeneous group felt the cliqueness was counterproductive, unstimulating, and unreal. Metro initiated small counseling groups in an effort to personalize the school; Community High had interest-based tribes; but not one of the larger schools was satisfied with its solution to integrating diverse groups of students. Some felt the staff lacked experience working with such groups; others felt such groups were not powerful enough to accommodate increased and frequently doubled size. Obviously it is much easier to develop and maintain a feeling of community in a group of fifty than two hundred (not to mention 1,500).

Expansion at Community High and Metro brought several changes. Students no longer knew each other as personally. They did not participate as much when they saw they were not crucial to the program and that others would carry that load. Although the feeling of newness and innovative risk-taking had begun to wear off by the second year, expansion divided the students between the old and the new. The new students, arriving in such great numbers, were understandably resented.

Expansion also meant meeting a greater variety of needs. It meant a more diverse staff, coordinating a pool of volunteer teachers, and finding ways to share resources with a variety of institutions. Larger programs, of course, could offer more diverse curricula.

Schools financed by public taxes, such as Metro and Community High, also felt pressured to demonstrate the viability of their programs for a large number of students in public school systems. But while the curriculum was expanded, energy was drained from creating ways to build community feeling. Thus expansion offered greater possibilities for some aspects of individual growth—through enlarged curricula and increased staff resources—but reduced members' feelings of community and group cohesion.

INDIVIDUAL VS. COMMUNITY GROWTH

The school that values both autonomy and community always finds itself pulled in opposite directions. Conflict is inherent, since the conditions that free an individual to be autonomous are the very ones that work against community and sharing.

The concept of "do your own thing" focuses on individual growth, with the understanding that accountability to others is not necessarily involved. At best, it means freedom from the crippling restraints of conformity that group life often imposes. At worst, it means a student does not have to do anything he doesn't want to and has no responsibility or accountability to anyone else, neither his teachers nor his peers.

In traditional schools, students generally are accountable to their teachers and are supposed to learn what the teacher expects them to. In innovative schools, accountability is often more broadly defined to include peer control. Students are responsible to themselves and one another; they depend on their peers to help make the programs work and to facilitate each other's learning.

Yet at times the rugged individualism of "do your own thing" strains the bonds of community. Students who chose to do nothing, for instance, were often resented by their peers. As a student leader at Community High said:

> Maybe they are not turned off by the school but just infatuated with not having to do anything. It has gone to their heads. They are probably enjoying it and it may not be bad, but I don't like to see people just sitting around.

Similarly, teachers were frustrated when students chose not to attend class in order to "do their own thing."

Nonetheless, staff members supported their students' efforts to define themselves more clearly, respected their need for autonomy, and tried not to dominate them. Again and again, they cited their conviction that self-motivation and self-reliance were crucial to learning. However, they also recognized that the development of community spirit required interdependence. Students, in contrast, were less certain of the need to balance individual and collective responsibilities. They wanted to be free to move in and out of classrooms and the community as they wished. They wanted maximum individual freedom with the option to invest in developing community if they so chose. Many, however, vacillated between the wish to explore "Who am I?" and "What can I do on my own?" with the wish to grow with the support of others.

In the initial phases of the programs, students wanted to build together. Later, however, the commitment sought by the leaders caused hard feelings. Strong leaders and builders of community were periodically out of grace and resented for pushing their ideas on others and interfering with the freedom of others. Some students did not want to be curtailed by rules of any kind or held accountable to anyone—students, staff, or themselves—for anything.

But individual freedom must be compromised at least somewhat if a group is to exist. A Milwaukee staff member put it this way:

> When a person joins a group, he has to give up some
> of his freedom, at least so that I know what he's
> thinking so I can proceed in the group.

He felt that quiet students should commit themselves to participating in conversations so that sharing and assessing could occur. In schools that valued community, there was considerable group pressure to be open and honest in order to maintain good community feelings. Many, however, were not willing to accept a commitment to openness and participation, preferring to depend on others' involvement.

Several schools used formal mechanisms to stimulate discussion and decision-making within a group. Sudbury Valley's judicial system and General Assembly laid out clear rules for mediating interpersonal differences and making decisions. Metro's counseling groups were the locus for discussion prior to decision-making at faculty meetings. Tribal meetings at Community High dealt with issues to be brought up at the Intertribal Council. Encounter groups were also used at Berkeley to explore sensitivity training and group dynamics.

To ease the strains between autonomy and community, most of the schools offered students a variety of ways to learn that included both individualized and group projects. In support of autonomy, all offered independent study and free time. Most allowed students to take apprenticeship jobs in specific subject areas or spend an entire semester on an individual project. In support of community, all used the school as a base and resource center, and half allowed students to take on group projects for a semester or a year. Milwaukee, Community High, and "Dillington" offered the most alternatives, and the abundance seemed to help lessen the conflict between autonomy and freedom. These three schools had strong community feeling as well as individualized curricula. Milwaukee and "Dillington" were small enough to involve most students in their governance structures. Thus, multiple options in group and individualized learning, coupled with a small size and widespread participation in governance structure, were characteristic of schools that had the least conflict between individual and community growth.

In some cases, size alone was the determining factor. For example, an institution's ability to tolerate broad autonomy was clearly related to its size. The larger the school, the more curbs there were on individual freedom. In addition, the larger the school, the less the overall commitment to community life.

But even in small schools, such as Milwaukee and "Dillington," the attainment of community spirit was, at best, sporadic. Group solidarity came and went as a function of the tasks, activities, and crises at hand.

The conflicting desires for individual growth and group identity are particularly painful for adolescents whose goals and values are not clearly defined. It takes time to learn what needs can be fulfilled through the group life and what needs must be developed separately. Usually it works both ways. The more secure their sense of group life is, the more they can afford to be autonomous, and vice versa. It is the same with institutions. The conditions that free an individual or an institution to be autonomous are not necessarily in conflict with community and sharing. Rather, it is a question of learning to recognize and balance the need for both. Institutions, like adolescents, can accumulate experience and come of age.

Pluralism
in Education

By *Glorianne Wittes and Joan Chesler*

If educational pluralism existed in the United States, each school would have its own culture and style, and each would define education's functions in terms of the interest group it served. Group distinctiveness would be an explicit organizing principle of each learning system.

But genuine pluralism in public education never has been established in the United States because American society has not been pluralistic. Blacks, Latins, eastern Europeans, Orientals, Indians, and other ethnic minorities have been excluded from power; the white English-speaking middle and upper classes have dominated and organized most American schools.

The WASP tradition is distinguished, in particular, by a managerial conception of schools: they are to produce skilled manpower to serve the institutions of society, especially the economic and military sectors, and they are to maintain the *status quo*. Teaching is a way of "managing the learning process" to "produce a certain kind of product," and counseling is the equivalent of "quality control." The tracking system is tied to job distribution and segregates students in order to maintain the *status quo*. Thus the academic track produces the country's professionals; the vocational track produces its blue collar workers and technicians; the general track produces its soldiers and its unskilled, unemployed dropouts. In this system, the prerequisites for success are: (*1*) whiteness, (*2*) competence in the school's language (standard English), (*3*) ability to maneuver in fairly complex urban school systems, and (*4*) a cosmopolitan cultural orientation. The system is self-perpetuating and self-reinforcing, since it rewards those who share the values of those who control it, that is, the students who are most successful in our public schools are white, upper middle-class, urban youngsters, whose backgrounds are most similar to those of their teachers, principals, textbook publishers, and other educators.

It may be, however, that the balance of power—which until now had permitted WASP leadership and dominance—is shifting. Forces have emerged that are challenging the status quo and are producing trends toward the development of pluralistic education. These trends orginate in the conflict over values in three areas: (*1*) majority vs. minority values (an ethnic conflict), (*2*) humanistic vs. minority values (a class conflict), and (*3*) professional vs. student and community values (a status conflict).

MAJORITY VS. MINORITY

Blacks and other racial minorities now are demanding, through student and community protest, that ethnic distinctiveness be made an explicit organizing principle of educational life. Because American culture has been "whitewashed" for too long, minority group members recognize the necessity to build, through the school's curricula, a sense of group identity and cultural pride in their young people. Such curricula, they believe, foster ethnic solidarity and will help them gain their fair share of political power and control of the local institutions that affect their lives. Without such power, white-run schools will continue to reflect only the majority culture and continue to portray minorities as inferior. Thus, minority group members, whether separatist or integrationalist, consider an educational curricula rooted in their own unique culture as both a right and a political necessity.

White community pressure for local control is different. Faced with bussing and desegregation, whites are clamoring to retain control of their neighborhood schools. They do not want to share control with any groups whose values and concerns differ from theirs and tend to identify such groups, in a racist way, as primarily nonwhite.

Whites who want their children to have an education that stresses their cultural identity can send them to parochial schools, for example, without being considered separatist or a threat to the white majority. But minorities in ethnic schools are not similarly accepted without considerable tension and conflict. The white majority views their demands for ethnic education and community control as a vicious form of militancy and separatism.

HUMANISM VS. TRADITION

The recent upsurge of interest in free schools and other alternative forms of schooling is largely a phenomenon of the urban middle and upper middle classes. Repudiating the managerial values of traditional education as dehumanizing, they are demanding more freedom and individual expression in their schools. They want more diversity of educational offerings and more individual control over substance and scheduling. Their demands, as David K. Cohen wrote in *Public Schools: The Next Decade*, may be seen as an "institutionalization of bohemia, which involves the expansion of values and life style which is radically different from, if not explicitly hostile to, the ethos of industrial capitalism." This life style values humanity, openness, and individual expression through creativity as opposed to market values that nurture closedness, conformity, and automatic behavior. Education is esteemed, but there is ambivalence or outright hostility towards the work-oriented and mechanical constraints of urban public schools.

In this humanistic view, schooling is not conditioned by the mechanical rhythm of the work place but by the unpredictable and spontaneous rhythm of individual discovery. The individualism stressed here is distinct from, and almost opposed to, the traditionalist's idea of individualized learning and teaching. The traditionalist approach, based on managerial values, aims to produce a certain set of skills, predetermined by the standards of someone other than the learner. Humanistic or counter-culture values are often antagonistic to the working class, whose security and survival lie in attachment to the traditional notions of authority and achievement.

PROFESSIONALS VS. STUDENTS AND THE COMMUNITY

Professional norms have long defined teachers as uncontestable sources of expertise and authority. As professionals, teachers are above politics. Neutral or nonpartisan, they keep a distance from their "clients" (students and parents).

Students and parents now challenging these norms claim that teachers cannot really be neutral, since not to advocate for students or ethnic minorities is to advocate against them. Teachers' lack of accountability to their clients removes them from any responsibility for their clients' victimization or failure. Furthermore, their "professional distance" from students and parents makes it easier for teachers to ignore the consequences of failure.

National teachers' associations resist community control not only because it threatens their values and jobs but also because it risks transforming the current nature of schooling.

THE "HUMANISTIC" SCHOOLS

Of the six schools in our study, all but one (Franklin) were committed to the new humanism with its emphasis on the individual. Sudbury Valley, Milwaukee, and Community High, for example, provided programs and curricula to enable the student to learn independently and to define for himself the resources he considered necessary. While this produced a *laissez-faire* atmosphere that distressed many students who needed more structure for their comfort and motivation, on the whole, it worked well for the majority.

There was, however, considerable ambivalence whether one's prime responsibility was to one's self or to the school community. Students did not consider the two in opposition; they yearned for both—at different moments in their school lives. Still, the ambiguity brought some anxiety, disillusionment, frustration, and profound mood swings, particularly at Community High where students and staff felt that self was frequently sacrificed for community, and vice versa, and were unsure which one to stress.

Where community is valued, it tends to "homogenize" the school as members come together, often lacking the skills to resolve their conflicts. When this happens, pluralistic individualism no longer sets the tone of the institution; shared majority values prevail instead. This was true, for example, at two schools, Milwaukee and Sudbury Valley, both of which placed a high value on community, while their curricula and programs stressed individualism.

At Milwaukee there was, from its inception, a certain intolerance of view. Its extremely loose, structureless program was designed to open the possibilities for individual growth, but "openness" masqueraded as pluralism. Only certain styles were accepted. Other points of view were treated as heresy, and dissenters were pressured to leave. The first to leave was one of the student founders who wanted more structure and requirements than his peers. The intolerance or inability to cope with conflict emerged again with the resignation of the school's director, when students found him too much "the director" and insensitive to their desires for independence in learning. He, in turn, predicted that the school would fail because of its inability to accept any vision, dream, or perspective besides its own.

Similarly, at Sudbury Valley most of the students who left in the large exodus, left voluntarily because they recognized the dominant group was unalterably opposed to their views and even considered them dangerous to the school's survival. Thus the pluralism envisioned by the school's focus on democratic governance and education became narrowly limited by the effort to ensure community.

Milwaukee and Sudbury are not unique. Communes, collectives, co-ops, and communities have been created and allowed to lapse over generations of American history. All too often they die because their survival as a community (with the cohesion this implies) becomes threatened by diverse values too far apart for reconciliation or by members' inability to deal with conflict. Further, the pull for individual rights frequently undercuts the desire for community, making the latter vulnerable to dissension.

While the new humanistic schools offer a model for reforming public education, they are unlikely to make it any more egalitarian or libertarian. Most humanistic schools remain an alternative for the privileged elite. The establishment of such schools is a political act—but not of significant dimension to provide genuine pluralism in American education. Members spend so much of their time and energy on their school's internal affairs that they have little left for any continuing communication or struggle with established schools or for effecting any significant changes in American education. Most find the challenge of humanizing their own institutions to be all they can handle.

Metro is an exception. Its struggles with the Chicago school system keep it in the public eye and alert to the necessity of creating change in the system as well as in Metro itself. Milwaukee is an exception, too. Its students consider it their obligation to politicize public schools, and they try to organize students, teachers, administrators, and parents in nearby schools. Milwaukee wants to humanize other institutions, not just its own. Still, Milwaukee represents a privileged enclave and is an unlikely model for public support, since taxpayers are not yet ready to finance schools, on a large scale, which are directed primarily by students.

Franklin, the one traditional school in our study, was attempting to humanize itself through a shared power governance structure. Ideally, the structure could have represented the interests of all groups in the development of policy and curriculum and promoted diverse, if not genuinely pluralistic, programs. While Franklin did provide some ethnic courses for minorities and special English-language instruction, it was not yet pluralistic. Its diverse groups had not defined their separate interests; as a result, their interests were not represented in the governing body (the Senate). There were black, white, and Oriental Senators, but they did not represent different interest groups.

MULTI-ETHNIC PROGRAMS

Only two of the six schools, Metro and Franklin, attempted to develop multi-ethnic programs. Metro, which had an equal number of black and white students, considered diversity in itself a sufficient basis for a multi-ethnic program. Students, for example, were heterogeneously mixed in small counseling groups in order to share their experiences and values. The curriculum was varied and individualized. Still Metro failed to become a genuinely multi-ethnic school. It favored middle-class white students and academically motivated blacks. Many black youngsters, and some whites, did not benefit. Yet those who lost out were enthusiastic about Metro because it allowed them to do their own thing, even if it meant skipping classes to rap all day, and it treated them with a respect they seldom received elsewhere.

Metro failed to become a genuinely multi-ethnic school because it was developed largely by whites in terms of a white perspective that did not recognize the blacks' need for racial consciousness. Only recently has a black staff member insisted on developing the group consciousness of Metro's black students as the first step in their education and school achievement. For Metro to become genuinely multi-ethnic, it would have to raise the group consciousness of white students and staff as well. It would need a curriculum that stresses both the differences and similarities of black and white history and culture. Race would form the content and the process of study as well, with pedagogical approaches developed to suit ethnic styles. Cross-group contacts would not be allowed to depend solely on individual friendships.

Concerned about its limited success with black students, Metro has sought to establish more black influence over its program. It increased the number of blacks on its staff (up by a third in a year) to equal the number of whites. It also drew black volunteers from the community. As the value of ethnic education grows among black participants, Metro may encounter racial divisiveness within its ranks, or it may move toward a more pluralistic, multi-ethnic program.

Franklin, with many black and Oriental students, has offered courses to appeal specifically to their interests. Many students, however, are dissatisfied with the range of options and the quality of these courses. In general the curriculum remains traditional and white-oriented in goals, style, and method.

While Metro and Franklin have attempted to develop multi-ethnic programs, the four other schools have not done so at all. "Dillington's" few black students, for example, sought their group identity beyond the school. Ethnic orientation did not exist in the school, even among the large number of Italians, who are Americans first and Italians second, in the melting pot tradition, and who did not seek programs revolving around Italian culture.

Community High is more directed by white values now than before, when it had more black students. The Berkeley school system, as a whole, has been attempting to become pluralistic by providing several distinct alternatives, one being

Black House, which has attracted many black students. Community High, nonetheless, hoped to develop a humanistic institution that cuts across racial lines and incorporates people as "brothers," and some black students have chosen it over Black House.

The Berkeley system is interesting. Providing educational pluralism through the establishment of separate schools, rather than trying to incorporate diverse values and orientations within a single setting, like Metro, may be a useful model. Blacks and whites can better define education for themselves, perhaps, in a system that does not regard integrated schooling as the highest good nor separated schooling as the greatest evil.

THE NEW PROFESSIONAL ROLE

In all the schools except Franklin, teachers have dropped their traditional role as professionals. They no longer pose as authoritative experts, above politics and advocacy. They no longer keep their students at a distance. Instead they see themselves as fierce advocates of students' rights and interests. Their attitude accounts for much of the schools' success as humanistic institutions, which would not have been possible had they clung to their professional norms.

Most of the teachers consider themselves "facilitators," persons with some experience and learning. They do not place themselves above the students. They believe that knowledge is a tool—not a means to exert authority. That students also teach in a number of the schools makes the distinction and distance between students and staff even less traditional.

There is a chance, however, that the old professional norms

could reappear if the school communities attempt to impose values the teachers may not support. What will happen if the authority of white teachers at Metro, Community High or "Dillington" is challenged by blacks who seek teachers particularly knowledgeable about their culture and needs? Or what will happen if Milwaukee's students go against staff preferences in hiring and firing teachers? Will the teachers remain open and vulnerable, or will they rush to defend themselves with their professional "rights" as "experts," not accountable to laymen's assessments? Usually, the past has demonstrated, when teachers' values conflict with the community, the high walls of professional norms have been raised in self-defense.

WHAT LIES AHEAD

Can educational pluralism ever be achieved? Indeed, can cultural pluralism ever become a reality in America? The day when all groups of society have equal status is still a long way off. Until then, it seems, we will be left with a sprinkling of educational alternatives available to a few, including some in minority groups, while the masses continue to attend the very schools that perpetuate the inequality of American society.

Recently various proposals have emerged that purport to widen the number of educational choices, given the absence of genuine shared political power in this country. In reality, none is likely to produce a pluralistic system. One is the Voucher Plan, which gives students tuition vouchers to attend schools of their choice. But how many local communities will be able to offer a significant choice? How many have, like Berkeley, a variety of alternative schools, each incorporating unique institutional arrangements, social climates, educational programs, and interpersonal relationships? A further problem with the voucher proposal is that in granting choice to some, it may deny it to others. For every seat taken, someone is turned away.

Another proposal is for community control and the redrawing of large school districts into smaller, homogeneous communities to ensure community control. This raises the basic question of whether the policy for the educational system should be based in the profession or in the local community. While many, on both sides, think the answer is obvious, the alternative schools of our study betray a certain ambivalence. The "deprofessionalized" teachers, favoring close attachment to the community, would share decision-making with students and parents. But most students, in contrast, are strongly against laymen affecting the direction of their schools, feeling more allied with their teachers than their often educationally conservative parents. The ambivalence leads to other questions. Will schools under community control become even more conservative? Will community control produce alternative forms of education, or will most schools be alike?

Contract performance programs farm out segments of the curricula (math or reading) to non-school agencies such as community corporations, profit-making firms, or nonprofit institutions, which agree to raise student performance to certain levels or forfeit their contract. However, since such programs entrench the reliance on standardized test scores, it is difficult to see how they can lead to an egalitarian school system or a pluralistic one.

Educational pluralism may be easier to achieve at a system-wide level than within a single school. To be unique, an educational subsystem needs autonomy and space to grow. When pluralistic subsystems are placed close together within a single school, they are apt to compete rather than collaborate. Their integration is difficult enough at the system-wide level, but there, at least, they are not as visible to one another, and their members are not forced into frequent interaction. The competition is less. Still, success, whether in a single school or system-wide, requires cooperation as well as separation. Such integration and differentiation require careful planning. A single multi-ethnic school, for example, might structure certain programs of specific import to black students (e.g., Black Studies); others of specific import to whites (e.g., White Culture and Racism); and still others of mutual interest to both (e.g., The New Society: Problems, Policies, and Plans). A pluralistic system might divide its high schools among separate programs. In 1971, Berkeley's system, for example, offered six alternatives: Community High Schools I and II, which were small, white, liberal arts and counter-culture oriented; Black House; Other Ways, which attracted Third World politically sophisticated students; Model A, whose students worked in the community a great deal; and Berkeley High School, college preparatory and comprehensive, the most traditional school of them all. How many separate programs a school or system offers, however, may well depend on how a community chooses to define its various interest groups.

Sometimes, it must be noted, the differences in viewpoints are too great to be integrated into a pluralistic system. Despite its democratic governance, for example, Sudbury Valley managed to force out students whose views and values were *too* disparate from those of the majority. Democratic structures are not infinitely flexible, and majority rule does not protect the right of groups to act however they choose. Thus Sudbury Valley is not developing a pluralistic program, except within the narrow framework of individual rather than group expression. Milwaukee, too, has similarly come to represent a single, rather than a pluralistic, orientation.

For a system to function pluralistically, people need to know how to use conflict creatively to protect minority interests. In each of the six schools studied, participatory governance was the decision-making style. Since this process tends to bring conflict of interests to the surface, it is worth looking at how conflicts were handled by the schools:

> 1. At Milwaukee and Sudbury Valley, conflict led to the forced exodus of dissenters and an increased homogenization of values and interests in those who remained.
>
> 2. At Franklin conflict has been almost nonexistent; the Senate has avoided dealing with issues that might arouse conflict of group interests; its members represented not constituents but themselves, as individuals.
>
> 3. Because Berkeley's alternative schools have been granted considerable autonomy, conflict between them has been minor. If many more are created, however, conflict over scarce resources is likely to emerge. Within Community High I the emphasis on individualism minimized group identification in the separate tribes formed around special interest; thus group conflict was minor. It could emerge, however, if the tribes develop more cohesion and more vision of themselves as culturally distinct from one another.

Whenever conflict mounted, the inevitable result was an attempt to reduce it by one of three ways:

> 1. Token gestures with no long-term impact.
>
> 2. Oppresion of dissenters, forcing them to leave or to submerge their point of view and drop their demands.
>
> 3. Compromise, which may please no one and erodes diversification.

None of these "solutions" is compatible with pluralism.

Better ways must be found to utilize conflict so that diversity is maintained at the same time as is integration and survival.

Unfortunately, schools cannot be any more pluralistic than society will allow. Only when diverse groups define their interests as distinct, separate, and legitimate can we distinguish the various needs our schools must meet. Definition alone is not enough, however. The separate interest groups must gain enough political power to make their needs known and met. Then, hopefully, we can make creative compromises to share our educational resources and enrich schooling for *all* students.